*Soldiers in
Zimbabwe's
Liberation War*

Soldiers in Zimbabwe's Liberation War

Edited by

NGWABI BHEBE
Professor of History
University of Zimbabwe

TERENCE RANGER
Rhodes Professor of Race Relations
University of Oxford

JAMES CURREY
London

HEINEMANN
Portsmouth, N.H.

UNIVERSITY OF ZIMBABWE PUBLICATIONS
Harare

James Currey Ltd
54b Thornhill Square
Islington
London N1 1BE

Heinemann
A division of Reed Elsevier Inc.
361 Hanover Street
Portsmouth, NH 03801-3912

University of Zimbabwe Publications
P.O. Box MP 203
Mount Pleasant
Harare

ISBN 0-85255-659-4   (James Currey cloth)
ISBN 0-85255-609-8   (James Currey paper)
ISBN 0-435-08974-9   (Heinemann cloth)
ISBN 0-435-08972-2   (Heinemann paper)
ISBN 0-908307-36-5   (University of Zimbabwe Publications)

1 2 3 4 5 99 98 97 96 95

British Library Cataloguing in Publication Data
Soldiers in Zimbabwe's Liberation War. –
I. Bhebe, Ngwabi II. Ranger, T.O.
III. Series
968.9104

Library of Congress Cataloging-in-Publication Data
International Conference on the Zimbabwe Liberation War (1991 :
   University of Zimbabwe)
   Soldiers in Zimbabwe's liberation war / edited by Ngwabi Bhebe and
Terence Ranger.
       p.   cm. --
   Chiefly papers presented at the International Conference on the
Zimbabwe Liberation War held at the University of Zimbabwe in
Harare, July 8–12, 1991.
   Includes bibliographical references and index.
       ISBN 0-435-08974-9 (Heinemann). -- ISBN 0-435-08972-2 (Heinemann : pbk.). -- ISBN 0-908307-36-5 (Univ.
of Zimbabwe Publications). -- ISBN 0-85255-659-4 (J. Currey). -- ISBN 0-85255-609-8 (J. Currey : pbk)
       1. Zimbabwe--History--Chimurenga War, 1966-1980--Congresses.
   2. Zimbabwe--Politics and government, 1965-1979--Congresses.
   3. National liberation movements--Zimbabwe--Congresses.
   4. Guerrillas--Zimbabwe--Congresses.   I. Bhebe, Ngwabi.
   II. Ranger, T.O. (Terence O.)   III. Title.   IV. Series.
   DT2988.158 1991
   968.91'04--dc20   95-4003
                                                                                            CIP

Typeset by University of Zimbabwe Publications
and printed in Britain by Villiers Publications, London N3

Contents

NOTES ON CONTRIBUTORS

Abiodun Alao, a Nigerian, is one of the few West African scholars to work on Zimbabwean history. In 1991 he obtained his doctorate from the Department of War Studies at King's College, London, with a thesis entitled 'The Defence and Security Implications of the Liberation War in Zimbabwe, 1980–1987'.

Teresa Barnes obtained her doctorate in 1994 from the University of Zimbabwe with a thesis entitled "We Women Worked so Hard': Gender, Labour and Social Reproduction in Colonial Zimbabwe, 1930–1956'. In 1992 she published, together with Everjoyce Win, *To Live a Better Life: An Oral History of Women in the City of Harare, 1930–1970* (Harare, Baobab).

Ngwabi Bhebe is Professor of History and Pro-Vice-Chancellor of the University of Zimbabwe. He is the author of many books and articles on the history of Zimbabwe, the most recent being *ZAPU and ZANU Guerrilla Warfare and the Lutheran Evangelical Church in Zimbabwe* which is now at press.

Jeremy Brickhill served with the ZIPRA Intelligence during the liberation war. He became a member of the National Army in 1980 and was entrusted with the preparation of ZIPRA's history in a projected collective account of all the elements constituting Zimbabwe's new army. He is working for a doctoral thesis at the University of Oxford on ZIPRA's role in the liberation struggle.

Dumiso Dabengwa's political history dates back to 1958 when he joined the African National Congress. He was sent by ZAPU for military training in the Soviet Union in 1964 to 1965. On his return he was appointed Head of Military Intelligence between 1965 and 1970 and in 1972 he combined that post with that of Secretary of the Revolutionary Council. Between May 1980 and August 1981 he served as Head of ZIPRA in the Joint High Command to implement the integration of the various forces in the Zimbabwe National Army. He was elected Member of Parliament for Nkulumane (Bulawayo) and appointed Deputy Minister of Home Affairs in 1990. He is currently Minister of Home Affairs and member of the ZANU (PF) politburo.

Henrick Ellert served in the Rhodesian Intelligence during the guerrilla war. He is the author of *The Rhodesian Front War: Counter-insurgency and Guerrilla War, 1962–1980* (Gweru, Mambo, 1989). Now working as a business consultant, he is also researching on white ethnic minorities.

Norma Kriger is a Professor of Politics at Johns Hopkins University. She is the author of *Zimbabwe's Guerrilla War: Peasant Voices* (Cambridge, CUP, 1992). She is currently working on ex-combatants.

David Moore is at Flinders University in Australia. He obtained his doctorate from York University, Toronto, in 1990 with a thesis on 'The Contradictory Construction of Hegemony in Zimbabwe'. He has published an article, 'The ideological formation of the Zimbabwean ruling class,' in the *Journal of Southern African Studies*, 1991, 17, 3.

Terence Ranger is Professor of Race Relations at the University of Oxford. He has written many books and articles about the history of Zimbabwe. Studies on the liberation war include *Peasant Consciousness and Guerrilla War in Zimbabwe* (London, James Currey, 1985).

Josiah Tungamirai received military training at Mgagao in Tanzania. Between 1977 and 1980 when Zimbabwe became independent, he was the Zimbabwe National Liberation Army Commissar. He became Major-General in the new Zimbabwe National Army between 1980 and 1982 but thereafter took over the command of the Air Force of Zimbabwe as Air Marshal in 1986. In 1992 he retired from the Air Force with the rank of Air Chief Marshal.

LIST OF ABBREVIATIONS AND ACRONYMS

ANC	African National Congress
BMATT	British Military Advisory and Training Team
BSAP	British South Africa Police
BSS	Bureau of State Security
Cde	Comrade
CID	Criminal Investigation Department
CIO	Central Intelligence Organization
COIN	Counter Insurgency
COMOPS	Combined Operations
COMPOL	Commissioner of Police
CP	Centre Party
DAI	Directorate Air Intelligence
DDG	Deputy Director-General
DEX	Director External
DG	Director-General
DIN	Director Internal
DMI	Directorate of Military Intelligence
DP	Democratic Party
DSBO	District Special Branch Officer
FISBY	Federal Intelligence and Security Bureau
FNLA	National Front for the Liberation of Angola
FRELIMO	Front for the Liberation of Mozambique
FROLIZI	Front for the Liberation of Zimbabwe

GC	Ground Coverage
GPSO	Government Protective Security Officer
HNP	Herstichte Nasionale Partie
INTAF	Ministry of Internal Affairs
ICC	Intelligence Co-ordinating Committee
JHC	Joint High Command
JMC	Joint Military Command
JOC	Joint Operation Commands
MCP	Malawi Congress Party
MNR	Mozambique National Resistance
MPLA	The People's Movement for the Liberation of Angola
NDP	National Democratic Party
NIS	National Intelligence Service
NRP	Northern Rhodesia Police
NSO	National Security Organization
NUF	National Unifying Force
OAU	Organization of African Unity
OCGC	Officer Commanding Ground Cover
OCSB	Officer Commanding Special Branch
PSBO	Provincial Special Branch Officers
PSYOPS	Director of Psychological Operations
RA	Republican Alliance
RAP	Rhodesian Action Party
RENAMO	Mozambique National Resistance
RF	Rhodesia Front
RIC	Rhodesian Intelligence Corps
RLI	Rhodesian Light Infantry
RNP	Rhodesian National Party
RP	Rhodesian Party
RRA	Rhodesian Republican Army
SADF	South African Defence Force
SASCON	Southern African Solidarity Congress
SAS	Special Air Service
SB	Special Branch
SFA	Security Force Auxiliaries
SRANC	Southern Rhodesian African National Congress
SRC	Students Representative Council

SWAPO	South West African Peoples Organization
UAC	Union Administrative Council
UANC	United African National Council
UDI	Unilateral Declaration of Independence
UNIP	United National Independence Party
USSR	Union of Soviet Socialist Republic
ZANLA	Zimbabwe African National Liberation Army
ZANU	Zimbabwe African National Union
ZANU/PF	Zimbabwe African National Union Patriotic Front
ZAPU	Zimbabwe African People's Union
ZDI	Zimbabwe Defence Industries
ZIMA	Zimbabwe Medical Aid
ZIPA	Zimbabwe People's Army
ZIPRA	Zimbabwe People's Revolutionary Army
ZIS	Zambian Intelligence Service
ZLC	Zimbabwe Liberation Council
ZNA	Zimbabwe National Army
ZP	Zambian Police

ACKNOWLEDGEMENTS

The editors wish to thank the Ford Foundation and the Swedish Agency for Research Co-operation with Developing Countries (SAREC) both of which supported the International Conference on the Zimbabwe Liberation War held in Harare on July 8–12, 1991, at which most of the papers appearing in these two volumes were presented. We are also grateful for the generous subsidy the two organizations have provided for the publication of the two books.

We are further grateful to Professor Carl F. Hallencreutz and his colleagues, the organizers of the Seminar on Religion and War in Zimbabwe and Swedish Relationships held at Uppsala on 23–28 April, 1992, for their permission to publish Ngwabi Bhebe's paper on the Healing of the Scars and Jeremy Brickhill's chapter on the Mafela Trust. The conference gave us an opportunity to finalize our editorial work.

We are thankful for the academic sponsorship we have enjoyed from the University of Zimbabwe and the Oxford University African Studies Committee during the conference itself and throughout our editorial work.

For the unstinted and efficient secretarial and administrative support, we are grateful to Phyllis Ferguson, who worked hard for the success of the conference from our Oxford end; to Miss Emerencia Naka, of the University of Zimbabwe, who provided the conference with all its secretarial support; Mr Bryan Thomas Callahan of Swarthmore College, Pennsylvania, who ran around to ensure that conference papers were produced in the right amounts and that they were delivered to the participants timeously; and to Mr Dumisani Vuma, who ferried participants between the airport and the conference venue at the University of Zimbabwe.

Finally, we are indebted to the University of Zimbabwe Publications Committee and the then Publications Officer, Roger Stringer and the Director of Publications, Samuel Matsangaise and the entire staff for well produced publications.

General Introduction

NGWABI BHEBE
TERENCE RANGER

In July 1991 the University of Zimbabwe was host to an international conference on Zimbabwe's War of Liberation. Two speakers at once threw down a challenge. The first was the Vice-Chancellor, Prof. Walter Kamba, who insisted that the conference was meeting at just the right moment:

> For us the war is still a living reality. But it is also history . . . We can look at it now clearly; look at it whole. The unity agreement makes it possible, and makes it necessary, to include the role of ZIPRA as well as the role of ZANLA, to extend the grassroots studies of the war from Manicaland and Mashonaland into Matabeleland. Ten years and more of Independence make it possible and make it necessary to look back and ask questions about the effect of the war and its legacy for what has followed. For the sake of Zimbabwe's understanding of itself we need to raise questions about social conflict during and after the war, about gender, about terror and counter-terror, about mobilization and demobilization, about combatants and ex-combatants, and even about dissidents.

> Zimbabwe needs to remember and to understand the war: to understand it at the level of high analysis and to understand it at the level of suffering and trauma. We need to understand it for reviewing policy, for making the record more complete, for healing memories. At the University here this week you can discuss everything and anything, raise challenging questions, dispute comfortable stereotypes. This is part of what we mean by academic freedom, a freedom for which this university firmly stands . . . Zimbabweans need knowledge about the war. It is your job to learn from them and make available what you have learned.

His challenge was pushed further by Dumiso Dabengwa, who urged that conditions be created for a new breed of social scientists to emerge in Zimbabwe.

We urge the emergence of a class of scholars capable of withstanding threats and intimidation and rising above racial, ethnic and tribal considerations . . . The new breed of Zimbabwean social scientists ought to stand up against the suppression of any information and should develop an ever-critical mind with respect to the facts, especially purported facts, and actions of political leaders. Anything short of cultivating a tradition of selfless enquiry and exposure of the truth will certainly lead to a nation of sycophants and robots without the necessary powers of independent thought which we should all cherish. A conference on the history of the liberation war is an excellent beginning.

It is a hard task for any conference — or for any subsequent publication — to live up to these demands for courage and rigour and independence of mind. But at least the conference attempted to do so. It brought together, for the first time and in an atmosphere of frankness, leaders and members of ZANLA, ZIPRA and the Rhodesian Security Forces; it brought together cabinet ministers from both ZAPU and ZANU/PF backgrounds, Zimbabweans and non-Zimbabweans, professors and graduate students, those who have already published books on the war and those who are setting out to write them, historians and anthropologists and literary critics and educationalists and theologians. Over four days of discussions this varied group remembered and probed and questioned.

These two volumes present most of the papers given to the conference, and the volume introductions draw on the conference discussions. We hope that their publication will mark another stage in our understanding of the war. However, it should at once be made clear that they do not set out to offer a full coverage of all aspects of the war or a full commentary on what has already been published. It is their intention to move on: to look at questions which have hardly yet been raised and to suggest others which are just beginning to be defined. So in order to make the best use of these two volumes, it is necessary to begin with a brief account of the existing literature on the liberation war.[1]

There is an odd paradox about this literature. Writing about most wars usually begins with descriptions of battles, accounts of armies, biographies of generals and autobiographies of soldiers. Only later do historians turn to the impact of those wars on civilians, on society, on older men and on women and children. But as far as Zimbabwe's war of liberation is concerned, the reverse has been true. The major studies of the war from an African perspective do not deal with armies or military tactics or the experience of fighting men and women. Instead they deal with the impact of the war on Zimbabwe's peasantries;[2] with the war experience of African women;[3] with ideology and religion;[4] and with the need for healing after the war.[5] Only from the White Rhodesian side of the war has there been a flood of books about soldiers and fighting — whether general accounts of the war,[6] or boasts of the triumphs of the Rhodesian Intelligence services,[7] or glorifications of the 'special forces',[8] or picture-books,[9] or White autobiographies.[10] Many of these have been published in South Africa. So it would be true to say that we know a great deal on the African side about civilians and about religion; a great deal on the Rhodesian side about military operations and 'dirty tricks'. But we still know very little about the guerrilla armies or guerrilla intelligence services, just as we know hardly anything about Rhodesian ideology and religion, or about the effect of the war on White civilians.[11]

There are several reasons for this imbalance. To quote again from Dumiso Dabengwa's contribution, from the perspective of the liberation movements 'the armed struggle was only part of the struggle'. The guerrillas always had a keen appreciation of the supreme importance of the social, ideological and political 'fronts'. But on the Rhodesian side — both during the war and in the retrospective literature — it often appears as if military factors only are significant: as if the war could (and should) have been decided purely by military superiority. Indeed, much of the literature published in South Africa claims that the Rhodesian forces could have 'won' the war in battle had they not been betrayed. The almost exclusively military focus of ex-Rhodesian literature on the war is a sign of continued failure of understanding.

But there are also research reasons for this imbalance. When academic work began on the war after 1980, researchers in Zimbabwe did not have access to the records of any of the armies. ZANLA's files were unsorted and closed to scholars.[12] ZIPRA's files were seized by the police.[13] Rhodesian army and police files were either burnt in a great holocaust of documents or smuggled to South Africa. So researchers in Zimbabwe went out into the rural areas, where the war had been fought, and interviewed the people who had experienced it. As a result they paid a great deal of attention to peasant grievances, or to peasant religion, or to the cleavages in rural society. But they interviewed few guerrillas since those who had fought the war were rarely any longer to be found in the areas where they had been combatants. However, at least some of those writing in South Africa had access to the smuggled Rhodesian army files.

Finally, there has been the strange silence of the guerrillas since 1980, with only one autobiography published.[14] Many reasons have been suggested for this. Some scholars — such as Richard Werbner in south-western Zimbabwe — have found ex-combatants reluctant to talk about traumatic war-time experiences. Others have argued that for ZIPRA veterans, at least, and even for former members of ZIPA or the 'left' groups within ZANLA, it has not until recently been safe to do so. Yet others speak of the marginalization of even ZANLA ex-combatants (a marginalization reflected in these volumes in Teresa Barnes's interviews with former guerrillas), and of the creation of an 'official' version of the war which gives all the glory to political leaders and to generals, many of whom are safely dead. For whatever reason, publishers have been reluctant to accept guerrilla life-stories. The result of all this has been that the guerrilla experience has come to us through fiction rather than through history and autobiography.

As we have suggested, there have been some positive benefits of this silence about the military aspects of the guerrilla war. It is no bad thing to *begin* with the experiences of civilians, peasants or women. It is important to see the war in social, political and ideological terms rather than just as a military operation. But, clearly, this imbalance has had many negative effects. We have been stuck with an orthodoxy — one version of the war which gives all the credit to ZANLA and none to ZIPRA, and which highlights some elements within ZANLA while denigrating others.[15] The time has certainly come, as Walter Kamba insisted, to look at ZIPRA as well as at ZANLA, and to look at ZIPRA and the 'Nhari' rebellion and the 'Vashandi' within ZANLA. The time has certainly come to review contrasting military strategies; to hear the voices of the combatants at least as clearly as those of the peasants or of 'the mothers of the revolution'. Even the Rhodesian side of the military struggle, about which so much has already been written, needs to be made into history rather than myth.

For these reasons our first volume will focus on 'Soldiers', bringing together chapters on ZIPRA, ZIPA and ZANLA; discussing the 'Nhari' rebellion and the 'Vashandi', the Fifth Brigade and the 'dissidents'; comparing Rhodesian Intelligence Services with guerrilla intelligence services; exploring the effects of Rhodesian 'dirty tricks' and poisoning on the guerrillas; looking at the integration of the armies after 1980; and giving a voice to ex-combatants.

Nevertheless, there is still much to be said about the social, political and ideological aspects of the war and these are the topics of our second volume, on 'Society'. This volume, too, will focus on questions which have not yet been explored in the social historical research already done. Thus there is no chapter on spirit mediums — so effectively discussed in David Lan's *Guns and Rain*. Instead there is a chapter exploring the hitherto neglected subject of the interaction between guerrillas and the Mwali shrines of the south-west. There are no chapters making the sort of generalizations which have already been established about the role of the Christian churches in the war. Instead there are detailed case studies which modify or complicate those generalizations or bring to the fore hitherto neglected denominations. There are no chapters on peasant ideology (about which so much has been written by Ranger and Kriger and Manungo); instead there are contributions on education and ideology in the camps in Zambia and Mozambique, and on Rhodesian ideology as reflected in fiction. Finally, there are three chapters which open up an important new topic: the continuation of the war after 1980 in some places and its continuing impact in others. These chapters look at the war of the 'dissidents' in Matabeleland; at the impact of the war on gender relations; and on what patterns of patriarchy have emerged from the war in the rural areas.

Yet we hope that in focusing on different topics in these two volumes we have not lost sight of the insights of the work that has already been done. Even in a volume on 'Soldiers' it is not really possible ever to forget civilians. Thus if Jeremy Brickhill's first chapter in the first volume deals with 'pure' military history, discussing ZIPRA's development of a conventional war capacity, his second chapter on the work of the Mafela Trust relates the documentation of the guerrilla dead to the sorrows and traumas of the whole of rural society. Moreover, there are many interactions between the two volumes, between 'soldiers' and 'society', which we seek to bring out in the two individual volume introductions. These volumes are not a repudiation of the best work of the first decade but are designed to add to and deepen them.

Finally, the conference was intended to be a stimulus to further research, so it may be useful to set out what does *not* appear in these volumes and which topics still need to be explored. So far as the first volume is concerned the main group of 'soldiers' missing are the 'Auxiliaries' of Abel Muzorewa and Ndabaningi Sithole. We make some initial comments on them in the volume introduction but the whole subject of the Internal Settlement and of the auxiliaries badly needs to be researched. We suspect that such research will add not only to our understanding of the war on the ground but also of gender and generation issues and of witch-killings during the war.

So far as 'Society' is concerned, the greatest absence is of urban society. Urban links with rural insurrection is a topic well explored in studies of the Mau-Mau but hardly touched upon for Zimbabwe. Were there urban supply networks? Were there urban sabotage cells? What about the refugees who flocked into the towns from the countryside? What of the urban unemployed youth recruited as auxiliaries? What of the 'traditions' of urban violence, beginning with the riots of the mass nationalist period, through the clashes between ZAPU and ZANU supporters in 1963 and 1964, to urban violence during and after elections in the 1980s? Is there any urban equivalent to rural religious developments during the war? Given the centrality of urban violence in South Africa and the sophistication of the studies made of it, this is a serious gap in the Zimbabwean literature.

There are also areas of the country about whose wartime experience we knew hardly anything. There has been no study, for example, of the war history of the peasant societies of Northern Matabeleland, which we badly need to balance Jeremy Brickhill's account of the fighting men and women in that province. Nor do we know much about civilian interactions along and across the Mozambique border, either during the war or in the post–1980 period of RENAMO raids. There is the lowveld — Tonga country in the north-west, or Hlengwe and Shangaan country in the south-east — a study of which would help break down the exclusive focus on the 'Shona' and the 'Ndebele'.

And even in those areas where studies *have* been carried out on the civilian experience in the war we need more attention to *class* as well as to gender and generation. Now that the 'indigenous businessmen' (or women) are coming into their own, we need studies of their role during the war. Of course, even now that indigenous businessmen and women are coming into their own, Whites still dominate much of the economy and possess the most productive areas of the land. We need to know much more about White society and ideology in the past and especially during the war.

Another conference in ten years time will be able to throw light on all these questions — and generate yet new ones in its turn. In the interim we offer these two volumes as, we hope, a provocative report on the state of the debate about Zimbabwe's liberation war.

Volume Introduction: Soldiers in Zimbabwe's Liberation War

NGWABI BHEBE
TERENCE RANGER

Studies of the military aspect of Zimbabwe's liberation war have been very incomplete and two major criticisms can be levied against them. These criticisms were enunciated by those presenting papers at the conference.

The first criticism is that the 'authorized' account by Martin and Johnson, *The Struggle for Zimbabwe*,[1] which was distributed to all Zimbabwean secondary schools, constitutes, in David Moore's words, 'a singular and celebratory narrative buttressing ZANU(PF)'s claims to power', and it suppresses or down plays the contributions of ZIPRA and ZIPA.

The second criticism was made by Teresa Barnes:

> Wars are often summed up as the decisions of leaders and the movements of armies. It is often forgotten that all of these depend on ordinary soldiers, who personally sacrifice to achieve advances and victories, and physically suffer the consequences of retreats and victories. But their experiences are usually obliterated in the manufacture of histories, and may even be lost to popular memory. The result is the propagation of an official mythology of war.

Barnes is also critical of Martin and Johnson's book, which she characterizes as a 'quasi-official history which depends solely on official accounts and the recollections of national leaders'. She adds that accounts of the Rhodesian side of the war have similarly ignored the role of the common soldier.

The conference's response to these two criticisms has given this volume its title and structure. Here, readers will find not only Josiah Tungamirai on ZANLA but also Dumiso Dabengwa and Jeremy Brickhill on ZIPRA, David Moore on ZIPA, and discussion of factions within ZAPU and ZANU. We have called this volume 'Soldiers' rather than 'Armies' so as to emphasize Teresa Barnes's point. The volume ends with three chapters: one by Norma Kriger on the politics of creating war heroes, which documents the state's attempts to monopolize the memory of the war, and two which focus on the guerrilla dead and on ex-combatants — Jeremy Brickhill's account of the work of the Mafela Trust which seeks to document the death and to mark the grave of every ZIPRA soldier killed in the war, and Teresa Barnes's presentation of the reminiscences of four ex-combatants. On the Rhodesian side we cannot claim to have elicited the experiences of individual soldiers, but at least Ray Roberts's analysis of the tension between police and military views of the war and Henrick Ellert's account of the infinite complications of Rhodesian Intelligence prevent the creation of any simplistic model of how the war was fought by the Rhodesians.

CONTRASTS AND COMPARISONS

What happens, then, when for the first time all these groupings are brought together? The conference began by considering *contrasts*. In the version hitherto established, there has been one simple contrast, that between ZANLA and ZIPRA: the first had many guerrillas deployed in the country and fought the war effectively; the second had fewer guerrillas inside Zimbabwe and pursued a baffling strategy of apparent inactivity. Now Jeremy Brickhill, himself a member of ZIPRA and researching its history for his doctorate, suggests a number of new contrasts which are much more favourable to ZIPRA.

He argues that there were three main differences between ZIPRA and ZANLA. Firstly, in patterns of recruitment: ZANLA, he says, was a peasant army; ZIPRA, however, could be described as proletarian in the sense that a high proportion of its recruits came directly from waged jobs in towns or in industry. The implications of this are that ZIPRA was more open to radical and secular ideas and more amenable to formal military and technical training.

The second contrast lay, he suggests, in the political character of ZIPRA's relationship to the civilian population in the operational zones inside Zimbabwe. Before ZAPU and ZANU were banned in 1964, ZAPU had enjoyed support in most parts of the country, and certainly in the zones which later became ZIPRA battlefronts. Brickhill believes that ZAPU party structures had survived underground in these areas and that, even where the main ZAPU branch had been driven out of existence, women's branches and youth leagues survived. When ZIPRA guerrillas arrived in their areas these groups organized logistical support and attracted recruits. Hence in ZIPRA-dominated zones there was no need for the guerrillas themselves to create support structures or to make new claims for legitimacy, as Brickhill thinks ZANLA guerrillas were obliged to do. ZIPRA did not need to select young *mujibas* and *chimbwidos*, nor to hold *pungwes* to mobilize or to politically educate the people. Nor did it need to ally with non-political sources of legitimacy such as spirit mediums or mission churches.

Thirdly, he argues, and this is the main thrust of his chapter in this volume, that ZAPU's political control and ZIPRA's proletarian character enabled a unique transition from guerrilla war to certain 'conventional' strategies. ZIPRA, alone among African guerrilla movements, had made this transition and was poised by the end of 1979 to implement it.

These contrasts were a stimulating reversal of the usual picture of ZIPRA as a do-nothing army finally forced into inappropriate militaristic tactics by its Soviet advisers. It must be said, though, that while Brickhill's data are impressive, the conference as a whole was not persuaded that the contrasts were anything like as sharp as he suggested. Numbers of ZIPRA's soldiers were certainly recruited from employment in South Africa, but it was argued that this had regional rather than ideological or class roots, given the peculiar dependence of the Zimbabwean south-west upon labour migration to the south. Comparing Brickhill's data on recruitment with those presented by Tungamirai in his chapter in this volume, the conference was struck not so much by the solidly 'peasant' nature of ZANLA's army as by its educational variety and layering.

There was general acceptance of the view that ZAPU had enjoyed wider support than ZANU in 1964, but several modifications to Brickhill's analysis were suggested. Firstly, there had been some areas of ZANU support and these were significant in the development of rural violence — as, for example, with the activities of the 'Crocodile Gang' in Chipinge. Secondly, some of the areas in which guerrillas first began to operate successfully, such as Hwange and the north-east, had been the least politically organized in the open nationalist period and it was hard to imagine underground party branches waiting ready to engage with the 'boys'. Thirdly, even in areas such as the mid- and south-west, where there had undoubtedly been very strong ZAPU branches, state repression and political confusion over the rise of Muzorewa's ANC certainly meant that ZIPRA guerrillas had a great deal of work to do to rebuild support structures. Fourthly, and this is argued in detail in our second volume, it seems that some ZIPRA guerrillas did seek access to other sources of legitimacy, such as the Matopos shrines, or work with missions where this was possible, as with the Spanish Burgos Fathers in Hwange.

In many ways the conference was struck more by the similarities than by the contrasts between ZIPRA and ZANLA — though to urge comparisons is in itself an important modification of the established view. Take the question of recruitment, for example. Fay Chung's contribution, which appears as a chapter in our second volume, begins with the recruitment dilemma common to both ZANU and ZAPU:

> There were few recruits to train as guerrillas in the early days. Zimbabwean youths preferred to go for further studies rather than to train as guerrilla soldiers. As a result of the dearth of volunteers, both ZANU and ZAPU engaged in a policy of forced conscription in Zambia. The Zimbabwean peasant families in Mumbwa formed the natural and easily available source of conscripts. Peasant youths, many of them poorly educated or even illiterate, were among the first to train as guerrillas. The end result was that a dominant and homogeneous group of guerrilla fighters

emerged, later to be known as the 'veterans'. Poorly educated and drawn mainly from the Karanga people, who had settled in Mumbwa, they developed a pride in their military vocation with a marked disdain for education and a distrust of the educated.[2]

Hence a 'veteran' group, very different from Brickhill's profile of ZIPRA, developed in both ZAPU's and ZANU's guerrilla forces, even if ZAPU conscripted Zimbabweans living on the Copperbelt as well as those living in Mumbwa.

Chung immediately suggested another similarity. The history of both ZAPU/ ZIPRA and of ZANU/ZANLA is filled, as these two volumes will abundantly demonstrate, with clashes between 'layers' of recruits: the March 11 movement within ZAPU in 1971; the 'Nhari rebellion' within ZANLA in 1974; the rise of ZIPA; the 'Vashandi' in Mozambique — all can be seen in terms of younger, more ideological, fighters challenging the dominance of the 'veterans'. Faction fighting within the exiled nationalist political leadership has often been analysed by political scientists in terms of 'generational' struggle. It began to look to the conference as though a similar analysis should be applied to cleavages among the guerrillas themselves. If so, it would make less sense to present a general and overall profile of the two armies and more sense to seek to establish a *sequence* of recruiting, as Chung briefly attempts to do in her chapter.

But, in addition to sequences, Chung also suggests that from the beginning both ZAPU and ZANU were building up disparate armies. She used the differential of education, since her topic was, after all, 'Educational Deprivation as an Issue in the Liberation Struggle'. She argues that, in addition to the peasant recruits from Mumbwa, there was:

> from the earliest days another fertile recruitment ground, and that was from the ranks of young students who had fled from Rhodesia in search of education . . . Both ZANU and ZAPU made it their custom to welcome such students at the airport, but instead of finding themselves in colleges and universities as they had intended, they found themselves whisked off to military training camps.

As Chung points out, one such student was Josiah Tungamirai himself. As she also points out, there grew up 'two largely disparate groups: peasant youths and educated youths'. This dichotomy was to be reproduced on a much more massive scale within ZANLA from 1973 onwards with a 'flood of willing recruits' into Mozambique, many of them secondary-school students, others 'peasant' youths and illiterate refugees. Later still, university students joined the recruits. These 'disparities' added to the 'generational' tensions within both guerrilla armies.

We may make some remarks on these apparent similarities between the recruitment and composition of ZIPRA and ZANLA. The first is that education clearly cannot be regarded as the only divisive factor within (or between) the guerrilla armies. Some commentators would stress *region*, with tensions between earlier Karanga 'veterans' and later Manyika recruits inside ZANLA, and tensions between 'Ndebele' and 'Kalanga' within ZIPRA. A regional emphasis might show a growing contrast between ZANLA and ZIPRA, no matter how common their early patterns of recruitment in Zambia may have been. By the 1970s the flood of recruits into Mozambique came overwhelmingly (as shown in Tungamirai's chapter) from the rural areas of eastern Zimbabwe, while ZIPRA recruits came from largely labour migrants into South Africa.

So it could be argued that it was after the early 1970s that contrasts such as those drawn by Jeremy Brickhill began to be established. The open frontiers into Mozambique allowed many more 'peasants' to join ZANLA than could make the complicated journey to Botswana and by air to Zambia to join ZIPRA. So at this stage, perhaps, the peasant/proletarian contrast began to develop. And one could add to this, taking account of Chung's data, a contrast at the other extreme between the larger number of university-educated people who joined ZANU and the smaller number who joined ZAPU. For the later 1970s, then, one might argue a modified Brickhill-style contrast between the very varied composition of ZANLA, from peasant youths, the urban educated, and a more homogeneous ZIPRA made up of 'proletarian' labour migrants.

But even at this stage the contrasts are not sharp. The chapters and oral presentations summarized in the introduction to our second volume show how anxious ZIPRA was in the later 1970s to match the numbers of recruits pouring into Mozambique. Paulos Matjaka Nare describes his own abduction and that of other teachers and children from Manama school by ZIPRA guerrillas:

> The escalation of the liberation war in Rhodesia at the beginning of 1977 assumed a new character. More and more young people started to desert the country with the intention of joining the guerrilla warfare. Thus in January of the same year Manama Secondary School became one of the first schools to move *ad hoc* out of the country. The harassments by the Rhodesian army, hovering above our heads with spotter planes and helicopters, caused untold trepidation. It triggered mixed reactions. Some took cover, others cried, while some took to haphazard stampeding. A few students and teachers took a chance to hide here and eventually returned home. The majority became even more resolute. We had two armed guerrillas in our company . . . We all cherished the popular idea that we would eventually train in guerrilla warfare and return to liberate our country.

This does not sound much like a focus on the urban employed — nor very different from mass school responses to ZANLA in eastern Zimbabwe.

Moreover, the Manama case was an extreme example of a much more general pattern. During his oral presentation to the conference, Ngwabi Bhebe handed out a map of the communal areas of Mberengwa, southern Gwanda and Beitbridge, which showed 'some routes used by ZIPRA recruits'. These routes ran from Mount Nhamande, in Mberengwa, south-west to the Botswana border. In the critically important Mberengwa zone, which was fiercely contested between the Rhodesian forces and ZANLA, ZIPRA did not mount military offensives as, said Bhebe, it desperately needed recruits so as to match ZANLA's numerical strength. So while ZANLA demanded logistical support in Mberengwa from peasants and missions, ZIPRA maintained a permanent base at Mount Nhamande solely for the purpose of collecting and dispatching recruits south-west to Botswana for onward transmission to Zambia. Here, then, was a deliberate recruitment policy, which took place at a time when ZIPRA was beginning to work out its transition to more conventional warfare, which did not focus on proletarian migrant workers but on a combination of peasant youths and half-volunteer, half-abducted school-children which was very similar to the combination of recruits going into Mozambique.

This makes a good moment to take advantage of Teresa Barnes's transcripts of ex-combatants' life-histories. Some of her informants conform exactly to the model of the easy crossing into Mozambique. 'TM' from Chipinge lived 'so close to the border' that he 'even attended the Mozambique Independence' celebrations, and was so exalted by doing so that he crossed the border to join ZANLA a month later. 'CM' from the Honde Valley lived only 15 km from the Mozambique border, used to shop on the Mozambique side, was inspired by FRELIMO, and crossed to join ZANLA with four friends. But her one ZIPRA ex-combatant, 'X', tells a story which throws useful light on our discussions, showing that it was possible to continue, or at least to revive, ZAPU branches far outside Matabeleland, and also that ZAPU recruited, when it could, deep in the eastern countryside:

> In 1973 I took a job with the Ministry of Education teaching primary school. I taught in Masvingo [Province] near the Mozambique border. There was quite a lot of political activity going on. It was near Gonakudzingwa, where a lot of our nationalist leaders were detained for quite a long time. At the time, the UANC led by Muzorewa was mobilizing people in the country. So I got involved in setting up branches [of ZAPU] with three other teachers at the school.

> I was actively involved. I remember recruiting so many people to join the armed struggle. We actually had a network whereby somebody would drive up to that place and then collect the people and drive them straight out to the Botswana border and take them across. The border to Mozambique was about ten kilometres away, but we were recruiting people to join ZIPRA . . . Then what happened was the president of our district was arrested . . . That is the main thing that forced me out of the country.

The interim conclusion, before further work is done on these patterns and periodizations of recruitment, is that the contrasts which remain between ZIPRA and ZANLA, though certainly significant, were not the result of deliberate policy, nor of class or ethnic preferences, but rather the results of specific historical and geographical factors.

To a certain extent this is true, too, for the contrast between ZIPRA and ZANLA tactics and strategy. Once again Brickhill's sharp contrast was modified by some of the other papers and discussions. Thus, just as Fay Chung had begun with the common dilemma of both ZAPU and ZANU in early recruitment, so Dumiso Dabengwa began, in his paper to the conference and still more in his spoken introduction, with the first faltering steps to violence. He described how the PCC/ ZAPU, after their split with ZANU, set up a 'Special Affairs' department to recruit volunteers and co-ordinate sabotage within the country. They obtained grenades left over from the Congo Civil War but did not know how to detonate them, so when they were thrown they failed to explode; then they stole fuses from the mines and achieved some explosions. And even after it became clear that more formal training was needed, and Dabengwa himself went to the Soviet Union, guerrilla thinking was still for a long time focused on infiltrating a few men into the country to co-ordinate and perform acts of sabotage. The story at that stage was essentially the same for ZANU.

It became clear at the conference that, even years later, and at the moment when ZANU/ZANLA were soon to make their breakthrough in the north-east — so often described as a triumph for a new, Maoist, doctrine of guerrilla war peculiar to ZANLA — there was still an inter-changeability both of men and ideas between the two armies. Dabengwa describes the opening of the north-eastern front thus:

> It was during [the 1971] crisis that ZAPU lost its important and strategic contact with FRELIMO. ZANU knew of the setbacks facing ZAPU to mount joint operations with FRELIMO. The information came from ZAPU commanders who were defecting to ZANU. Among them were Rex Nhongo (now Solomon Mujuru) and Robson Manyika. Manyika had first-hand knowledge of all of ZAPU's plans with FRELIMO since he was ZAPU's Chief of Staff before his defection. Manyika gave the plans to ZANU which then exploited the situation and attempted to approach FRELIMO but did not succeed because ZAPU had asked FRELIMO to give it some time to sort out its internal problems. ZANU then went to Tanzania where it was introduced to FRELIMO. After this introduction Robson Manyika went to the Tete corridor with ZANU functionaries at the expense of ZAPU . . . This is how ZANU first got its sizeable number of recruits.

According to Dabengwa's oral presentation, preparations for this north-eastern offensive had been on hand between ZAPU and FRELIMO since 1969 and ZAPU emissaries had made contact with underground agents in the area in readiness for infiltration. These agents were later mobilized by Robson Manyika, now acting for ZANU.

One might take with a pinch of salt this claim that the successful north-east offensive was really planned by ZAPU. But two points can be made here. One is that Fay Chung confirmed in discussion the importance to the fortunes of ZANU's army of the 1971 split in ZAPU: 'Before the split ZIPRA had 800 guerrillas and ZANLA had 12; after the split ZIPRA had 600 and ZANLA had 212.' The other is that, whoever was responsible for the strategy of carefully prepared infiltration and the political education of the people in the north-eastern part of the country, Dumiso Dabengwa was clearly not distancing himself from it nor comparing it unfavourably with some superior ZIPRA programme.

Even with the great contrast of strategy in 1979 we can see some similarities. In his oral presentation Jeremy Brickhill cited a ZIPRA commander on the danger of getting too many guerrillas crammed into one area — by late 1978 there were 'far too many' ZIPRA soldiers on the Khami river for the health of a guerrilla war. This was one of the incentives to moving towards a strategy of 'conventional' warfare. When David Maxwell spoke to his paper on the war in Nyanga, which appears in the second volume, he quoted local people there as making the same point. They had got on well with the ZANLA guerrillas when there were not too many of them and they lived away from the villages, but by 1978/9 there were 'too many' and 'they even lived in the houses'. Again, it is illuminating to compare the end of Dumiso Dabengwa's chapter with the end of Fay Chung's:

> In 1978 [writes Dabengwa] ZIPRA started training regular forces. There were some ZAPU critics and detractors who deliberately misinterpreted this concept and argued that it was impossible for a regular army to take over any country . . . The fact of the matter is that, in the liberated zones, ZAPU's objectives were to set up some civil administration and to open schools which had been closed because of the war. The regular ZIPRA army was to complement the presence of the guerrilla army by bringing back the regular administration . . . It was unthinkable that there could be a semblance of civil life in these areas without providing the necessary defence which could only come from well-trained regular army units.

Now Chung about ZANU and ZANLA:

> There was also planning for education in semi-liberated zones where the Rhodesian authorities had closed down schools. By mid-1979 ZANU believed that, because certain operational zones were now seldom entered by Rhodesian forces, it was appropriate to re-open schools under the jurisdiction of ZANU. A number of educational personnel were sent to the war front to prepare for the re-opening of schools. However, the plan was never effected as the war came to a sudden halt as a result of the Lancaster House negotiations towards the end of 1979.

Lancaster House, of course, frustrated the realization of ZIPRA's plans, too. We shall never know how successful they might have been in making Brickhill's unique breakthrough, or how ZANLA could have protected schools in semi-liberated zones without well-trained regular units to protect them. Of course, very significant contrasts remain, but at least it seems that the two guerrilla armies were living in the same world of problem and response.

Once again we can draw on Teresa Barnes's informants for some additional illumination. As it happens her three ex-combatants do not fit either the simple ZIPRA or ZANLA stereotypes. In contrast to the view that ZIPRA guerrillas held back from fighting, her 'X' fought continuously inside Zimbabwe from mid-1977 to the ceasefire, moving south from Chirundu and Mana Pools to Karoi and Hurungwe, and then to Zvimba and parts of the Midlands. Instead of informally trained quasi-bandit ZANLA infiltrators, her 'TM' sees himself as a proper soldier. He, too, operated inside the country continuously from 1977, in Zimunya, Buhera, Charter and Mhondoro. 'We were advancing towards Harare with the mission of blowing up the Harare–Bulawayo railway line'. And to complicate the formal/informal military contrast further, 'TM' had in his detachment some sections 'composed of a combination of FRELIMO soldiers and ZANLA forces. They couldn't even speak Shona. But military language we could speak a bit, so we understood each other'. For the soldierly 'TM' it was 'just a surprise at the end of 1979 when we heard about the ceasefire . . . We did not even think of ending at that time because we had gathered a lot of weaponry and a lot of targets were on the books.'

What emerges, of course, both from Brickhill's original contrasts and from these modifications, is ZIPRA's re-entry into the light of history, which ZANLA has occupied since 1980. Whether ZIPRA was different in the ways that Brickhill claims, or similar in the ways that we have been suggesting, or different in yet other ways, at least it was significant. Clearly, a full history of the war needs to take ZIPRA and the questions we have been raising about it very much into account.

But a further contrast emerged during the conference: that between the guerrilla armies as a whole and the Rhodesian security forces. Take, for instance, Henry Ellert's chapter in this volume on 'The Rhodesian Security and Intelligence Community'. The conference listened to it in astonishment at its elaboration; at the sheer indigestible amount of information Rhodesian Intelligence collected; at the confusion between the operations of its various branches. Dumiso Dabengwa, himself the head of ZIPRA Intelligence, commented that this over-proliferation of information must have been counter-productive. There was too much information and too little intelligence. All ZIPRA intelligence gathering, he said, was operationally, not politically or ideologically directed. ZIPRA depended on direct field observations and on agents infiltrated into the Rhodesian army and police.

This leads to an apparent paradox. We have contrasted in our 'General Introduction' the guerrilla appreciation that 'the armed struggle was only part of the struggle' with the White Rhodesian emphasis being on a purely military victory. Yet Rhodesian Intelligence ranged much more widely than the guerrillas'. Maybe the answer is that for the Rhodesians ideological, personal and political factors were all thought to be 'operationally directed' while for the guerrillas these matters were more important than war. Yet Prof. Ray Roberts's paper on the Rhodesian forces raised other problems. Far from being too militaristic, he argued, White Rhodesian thinking during the struggle was not militaristic enough.

Since Roberts's paper is unfortunately not available for this publication, we summarize it here at some length. He asserted that, since the conference was in the business of destroying myths, it ought also to destroy the myth of 'the long Rhodesian military tradition' and of the Rhodesian army as 'the White electorate in arms'. It should also view sceptically the idea that Rhodesian power always rested on naked force which readily developed into repression, militarism and martial law. Discussion of Rhodesian ideologies of legitimation, order and violence we shall reserve to the introduction to our second volume. Here we summarize Roberts's argument on the Rhodesian forces.

There is, he said, very little evidence of a Rhodesian military tradition: Rhodesian troops had displayed little of their boasted aptitude for bush-fighting in the 1914–18 war; the fact that White Rhodesians took part in both World Wars was more a function of the simplicity of Rhodesian agrarian operations than of any inherent military qualities in Rhodesians; there were always deep fears of the settler manhood being wiped out in some great military catastrophe, so the preferred strategy was the dispersal of Whites as officers in Black units. In any case, after the Second World War the Rhodesian army was virtually disbanded. Thus any 'military tradition' is very, very recent, beginning in fact only in 1951, when the demands of British imperial strategy called for Rhodesian troops ready for deployment across colonial borders. A 'real' army, with specialists, tanks and war-planes came only with Federation. In 1961 the Rhodesian Light Infantry was formed, but even that was at first composed largely of British ex-army men, just as the Special Air Service was also largely British. Even after the break-up of the Federation in 1963, Britain still saw Southern Rhodesia as a vital imperial military resource and ensured that the territory got most of the Federal military resources.

UDI, of course, broke this imperial link. The question now was what Rhodesia's own 'military tradition' was going to be. The army was still not developed. The police, that semi-militarized first line of defence, still opposed the creation of a distinct military force, and in particular saw African protest and resistance as 'civil disobedience' to be punished by prosecution in the courts. Hence most 'intelligence' was collected for police and judicial purposes rather than for military ones. The police did not even tell the army about the Chinhoyi incursion and dealt with it themselves — in chaotic fashion, with no air support, no radio control, and nearly ultimate failure. After this, there had to be a Joint Operational Command, but a police view of intelligence persisted. 'Never', said Roberts, 'has so much intelligence been collected to so little point'.

Even when the army was called in it had no 'tradition' of its own to draw on, but slavishly applied techniques learned during its Malaysian experience. The only real Rhodesian innovation was the use of light-weight radios to maintain contact between 'sticks' of soldiers. Moreover, up to late 1977 the police and air force had an equal voice with the army in all decisions. Smith himself did not listen to military advice but gave his trust to his Secretary for Internal Affairs, Hostes Nicolle, who represented the old Native Department tradition and who could 'misunderstand Africans in three languages'. Internal Affairs never realized that their ground-level network had been completely subverted by the guerrillas.

So the civilians — Internal Affairs and the Police — believed that 'unrest' could be 'suppressed'. The army, claimed Roberts, had a much more realistic perspective. It realized that there must be a political solution but never got permission for a full-scale Malaysian-style 'hearts and minds' campaign. Protected Villages surrounded by a guerrilla-dominated countryside could never match the effectiveness of Malaysian-style transfers of population; Rhodesian 'psychological warfare' was half-hearted and ineffective. Even when the Internal Settlement came there was division, with Internal Affairs backing the 'Guard Force', the army backing Ndabaningi Sithole's 'Auxiliaries', and the police backing Abel Muzorewa's 'Auxiliaries'. And in the end the Rhodesians did not really fight a war to its full consequences. They were reluctant to suffer devastating casualties or to see property massively destroyed. The whole thing was, in Roberts's view, a 'holding operation' rather than a war — and maybe, he ended provocatively, the Rhodesians lost a war that they did not fight but won their holding operation, retaining White control of farming and industry.

Dumiso Dabengwa commented that it had seemed like a war to him: the SAS and the Selous Scouts had shown plenty of aggression and commitment; the regime had been prepared to use any 'dirty trick' against the guerrillas and to carry violence indiscriminately into neighbouring states. But, whatever one's reaction to Roberts's argument, the contrast between the Rhodesian forces and the guerrillas emerges more clearly from his paper than from Ellert's. Maybe one can state it, in Roberts's terms, as a contrast between 'civilians' who thought that a purely military answer was possible and soldiers who knew that it was not.

Roberts's analysis goes some way towards historicizing the Rhodesian side of the fighting rather than mythologizing it as most of the material published in South Africa has done. Perhaps further historical work on the Rhodesian forces could pose some of the questions we have raised about the guerrilla armies. The question of recruitment, for instance, is worth pursuing. How far were the Blacks who fought in the Rhodesian forces conscripts or 'volunteers'? How far were the Whites, for that matter? Were there some of the same tensions between 'veterans' and subsequent 'generations' of soldiers; between the educated and the not so educated? And just as there was within the guerrilla armies — and in ZIPRA in particular — a tendency towards 'conventional' war, so within the Rhodesian forces there was a tendency towards 'guerrilla' war. Roberts's assessment puts the bloody exploits of the SAS and the Selous Scouts (such best-sellers in South Africa) in perspective, but they remain interesting as a dreadful sort of tribute to the guerrillas. One of the bitter ironies of the war is the training of the first RENAMO recruits in how to be guerrillas by the Rhodesian CIO and SAS, complete with instructions on how to use spirit mediums and compose *chimurenga* songs in the style of ZANLA.[3]

DISUNITIES

A common theme to both ZAPU/ZIPRA and ZANU/ZANLA has been disunity — both their failure to come together to form a single front and the regular cleavages within each of them. Dumiso Dabengwa's chapter in this volume offers a salutary example of frank disclosure on this subject. He describes how the frontline states called a unity meeting in Mbeya, Tanzania, in 1967, a time when 'ZAPU was very active militarily'. The unity accord involved a Joint Military Command and the deployment of ZANU cadres in the country alongside ZAPU fighters. This was formally agreed by the political leaders of ZAPU and ZANU but 'the major commanders of ZAPU did not participate in the implementation of the agreement'. They were deliberately left out in a move which 'amounted to deliberate sabotage . . . on the part of ZAPU'. This was because ZANU had at that time 'a very small number of trained men and little support inside Zimbabwe'. The ZAPU leadership expected soon to be able to open up the north-eastern front in alliance with FRELIMO and thus be able to tap 'large numbers of recruits'. So 'our view at that stage was simply that ZANU must disband and rejoin ZAPU'. In retrospect, Dabengwa admits, 'it was not correct for ZAPU to have taken such a decision'.

But Dabengwa still finds it difficult to do historical justice to those who split ZAPU itself. His account of the original ZAPU/ZANU split, for instance, depicts the founders of ZANU as 'those who harboured secret agendas and who had been waiting for an opportunity to promote their personal ambitions by dividing the organization'; those who, like himself, remained loyal, on the other hand, were 'those who interpreted set-backs in the struggle as normal in the dialectic of change . . . requiring patience, study and occasional adjustment of strategies and tactics'. His discussion of the March 11 movement within ZAPU in 1971 suggests that the young 'left' critics were 'under some external influence'. His account of the emergence of ZIPA in the mid-1970s, first as a united army and then as the so-called 'Third Force', sees the whole episode essentially as a hindrance to the logical development of ZIPRA. ZIPRA elements within ZIPA found the ZIPA strategy 'to be completely disjointed'; they resented having to work with ZANLA cadres who 'were not trained at all'; ZIPRA men were then victimized and some shot in cold blood as 'ZIPA started collapsing in 1975'. These were 'bitter experiences'.

Of course, ZANLA leaders have been no more — and often even less — generous to their own internal oppositions. Thus the Nhari 'rebels' of 1974 have been portrayed as the tools of Rhodesian Intelligence, the ZIPA leaders have been seen as ultra-left fanatics, and so on. The conference, however, was concerned to test all these propositions and to try to understand such internal oppositions in their own terms. We did not get far with Nhari or with the 'Vashandi' workers group in Mozambique, though Fay Chung has some interesting things to say about them in her chapter in the second volume and had yet more interesting things to say during the discussions, some of which are reflected in our introduction to that volume.

But David Moore's paper on ZIPA, which appears in revised form as a chapter in this volume, was a major work of rehabilitation. He saw ZIPA not just as a failed attempt at unity between ZIPRA and ZANLA, not just as an obstacle to the logical development of the mainstream guerrilla armies, not merely as an ultra-left deviation, but as an immensely promising innovation. The 'libels' against ZIPA he saw as prefiguring much contemporary ideological confrontation.

> Such oppositions are apparent today in the confrontations between the university students' contemporary dissent and the reaction of the ruling party and the state to it. ZIPA was composed of young and idealistic members of a state or ruling class in the making . . . They were condemned as 'know-alls' and quelled with the violence of a nascent state . . . A study of ZIPA might illustrate important tendencies within the Zimbabwean state class in the ways in which it deals with threats to its ideology and its hold on power.

But he also sees ZIPA as illustrating the potentials in an alternative ideology. ZIPA leaders were trying to base an effective unity which could win the guerrilla war on the foundation of shared ideology, explicitly on 'Marxist principles'. This meant a determined effort, first at self-education and then at ideological diffusion through the whole army. Such ideological unity would overcome ethnic differences and the factional legacies of past in-fighting. It would sweep away the sort of pragmatic reservations which had sabotaged the Mbeya Accord. Alas, ZIPA had no time: its apparent élitism created resentment; the 'old guard' were able to break it and imprison its leaders.

There is no need for us to summarize a chapter whose argument is set out fully in this volume. Whether or not readers agree with it — and Moore himself stressed the contemporary political function of propositions about the past — there is no doubt that it reinstates ZIPA as much more than a side-show. Indeed ZIPA dominated the fighting in eastern Zimbabwe during several months in 1976, and much of the discussion in our second volume about the interaction of guerrillas and rural society hinges around the contrast between the attitudes of ZIPA and earlier, and later, ZANLA approaches to rural culture and religion.

OVERLAPS

ZIPA sought to detach ZANLA and ZIPRA soldiers from their specific 'traditions' so as to combine them in a single force. There was, however, another sort of interaction between ZIPRA and ZANLA on the ground which does not appear in any of the chapters in this volume. This is the simultaneous operation of the two guerrilla armies, as distinct forces, but in the same regions. Dumiso Dabengwa made reference to such interactions when answering a question about ZIPRA's intelligence reports. This, he said, was not concerned with providing information about ZANLA or ZANU, except when guerrilla groups overlapped. Then reports came in about clashes and tensions which, as he wryly admitted, 'always blamed ZANLA for the difficulties'. Sister Janice McLaughlin, who has had access to the ZANLA archives, said that she had seen similar reports from the other side. Returning for a moment to the question of the perceived differences between the two armies, it would be interesting to study the stereotypes of each other which emerge from such reports.

The practical consequences of such overlaps plainly varied greatly from war zone to war zone. We have already mentioned Mberengwa, as described by Ngwabi Bhebe, where ZANLA waged war and ZIPRA concentrated on recruitment (with an additional detail supplied by Jeremy Brickhill that the ZIPRA cadre who set up the recruitment base at Mount Nhamande was a deserter from a ZIPA detachment which had entered the country from Mozambique). Bhebe showed that the Mberengwa zone was extraordinary. It was 'the most highly contested' of all zones between the guerrillas and the Rhodesian forces, containing as it did key economic resources (chrome, asbestos, emeralds, ranching, citrus) and straddling key routes to the south. The Rhodesians never abandoned this zone to the 'auxiliaries' and did not allow even 'semi-liberated' areas to the guerrillas. So it was a zone in which ZIPRA did not fight but recruited — very different from the semi-liberated zones in the north-west where ZIPRA's dominance was so total that it became necessary for them to install regular forces; and very different, too, from the area described in the only other conference paper to discuss the overlap of ZIPRA and ZANLA — Ncube and Ranger's chapter in volume two on the war in the Matopos. Here, in ideal guerrilla territory, both ZIPRA and ZANLA operated; here, the incursion of ZANLA into the very heartland of ZAPU's cultural nationalism and political symbolism provoked special tensions. Some of the consequences of this are discussed in our introduction to our second volume.

LEGACIES

The conference asked what have been the legacies in independent Zimbabwe of these patterns of violence: of the actions on the ground of ZIPRA and ZIPA and ZANLA; of the 'dirty tricks' of the Rhodesian forces; of the bitter experiences of attempted unity. There is much discussion of some of the legacies for society in our second volume; here we are concerned with the legacies for armies and for soldiers.

One such legacy, of course, is the Zimbabwean National Army. For once we may allow Teresa Barnes's ex-combatants to have the first word, before coming on to Abiodun Alao's treatment of the integration of the armies. Her informants reveal the immediate reservations felt by so many guerrillas:

> I decided to quit the army and not to join the [new national army]. Not because I was injured. In fact I was not interested in the way the integration was taking place, whereby the ZANLA forces were to be trained by the Rhodesian forces as not having achieved enough military training. They said that we were guerrillas and not soldiers. Yet I knew I could do as much, the same as they did. My expectations were . . . that we would be attested into the army without facing any difficulties . . . that as trained soldiers we were going to start earning salaries for being soldiers. I also expected ZANLA and ZIPRA forces to be regarded as the super-army for the country — those who would be called when things were very tough. I didn't expect the kind of integration which took place.

Her ZIPRA informant, 'X', was caught up in the fighting between ZIPRA and ZANLA at Entumbane and hence lost any chance he had to become part of the new army.

Despite these difficulties, Alao's presentation to the conference hailed the integration as an extraordinary achievement. He laid stress on the development of a 'professional' ethos which had largely over-ridden 'primordial alliances and pre-Independence divisions'. He remarked that the major 'blow' to integrating professionalism was the 'initial creation of the Fifth Brigade', with its exclusively ZANLA recruitment and its Korean training. But at once he went on to add that 'the political controversy arising from the activities of the brigade in Matabeleland is outside the consideration of this paper' and to assert that 'the activities of the army in Matabeleland were largely the activities of a brigade', and hence not 'a sufficient criterion to measure the army as a whole'.

These judgements were challenged in the ensuing conference discussion. Delegates asked whether the 'political controversy' arising from the anti-dissident campaign in Matabeleland was not also a controversy about the legitimate use of force and appropriate army tactics. Could one blame the Fifth Brigade alone for what seemed an extraordinary failure to carry the lessons of the guerrilla war into Independence? In the army's use of force there seemed to have been an odd mix of continuities. On the one hand there was the apolitical 'professionalism' of the old Rhodesian forces, with many of their tactics being deployed, together with the same notion that violent repression alone could resolve the problem. On the other hand there were the techniques of ZANU mobilization so that the Fifth Brigade used the liberation war nickname, *Gukurahundi*, and organized *pungwes*, though now as the forces for the state rather than as insurgents. Both responses seemed equally ill-conceived. The military repression inherited from the Rhodesian forces could no more break the 'dissidents' than it had been able to break the guerrillas. As for the Fifth Brigade's politicization techniques, so successful during the liberation war, they could not succeed when used in combination with state terror. It was, in short, politicization without politics.

Now that unity and amnesty have compelled us to re-examine the history of the liberation war itself, should they not also compel us, it was asked, to examine what happened in Matabeleland in the 1980s and to ask whether it is possible to break out of these kinds of distorted continuities? It seemed that this task was all the more urgent in view of the continuities still visible along Zimbabwe's eastern border, where Protected Villages have been revived in the war against RENAMO. One day it would be fascinating, it was thought, to examine how the Zimbabwean National Army had dealt with an enemy inside Mozambique originally trained to copy the techniques of ZANLA.

We can sandwich Alao's presentation between the voices of ex-combatants because Barnes's 'X' has pertinent things to say about what happened in Matabeleland:

> At the time of demobilization in 1982 we formed a co-operative with some of my colleagues who were staying together at the assembly point. We had been fighting together . . . I stayed there up to 1984. My stay there was not really nice; I eventually decided to leave. On several occasions I was arrested, suspected of being a dissident; I was arrested, detained for some months, sometimes for weeks, sometimes for days, beaten up and things like that. Just because I was a former combatant and I belonged to the other party. So most of the combatants were actually suspect . . . I was picked up, detained and tortured.

There was little discussion at the conference about the 'dissident' side of the violence in Matabeleland in the 1980s, but evidence has recently become available which allows us to make an initial reconstruction for the sake of balance. On the 'dissident' side, too, it seems as though similarly distorted continuities from the war prevailed. Some 'dissidents' were indeed ex-ZIPRA combatants but they now operated in a context very different from that evoked by Jeremy Brickhill. Although the state suspected ZAPU of backing the 'dissidents', in fact the party structures tried hard to keep aloof from them. The 'dissidents' certainly no longer operated within the political guidelines laid down by rural party representatives, as Brickhill argues for the ZIPRA guerrillas. The result was a recourse to terror and the recruitment or coercion of *mujibas*. Both 'dissidents' and the Fifth Brigade coarsened and misused guerrilla traditions from the liberation war. In Botswana, among the young hot-heads who gathered at Dukwe Camp, the divorce between violence and politics was yet more extreme. Some of them were ready to accept South African support for the so-called 'Super-ZAPU' on the grounds that in order to cross a river one has to ride on the crocodile's back. When rebuked by ZAPU elders in Dukwe the youngsters repudiated their authority, claiming that they themselves had been 'born ZAPU'. The ZAPU elders scoffed at the very idea: no-one could be born ZAPU, they replied: one became ZAPU through political education and experience. But with many of the young, violence overrode politics: ZAPU elders in Dukwe were assaulted, and alliances were made with South Africa.[4]

The result for the people of the rural areas of Matabeleland, caught between the 'dissidents', the Fifth Brigade and Super-ZAPU, was terrible. For a record of their experience readers should turn to Richard Werbner's chapter in the second volume of this book and to his recently published book.[5]

There remained one further question about 'legacies': what happened to the soldiers after 1980, particularly to that great majority who were not integrated into the national army or detained and beaten as suspect 'dissidents'? This question is addressed by two chapters in this volume. Norma Kriger writes on the politics of war heroes — the elevation of some of the soldier dead into national heroes and a political resource. Teresa Barnes's 'Life After the Liberation War', which we have cited so often in this introduction, expresses the view of the living ex-combatants and their sense of exclusion. We do not propose to quote it any further but to let its eloquent text speak for itself for the feelings of ex-combatants about demobilization in all senses of that word.

TERROR, TRAUMA AND THE HEALING OF MEMORIES

Norma Kriger presented one paper to the conference — an initial comparison between ZANLA and SWAPO guerrillas in Namibia. She has contributed another to this volume. But it was neither of these papers which the conference wanted to discuss with her. Participants were anxious to discuss her views on guerrilla violence and intimidation as first presented in her doctoral thesis and as expressed in her revised and recently published book.[6] She defended herself against the misapprehension that she had ever explained civilian interactions with guerrillas solely in such terms, pointing out that the core of her work dealt precisely with groups within rural society which took advantage of the guerrilla presence so as to resolve inequalities and grievances. This theme is explored in our introduction to the second volume. Meanwhile we must note that a lively discussion ensued at the conference about the significance of 'terror' as a historical topic.

It is possible, of course, to take the position that all wars necessarily involve violence and horror and guerrilla wars more than most, as regimes strike at civilian populations and guerrillas search for 'sell-outs'. But a number of conference participants urged that beyond this inevitable violence there was a need to look at terror — the purposive but illegitimate violence deployed in various ways by both sides in the war. There was a need to look at Rhodesian poisonings, mass graves and public displays of bodies; at guerrilla killings of 'witches' and refusals to allow the dead to be buried. If we did not remember such instances of terror, it was argued, there was a danger that illegitimate violence might survive as one of the legacies of the war. As Jeremy Brickhill dramatically put it, 'complicity in silence allows Rhodesian terror and guerrilla terror to meet in the darkness and mate'. Certainly Brickhill himself had no intention of being complicit in silence about Rhodesian or South African 'dirty tricks', and immediately after the conference became involved in making a remarkable television documentary about the Rhodesian regime's poisonings and assassinations.

Moreover, the experience of terror sets up severe traumas which carry on long after the war. In our second volume we discuss the question of societal trauma and healing; here we deal with the traumas of the soldiers themselves. In Richard Werbner's chapter in the second volume he tells us that he found ex-combatants in the south-west unwilling to talk about their war experiences, since they had seen so many terrible things. Barnes's informants admittedly show no such reluctance, but one has only to turn to novels and poems to see that coming to terms with the memory and significance of terror has developed into a major theme of Zimbabwean imaginative confrontations with the war. Even if there have not yet been many guerrilla autobiographies, in fiction guerrillas confront not only the brutality of the enemy but of themselves. Of course, there is a dialectical relationship between the two. Brickhill himself argued that guerrilla fear and execution of 'witches' was largely a result of the Rhodesian campaign of distributing poisoned clothing to guerrillas, thus ensuring a lingering and mysterious death. Others urged that the balance of terror, so heavily weighted on the Rhodesian side, should always be remembered.

A NOTE ON THE AUXILIARIES

As we said in the 'General Introduction', no presentation was made at the conference, nor has anything been written, about the Security Force Auxiliaries (SFA); but UANC papers recently made available allow us to make a few remarks. UANC propaganda, of course, contrasted guerrilla force with SFA legitimacy. The SFA, it was claimed, did not execute witches, since even *varoyi* were in favour of majority rule; they did not interfere in domestic disputes. A brightly coloured poster in English and Shona contrasted oppressive ZIPRA with protective SFA:

> See the ZIPRA comrades and stooges of power-hungry Nkomo close your clinics and send you away without medicine. They do not care for you or for your children. ZIPRA are closing your schools so that your children cannot learn lest they become cleverer than they are. They are frightened of elections in April. They will try to stop you people from voting . . . See now the men of the SFA. They are helping you people with medicine and looking after the children. They are here to fight ZIPRA so that the children can go back to school to learn how to become voters for the Majority Rule Government which is coming in April.

Yet even within the UANC papers themselves there is plenty of evidence of another reality. One striking letter may suffice to make the point. Thus on 2 February 1979 the Headmaster of Gora Council School, Mhondoro, wrote to the General Secretary of the UANC. The day before, he said,

> the Auxiliary Forces entered the school and forced all pupils and teachers to assemble outside the classrooms . . . Two male teachers on the staff were forced to give political speeches to the pupils. Later the pupils were forced to chant political songs and slogans. The pupils were ordered forcibly to ridicule their teachers by saying together in a chorus: 'This teacher is a sell-out', etc., taking each teacher in turn. A female member on the staff was taken aside for questioning and was then shamefully beaten up in front of the school. The Auxiliary Forces openly boasted that all laws were in their hands and that they could do anything they wanted. They also issued a threat that some of us who were present were going to die at the last moment and yet majority rule was just round the corner. The school pupils were frightened and intimidated by the holding up of guns and the shouting of the Auxiliaries.

There is much more to be discovered about the Auxiliary forces' use of terror.

HEALING

But the study of terror is not so much a matter of assigning blame. The point is rather the *effect* of being the victim or perpetrator of terror. That is why we end this introduction, as we shall end the introduction to the second volume, with the topic of healing. There we shall look at religious and ritual healing. Here we end with healing through historical inquiry — with Jeremy Brickhill's chapter on the work of the Mafela Trust. In this chapter, so different from his formal discussion of ZIPRA military strategy, Brickhill deals with an enterprise both to right the record and also to heal memories.

Essentially the work of the Mafela Trust is an attempt, through field research, to list the names, next-of-kin and places of burial of the ZIPRA dead. But it has become much more than a commemoration of neglected heroes: it responds to the grief of survivors and their desire to carry out burial rites or to obtain certificates of death. In their inquiries the researchers have heard much of guerrilla heroism, much about Rhodesian terror, and something about guerrilla brutality. They have found guerrilla graves already established and tended by the people. They have also found memories of unmourned guerrilla dead remembered for violence rather than for heroism. They have come under much pressure to investigate the 'disappearances' of the 1980s. Above all, they have encountered the continuing suffering of those who were either civilians or guerrillas during the war.

The Mafela Trust responds to this need not only by identifying the dead but also by restoring the sense that, despite many appearances, the violence and suffering were significant. Teresa Barnes's informant, 'X', himself a ZIPRA guerrilla from Gwanda and himself a victim of irrational violence after 1980, nevertheless remains illumined by this sense of significance:

> I don't regret that I joined the liberation struggle. Not at all. I don't. I think that was part of my contribution to the liberation of this country. If I say I regret having joined the liberation struggle, then I would be saying that I regret having liberated my country, which I don't think is right. Things are not OK now, but the fact is that we liberated ourselves (although some people actually hijacked the revolution). I think I made an important contribution, and I'm proud of it.

This is certainly a healthy memory of the war. But we think that what the work of the Mafela Trust shows, and what the discussions of the conference showed, is that there can be no triumphal short cut to such a healthy mind. The experience of the war has to be confronted in its entirety — as 'X' confronts the totality of his experiences — before this sort of health can be achieved.

1

ZIPRA in the Zimbabwe War of National Liberation

DUMISO DABENGWA

INTRODUCTION

The definitive history of Zimbabwe's liberation struggle is yet to be written. So far most attempts have been either lacking in objectivity (even openly biased in some cases) or have been merely brief sketches of events. This is unfortunate because the liberation war has had and will continue to have profound consequences for the future of Zimbabwe and other countries in the Southern African region. A complete history of the struggle for national liberation is a long way from being produced and will only be achieved when the chroniclers of the struggle are no longer afraid to confront the truth head-on and openly, and have rid themselves of biases resulting from our recent political past — a past which saw the brutal killings of innocent people in the name of unity, peace, stability and progress. Unless our scholars can rise above the fear of being isolated and even victimized for telling the truth, we shall continue to be told half-truths or outright lies which will not help unite our nation or encourage a common effort at national development.

For too long historians have failed our people because of their timidity, sectarianism and outright opportunism. Conditions should be created in Zimbabwe wherein a new breed of a social scientist (historian, political scientist, economist, sociologist, and so on) can emerge. This class of scholars should be capable of withstanding threats and intimidation and will rise above those racial, ethnic and tribal considerations which are inimical to national and regional development. This new breed of Zimbabwean social scientist ought to be able to oppose the suppression of any information, and should develop an ever-critical mind with respect to all facts, especially purported facts, and towards the actions of political leaders. Anything short of a tradition of selfless inquiry and exposure of the truth will certainly lead to a nation of sycophants and robots who do not possess the power of independent thought which we should all cherish. This conference on the history of the liberation struggle in Zimbabwe is an excellent beginning of the articulation of a comprehensive history of our country and our nation.

The writing of the history of our national liberation struggle requires conferences such as this to help stimulate thinking and to promote the sharing of both the data and the research methodologies on the struggle for national liberation. In this context, my contribution on the role of ZIPRA in the Zimbabwe War of National Liberation is only a preliminary draft which covers only one aspect of the history of the struggle: that of the armed conflict. I expect that my contribution will be informed and improved by new data which may come to light from the comments of other conference participants.

The initial phase of the struggle

The Zimbabwe African People's Union (ZAPU) was formed on 17 December 1961 as a direct successor to the National Democratic Union Party (NDP) which had been banned by the settler regime barely nine months after its formation in 1961. The NDP's predecessor was the Southern Rhodesian African National Congress (SRANC), the first national political organization to struggle for the democratic rights of Africans in Rhodesia. Prior to SRANC there had been various localized and much smaller organizations fighting for a political voice for the Black people of this country. However, it was not until the formation of SRANC that a united political organization with a national character appeared, calling for independence and majority rule.

This call for independence and majority rule was continued by the NDP and was more clearly enunciated by ZAPU. Both these organizations appealed to, and had membership across, ethnic and tribal groupings throughout the country. At that time the language one spoke did not seem to matter: people made a conscious effort to understand languages other than their mother-tongue. The unity of the people against settler rule was taken for granted. Everybody was referred to as 'mwana wevhu' ('son of the soil'). This Shona phrase was used untranslated because its meaning was comprehensible to all.

Although there were a number of smaller political parties such as ZNP, PASU and others which also called for an end to White rule, they were not national in character. Because of the overwhelming authority of, first, the NDP and, later, of ZAPU, many of the smaller parties soon disappeared from the political scene. It is interesting to note that most of Zimbabwe's post-Independence government leaders were members of ZAPU in the early 1960s.

Throughout the struggle the settler regime routinely attempted to crush political parties and divide the people in order to weaken their resolve for independence. The first such attempt came with the banning of SRANC in 1959 and the arrest of some of its leaders. Forbidding open mass political activity was calculated to destroy support for the freedom movement and to diminish the possibilities for a united movement against colonialism. However, when NDP was formed and mass political rallies resumed, there was an even greater unity among the people. The same pattern was repeated with the banning of the NDP and the subsequent formation of ZAPU. However, when ZAPU was banned, developments took on a new turn — to the detriment of unity within ZAPU. The settler establishment had correctly calculated that the repeated banning of opposition political organizations and the detention of their leaders would sooner or later have an effect. One such consequence, which was to bedevil the nationalist movement well into Independence, was the formation of the Zimbabwe African National Union (ZANU) on 8 August 1963.

The repeated banning of nationalist movements meant that many people feared that the struggle was not making any progress. There were four types of people who were affected by the severe measures taken by the colonial regime against the nationalist movement. Firstly, there were the impatient who were upset by anything that appeared too conservative — even though they were often unable to find an alternative course of action. Secondly, there were the opportunists who, because they harboured secret agendas, were ready to use any normal difficulties in the nationalist movement as an opportunity for division. Thirdly, there were the ignorant who fell prey to the manipulation of information by the impatient and the opportunistic. The fourth group consisted of those who interpreted setbacks in the struggle as normal and who accepted change as being a long and protracted process requiring patience, study and an occasional adjustment of strategies and tactics without, however, destroying or renouncing the nationalist movement.

The 1963 split in ZAPU was engineered largely by those who harboured secret agendas and who had been waiting for an opportunity to promote their personal ambitions by dividing the organization. The opportunity for the split was facilitated by two related developments. One was the repeated banning of nationalist parties by the settler regime. The other was ZAPU's response to the constitutional talks held in London between the Rhodesian delegation led by Whitehead and the British Government.

After the failure of the London talks and the banning of political parties, it became clear that we had to prepare for a different approach to our struggle. It was decided that the only way left was for the African people to liberate themselves through forceful means as all peaceful methods had failed. Thus in 1963 we started building up a fighting force that would be able to initiate the armed struggle.

Cde James Chikerema was appointed as head of the Department of 'Special Affairs' which was mainly concerned with the armed struggle. Cde Chikerema started recruiting young people throughout the country for military training. I was among one of the first groups that left the country for Zambia in 1963. Towards the end of 1963 we left Zambia for Tanzania *en route* to various countries in the then socialist block. My group, for instance, went to train in the Soviet Union. After training most of the groups assembled in Zambia toward the end of 1964 and in early 1965.

Discussions were held with Cde Chikerema who was still head of 'Special Affairs' to work out a programme of military operations. Three clear recommendations arose from the planning meetings; these were:

a) We needed to operate as a force and not just a department.
b) We needed to create a base for an army.
c) We needed to deploy small units of two to three men and women inside Rhodesia to infiltrate different parts of the country in order to:
    i)   Carry out further recruitment;
    ii) Reconnoitre and sabotage small economic targets such as post offices, communication networks, electricity supplies, and so on.

As a result of these resolutions which were adopted by ZAPU's Special Affairs department in early 1965, we created what was called the 'Armed Wing' of ZAPU with a small command structure (the commander, the head of logistics, the head of intelligence and reconnaissance and the head of operations and personnel). This was followed soon after by the deployment of small units into Rhodesia. The idea at this stage was simply that groups of two or three men should infiltrate different parts of the country to carry out further recruitment and to reconnoitre targets such as telecommunications systems, electricity supply installations, and so on. As a result of our efforts, there were many acts of sabotage of enemy interests in 1965.

In 1966 we started recruiting larger numbers of trained personnel and decided to increase the size and number of our operating units. We began sending units of seven or eight men into Rhodesia to join the smaller groups which were already inside the country. The new, larger groups had to first liaise with groups already inside the country, especially those in the area of entry before mounting any operations. Not all of these units succeeded in linking up with the small groups before they were intercepted by the enemy. Some groups had to fight in self-defence and a few individuals were captured. Others managed to slip through and carried out their assignments. Contrary to claims that ZANU started the armed struggle in 1966 in Chinhoyi, the fact is that ZAPU's armed struggle started in 1965 when the small units were sent into the country.

In 1967 ZAPU was approached by the African National Congress (ANC) of South Africa with a proposal for joint operations. This was because the ANC had trained a large number of *Umkhonto we Sizwe* cadres. They had tried to infiltrate their trained men into South Africa through Botswana but most of them had been intercepted and their weapons confiscated by the Botswana Security Forces.

In addition, by this time (1967) there were already units of the South African Army operating together with the Rhodesian army along Rhodesia's border with Zambia. It is important to emphasize this fact because it became an important consideration in ZAPU's evaluation of the ANC's proposal for joint operations. The strategy of the South African Army was to stop the ANC at the Zambezi. They had, therefore, joined forces with the Rhodesian Security Forces before we considered joint operations with the ANC.

It was because the South Africans were already assisting the Rhodesians together with their problems in Botswana that the ANC approached ZAPU for help. In the circumstances, ZAPU thought that the ANC should be assisted by the ZAPU Armed Wing to cross through Rhodesia. However, it should be pointed out that there were those within ZAPU who thought any assistance to *Umkhonto we Sizwe* would result in a greater South African army presence in support of the Rhodesians. The counter argument to this position was that, even if ZAPU refused to assist, the ANC could and would cross through Rhodesia without ZAPU's permission and ZAPU would not know what was happening. Rhodesia was as much enemy ground to the ANC cadres as South Africa itself. Moreover, ZAPU could not claim to be in control of the country at the time.

In view of these considerations, ZAPU agreed that it would be prudent to allow the ANC passage through Rhodesia assisted by ZAPU. There were several advantages to this strategy. Firstly, ZAPU did not want the people to misunderstand the position of the ANC if *Umkhonto we Sizwe* should clash with the enemy while in transit. It was, therefore, necessary that ZAPU accompany them to explain to the people why the ANC cadres were in the country and why they could fight on Rhodesian soil. Secondly, the cadres could not go through the country without relying on the local people. We had no doubt that if ANC cadres tried to obtain assistance from our people on their own, our people would probably not understand why the ANC was in the country and would not co-operate with, and might even betray, them. It was necessary that ZAPU cadres be on the spot to give the necessary explanations.

The joint ZAPU/ANC 'Batoka Gorge Campaign' was undertaken in August 1967 as part of the above strategy. A joint ZAPU/ANC unit of 100 men was sent into Rhodesia. Their instructions were precise. Once they were inside the country the majority of the ZAPU men would split up into smaller units and proceed to their designated places of operations in Matabeleland North while one group of ZAPU men would escort the ANC comrades to the Limpopo.

Despite what others have said to the contrary, I am still convinced that our decision to work with the ANC in this way was correct. If we had to do it again we would do exactly what we did then. Our analysis of the situation was correct. It is absolute nonsense to suggest, as our critics and detractors have done, that the South Africans came into Rhodesia in 1967 because of ZAPU's 'joint operations' with the ANC. To the contrary, there is solid evidence that the South African army had been deployed in Rhodesia long before the ZAPU-ANC alliance and they remained until the end of the war. In fact the number of South African troops in Rhodesia continued to increase throughout the war although the last large group of *Umkhonto we Sizwe* members to use Rhodesia was in 1968 when the ZAPU-ANC alliance launched another major operation, this time through Sipolilo (now Guruve).

On this occasion an even larger infiltration was accomplished. This time the majority of ZAPU men remained in the north-east of Mashonaland while a section of ZAPU soldiers accompanied the ANC cadres to the Limpopo. It was understood that the ANC would, as far as possible, avoid contact with the Rhodesian Security Forces and were to fight only if attacked. It is important to emphasize that at this stage we were not thinking of creating an international fighting force. We saw the Zimbabwean and South African struggles as being properly carried out by the indigenous peoples of the two territories. However, we recognized the common nature of these struggles and the need for mutual support. Hence we gave logistical support to the ANC. We did not intend at that stage that ZAPU fighters should fight in South Africa for the ANC nor did our comrades in the ANC want to have their guerrillas fighting in Rhodesia for ZAPU. When the ANC did fight in Rhodesia it was because they were attacked by the Rhodesians and South Africans. We were completely against internationalizing our military campaign. The struggle was internationalized by the co-operation of the South African and Rhodesian regimes.

The ANC rarely used Rhodesia as a transit route after 1968 but, as already pointed out, the South African Army remained in Rhodesia until Independence. Indeed, as some observers have pointed out fairly convincingly, elements of this army remained after Independence and played a destructive role during the so-called 'dissident' period. During the struggle for independence, the basic premise of the South African government was that, rather than allow Rhodesia to fall, they would fight alongside Rhodesian forces to keep the ANC at bay in Zambia. The strategists of the South African army reasoned that, if Rhodesia was to fall, South Africa would soon be fighting its battles on the Limpopo and inside South Africa.

Their idea was not merely to intercept ANC fighters but to ensure that Rhodesia did not fall. Our reasoning was, therefore, that if *Umkhonto we Sizwe* cadres were not assisted to enter South Africa, the South African army would be able to concentrate its forces in Rhodesia to our detriment but if *Umkhonto we Sizwe* were well established in South Africa, the army would have to shift its attention onto developments inside its own borders. This is in fact what happened after the ANC established alternative routes, such as through Mozambique, for its returning fighters.

The Batoka Gorge and Sipolilo ZAPU/ANC campaigns created a certain confusion about what was going on in the struggle for Zimbabwe. Certain African leaders questioned the wisdom of ZAPU engaging in joint campaigns with the ANC while remaining at variance with ZANU. It was against this background that the OAU Liberation Committee organized a meeting at Mbeya in Tanzania to discuss the unification of the military wings of ZAPU and ZANU.

MBEYA AND ITS AFTERMATH

The prevailing opinion within the OAU at that time, especially among the Frontline States, was that the organization could more or less impose unity on the Zimbabwe liberation movements because the movements depended on the OAU and Frontline States for practical and diplomatic support. Caught between the wishes of their host countries and the demands of the struggle for the independence of their homeland, the liberation movements at times entered into pacts without thinking them through, or without first establishing their material basis. The Mbeya accord was one such pact. We met at Mbeya in 1967 while ZAPU was very active militarily. A loose unity arrangement under what was called a Joint Military Command (JMC) was reached. Under the terms of the agreement, ZAPU fighters were to be deployed to fight inside Rhodesia together with ZANU cadres in more or less the same way as ZAPU and *Umkhonto we Sizwe* had done. The implementation of this programme was left to the JMC which was headed by both ZAPU and ZANU commanders.

The political leadership of both ZAPU and ZANU was present at Mbeya and jointly appointed the JMC. It was agreed that both parties would field their fighters under the JMC and that a joint military leadership would implement the Mbeya agreement. But very little was actually achieved and the objectives of the agreement were not realized.

There were a number of reasons why the Mbeya agreement collapsed at its outset. One of the major reasons was that the main commanders of ZAPU deliberately chose not to be involved in the implementation of the agreement and decided to appoint junior command elements to work with the senior command elements from ZANU. Obviously, this made it impossible for the programme to be implemented. ZAPU's decision amounted to a deliberate sabotage of the Mbeya agreement.

The rationale behind this decision was that ZAPU was being forced to join hands with ZANU at a time when ZANU possessed a very small number of trained men and had little support inside Rhodesia. At that time, ZANU was not able to attract many recruits from inside the country nor from the community of exiles in Zambia. ZAPU was of the opinion that it would be imprudent to unite with an organization whose armed wing consisted only of the command element and a few soldiers who were continually being sent for training and re-training without doing any actual fighting. Thus, from ZAPU's point of view, it was necessary to sabotage the JMC by ensuring that the party's senior commanders did not participate in the implementation of the Mbeya agreement. This meant the collapse of the JMC. ZAPU did not want to have the bulk of the fighting army (consisting of ZAPU cadres) under the command of ZAPU/ZANU commanders. The ZAPU political wing was particularly opposed to unity at this stage. Cde Chikerema refused to attend the Mbeya meeting to found the JMC and sent J. Z. Moyo instead, with instructions to find a way to ensure that the JMC proposal did not succeed. If the OAU insisted on a unity agreement, Chikerema's instructions were to let ZAPU junior officers sit with Josiah Tongogara and see what they could do. He instructed his senior commanders Akim Ndlovu, myself and others to continue concentrating on the armed struggle as the armed wing of ZAPU and not as part of the JMC. Rightly or wrongly, this was the politics of the day. In retrospect, it was not correct for ZAPU to have taken such a decision.

Another reason why ZAPU was very reluctant to implement the JMC was that the party had by then started on a programme of joint operations with FRELIMO to open the Tete Front. Through field commanders such as Robson Manyika, ZAPU was actively assisting FRELIMO with the logistics of transporting its personnel. We were looking forward to the completion of this exercise because we were getting regular reports from the survivors of the Sipolilo Campaign (who were working as farm-labourers throughout the north-eastern part of Rhodesia) that they had completed their reconnaissance and had large numbers of recruits waiting to be sent out of the country for military training.

ZAPU had worked very hard to make sure that FRELIMO succeeded in opening the Tete Corridor and was most reluctant to give the north-eastern part of Rhodesia to ZANU which was not pulling its weight. ZANU at this point was doing very badly. It was trying hard but was not making any headway while ZAPU seemed to be forging ahead. We saw the JMC as a means of forcing us to carry ZANU on our backs. There were some African leaders who, by virtue of their own role in the split in ZAPU in 1963, would not countenance ZAPU successes — especially if ZANU could not also bask in the sunlight of such successes. Our view at that stage was that ZANU must disband and rejoin ZAPU. That was the thinking. It was not that we did not want to work with ZANU but that we thought ZANU needed to confess its failure as a splinter party.

CONSEQUENCES OF THE 1971 ZAPU SPLIT

In 1970 and 1971 ZAPU began a process of appraising the results of its military campaigns between 1965 and 1969, finding out if the party's strategy was correct, looking back at the operations carried out up to that point, and finding out if and where mistakes had been made. This self-evaluation exercise triggered serious problems inside ZAPU. J. Z. Moyo issued a paper 'On the Observations of our Struggle' which was critical of the manner in which certain operations had been carried out, notably Chikerema's publicity methods such as the filming of freedom fighters crossing the Zambezi. Moyo felt that such publicity jeopardized our entire strategy as much as it compromised the security of Zambia. This paper aroused severe disagreement among ZAPU's political leadership which at that time was composed of James Chikerema, George Nyandoro, J. Z. Moyo, Edward Ndlovu, T. G. Silundika and Jane Ngwenya. Chikerema emphasized that the political leadership had no right to decide on a military matter which was an issue to be resolved by himself alone as head of ZAPU's Department of Special Affairs. He did not accept the criticisms made by J. Z. Moyo.

In the meantime Chikerema had organized a group led by Walter Mthimkhulu within the army to safeguard his own interests. However, Mthimkhulu's group mutinied against Chikerema and arrested both military and political leaders such as J. Z. Moyo and T. G. Silundika. They also wanted to arrest Chikerema and Nyandoro but could not find them. When the crisis spread to combatants in ZAPU camps in Zambia and Tanzania, the Zambian Government intervened and succeeded in putting down the mutiny. The Zambians took the ZAPU political leaders to a remote place in Northern Zambia where an attempt was made to resolve the dispute. The attempt failed and ZAPU split into three groups:

a)   Chikerema founded a separate political party, FROLIZI, which had a military wing.

b)   The Mthimkhulu group which claimed to be neutral and independent.

c)   The rest of ZAPU now led by J. Z. Moyo.

Many of us strongly believed that the events leading up to the 1971 split did not arise merely out of disagreements between our political leaders but were also a result of external influence. For example, we suspected that the Mthimkhulu group was influenced by Britain.

We also suspected that some African countries had played a part in the split, particularly in the formation of FROLIZI which was marketed as a party that was going to unite ZAPU and ZANU. Our suspicions were based on the knowledge that certain people were still angry at the failure of the JMC and that they knew very well it was because of ZAPU that the JMC had failed. When the split took place these people used the opportunity to the full, saying 'Let them have it. After this they will be more accommodating and they will be forced to unite with ZANU'.

It was during this crisis that ZAPU lost its important and strategic contact with FRELIMO. ZANU knew of the difficulties that ZAPU was facing in mounting joint operations with FRELIMO. The information came from ZAPU commanders who were defecting to ZANU. Among them were Rex Nhongo (now Solomon Mujuru) and Robson Manyika. Manyika had first-hand knowledge of all ZAPU's plans as he was ZAPU's chief of staff before his defection. Manyika gave the plans to ZANU. ZANU then attempted to approach FRELIMO but did not succeed because ZAPU had asked FRELIMO to give it some time to sort out its internal problems. ZANU representatives then went to Tanzania where they were introduced to FRELIMO officials. Robson Manyika went to the Tete corridor with ZANU functionaries as a ZAPU leader when in fact he had defected and joined ZANU. This is how ZANU got its first sizeable number of recruits.

THE AFTERMATH OF THE 1971 ZAPU SPLIT

After the 1971 crisis Chikerema broke away and formed FROLIZI. Others such as Ambrose Mutinhiri who left with Chikerema later rejoined ZAPU. The Mthimkhulu group refused to join either FROLIZI or ZAPU and were detained by the Zambian authorities. The Zambian government said it took this action because the lives of the Mthimkhulu group were at risk.

The British government asked for the release of the Mthimkhulu group (which was also known as the 'March 11 Movement') and many members of the group were flown to Britain confirming pre-1971 intelligence information that the group did have contacts with Britain through some individuals who had influenced the group. This meant, however, that the Mthimkhulu group failed to achieve whatever mission they had had whereas Chikerema's group succeeded in pulling out of ZAPU and forming FROLIZI.

After the split J. Z. Moyo held a week-long consultative meeting. At that meeting ZAPU reviewed its entire party structure and its military activities from 1965 to 1969. The meeting concluded by drawing up a new strategy for the armed struggle and created a Revolutionary Council which was to be the main body of ZAPU outside Rhodesia. The council included all members of the national executive committee and members of the entire command structure of the party's military wing. It was under this structure that ZAPU's Zimbabwe People's Revolutionary Army (ZIPRA) was formed.

The task of the Revolutionary Council was to:

a)   organize the entire liberation campaign and ZAPU's political strategy inside and outside the country and gather the resources required for a successful armed struggle.

b)   review from time to time the military strategy of the party and to align it with the political objectives of the national struggle for independence.

Between 1972 and 1974, ZAPU, with the Revolutionary Council in control, was reorganized and its army (ZIPRA) was strengthened. There was massive recruitment and support from inside Rhodesia. In 1973 ZAPU started making friends with socialist countries after it had explained to them the new developments and what had happened during the 1971 crisis.

Operations between 1972 and 1973 were mainly concentrated on sabotage and planting land-mines along roads. The strategy was to carry out sabotage without full engagement with the enemy. The strategy involved a continuous cycle of retreating, planting land-mines and hiding. This strategy was designed in order to enable ZIPRA to retrain and reorganize its forces, which had been idle since the 1971 crisis, for intensive operations planned by the Revolutionary Council.

TOWARDS THE FORMATION OF THE PATRIOTIC FRONT

In 1973 an attempt was made in Lusaka to bring some common understanding between ZANU and ZAPU under the umbrella of what was called the Zimbabwe Liberation Council (ZLC). This effort failed because, while ZIPRA had reorganized itself after the 1971 crisis, ZANLA was experiencing serious internal problems. The ZLC also failed because ZANU thought that it had made important and strategic gains in the Tete Corridor and that unity with ZAPU through the ZLC would negate these gains. Ironically, ZANU's position was similar to that taken by ZAPU in 1967 when the latter sabotaged the Mbeya agreement by refusing to implement the JMC. This time, ZANU decided to sabotage the ZLC in the belief that as ZAPU had been so weakened by the 1971 crisis, unity would enable ZAPU to reap ZANU's successes.

When the internal political leaders of both ZAPU and ZANU were released from prison in Rhodesia in 1974 to attend the 'unity talks' in Lusaka, they found ZANU experiencing a great many problems, many of which came to the fore during the 'Nhari Rebellion' and the assassination of Herbert Chitepo in March 1975. Later that year the Zambian authorities detained a number of ZANU leaders implicated in the assassination of Chitepo. All this adversely affected ZANLA.

In contrast, ZIPRA had successfully reorganized itself and was geared for serious operations within the country but the release of the political leaders disrupted these plans. The external leadership of ZAPU had to listen to what the released leaders had to say about what was happening inside Rhodesia. The subsequent period of détente also greatly slowed down the momentum which ZIPRA had created as the Frontline States wanted to see that the détente period was free of military operations. As a result, all the material resources which had been assembled for the big operation were held either by the Liberation Committee in Tanzania or in Zambian stores.

During this time Bishop Muzorewa attempted to unite all parties under his United African National Council (UANC) which, among other things, had the objective of creating a single army. Muzorewa's attempt to unite the parties also collapsed.

Meanwhile ZAPU had started assembling its own cadres in Botswana for transit to Zambia for training. At that time all recruits in Mozambique, Botswana and Zambia were not defined as being either ZANU or ZAPU. Later, however, ZANU declared all the people in camps in Mozambique to be ZANU cadres without discrimination whereas in Botswana ZAPU continued to differentiate between its recruits and ZANU's and processed them accordingly.

The efforts at rebuilding the armies were frustrated by the OAU Liberation Committee which continued to refuse to release ZIPRA's weapons held in Zambia until the parties united. Some Frontline States were keen to create a united movement and ZANU, whose political leaders were in prison at the time, was anxious to co-operate. At this time ZANLA was enjoying strong support from the governments of Mozambique and Tanzania but was finding it difficult to operate because its commander, Josiah Tongogara, was in prison. Simon Muzenda, as ZANU's spokesman, approached ZAPU in an attempt to forge a unity arrangement. J. Z. Moyo, Nikita Mangena and myself were involved in the discussions. We finally agreed that ZIPRA and ZANLA would be brought together to form ZIPA (Zimbabwe People's Army) which was to be led by ZANLA's Rex Nhongo as Commander with Nikita Mangena as Deputy Commander and Jevan Maseko as Chief of Staff. ZIPA was to operate from Mozambique. It was agreed that ZIPRA elements in Zambia would operate under the auspices of ZIPA to persuade the

OAU Liberation Committee to release the weaponry which it was withholding pending the unification of the liberation movements.

Later Samora Machel called the ZIPA high command to Mozambique and told them that from then on they were to spearhead the revolution in Zimbabwe and that they would become the leaders of a liberated Zimbabwe. Machel informed ZIPA's high command that if they continued with their divided loyalty to Mugabe, Nkomo and Sithole, they would not achieve anything. He emphasized that, in order to obtain total support from Mozambique, the ZIPA high command would have to assume leadership of the struggle.

It was against this background that the OAU came to view ZIPA as a 'third force'. Nyerere called it 'a new force that has emerged in Zimbabwe'. At OAU meetings ZIPA was projected as the military liberator of Zimbabwe but not as a political party. The assumption was that, because the political parties were dead, ZIPA commanders had to continue the struggle on their own while politicians reorganized the parties.

Despite this optimism, ZIPA developed problems soon after its formation largely because of disagreements over strategy. ZIPRA command elements found the ZIPA strategy to be completely disjointed. For example, disciplined ZIPRA commanders were shocked to find that ZANLA deployed people inside Rhodesia who were not well trained or even completely untrained. Some recruits were trained using sticks and were only given a gun on the day of crossing into Rhodesia. Most of these people were literally butchered by the enemy. This partly explains why there were larger numbers of mass graves in ZANLA operational areas than in those areas where ZIPRA cadres operated. ZIPRA totally opposed ZANLA's strategy which led the latter to think that ZIPRA was trying to force ZANLA to adopt ZIPRA tactics. As a result ZIPA began to collapse in 1975 and ZIPRA elements were victimized, some of whom were deliberately shot in cold blood by ZANLA forces in Mozambique and Tanzania. Others who managed to escape returned to their original bases in Zambia.

In 1976, after these bitter experiences, ZAPU re-organized itself once again and worked very hard to strengthen ZIPRA operations across the Zambezi river. As part of this renewed effort ZIPRA opened a new front through Botswana without the permission of the Botswana government. At times the Botswana army intercepted ZIPRA forces who were using the front but at others they were ignored and permitted to proceed.

Efforts at reaching a negotiated settlement to the 'Rhodesian problem' continued against the background of an intensified military campaign by ZIPRA inside Rhodesia. In 1976 the Geneva Conference collapsed soon after it started. Before this conference ZAPU leaders, particularly Joshua Nkomo, had pleaded with Zambia to release the ZANLA leaders who were in detention so that they could participate in the Geneva Conference.

Despite the collapse of the joint effort of ZANLA and ZIPRA in Mozambique and Tanzania, ZIPA elements were present at the Geneva talks to represent the 'third force'. After the Geneva Conference, ZANU's political leaders, who had become increasingly isolated from the struggle because of their squabbles, went to Mozambique and were reluctantly accepted by ZANLA commanders. These commanders were influential in ZIPA. Some ZIPA leaders, such as Dzinovengwa, were then arrested in order to pave the way for an all-ZANU leadership of ZIPA.

This development marked the death of ZIPA. After ZIPA's collapse and the failure of the Geneva talks, Samora Machel called ZAPU and ZANLA to a conference and asked them to form a single party or to combine under one umbrella organization. This marked the beginnings of what was later to be called the Patriotic Front.

In 1977 ZAPU reviewed its strategy as had been agreed upon when the Revolutionary Council was created after the 1971 crisis and decided to embark on a new course. This new course involved not only producing guerrilla units but training regular units for the first time. The idea was that regular army units would establish themselves in the 'liberated zones' in which the guerrilla units had entrenched themselves and which were 'no-go' zones for enemy forces. Guerrilla units would then move forward towards other areas while the regular army would remain to defend the liberated zones.

ZIPRA started training regular forces in 1978. There were some ZAPU critics and detractors who deliberately misinterpreted this strategy and suggested that ZIPRA was intending to train a regular army which would overthrow any elected, post-Independence government which was not ZAPU dominated. Of course, ZAPU denied these allegations. ZAPU's objective was to restore civil administration in the liberated zones and to reopen schools which had been closed because of the war.

The new strategy also involved the training of non-military personnel to provide legal, medical, educational and administrative services. The need for these services was obvious to anyone familiar with life in the liberated zones. It was impossible to have any semblance of civil life in these areas without the necessary defence which could only be provided by well-trained regular army units. This is why ZAPU found the allegation that the units were designed for use in a post-Independent Zimbabwe nonsensical.

In 1979 the formation of the Patriotic Front was actually completed. By then ZAPU and ZANU leaders had talked to all the military commanders of the two parties and had visited both ZANLA and ZIPRA camps in Tanzania, Mozambique and Zambia addressing cadres to find out their attitudes towards the Patriotic Front. In most cases, cadres showed appreciation and understanding as long as their leaders were united. The military and political structures of the Patriotic Front were set up and a constitution was debated.

After the 1978 Commonwealth Heads of Governments meeting in Lusaka the Patriotic Front agreed to attend the Lancaster House Conference. The Patriotic Front tried to complete the restructuring of the political and military hierarchies of ZAPU and ZANU so as to negotiate as a single organization. However, some elements in ZANU vigorously opposed this process because they feared Nkomo would emerge as the leader of the Patriotic Front. Nevertheless, ZAPU and ZANU did negotiate at the Lancaster House Conference as a united Patriotic Front. This unity lasted only as long as the conference. Afterwards, the earlier fears and suspicions came to the fore again. The result was that in 1980 ZAPU and ZANU contested the Independence elections as independent organizations and not as the Patriotic Front. What happened after that is another story.

2

Recruitment to ZANLA: Building up a War Machine

JOSIAH TUNGAMIRAI

INTRODUCTION

Once the ZANU Gwelo Congress had concluded in May 1964 that the only way to attain majority rule in Rhodesia was through an armed struggle, the party focused on the problem of raising a trained army of guerrillas. Military training and the actual organizing and launching of the struggle had to be carried out outside the country because of the tight internal security surveillance against nationalist activities. Recruitment of guerrillas also had to be done in the neighbouring independent countries, especially Zambia, as well as inside Rhodesia. Both exercises were at first very difficult. At first those few individuals who left the country voluntarily seeking educational and employment opportunities in neighbouring countries were recruited and, in exceptional circumstances, some individuals left the country to train in guerrilla warfare after being recruited by the underground party structures and officials. But in the initial stages of the struggle these sources of recruits remained unreliable and produced very few cadres.

Slightly more recruits came from Zambia and Malawi. There were many African families resident in Zambia who had immigrated there from Southern Rhodesia during the heyday of the Federation of Rhodesia and Nyasaland. Many of them remained staunch supporters of their home nationalist parties, especially of the older ones such as the National Democratic Party (NDP) and ZAPU.[1] But when ZANU was banned in Rhodesia and resurfaced in Lusaka, its aggressive recruitment drives, under the leadership of the National Chairman, Herbert Chitepo, began to pay dividends. In 1967 the OAU, influenced by the rival ZAPU lobby, made it clear that, unless ZANU showed greater military activity it would lose the recognition which had followed the highly publicized Battle of Chinhoyi (28 April 1966). In order to increase its recruitment the Revolutionary Council had no option but to use the same method as that employed by ZAPU; that is, of press-ganging.[2]

SOCIO-ECONOMIC CONDITIONS FAVOURING RECRUITMENT

All ZANU's recruitment efforts, methods and successes must be understood in the context of the prevailing socio-economic and political disadvantages suffered by Africans in Rhodesia. The intensification of the war in the latter part of the 1970s was another contributing factor.

Land hunger
The unequal distribution of land was the main reason why the African people fought the settler regime. The land issue was so crucial that it even put the Lancaster House Constitutional Conference into disarray in 1979. The Conference was salvaged only when the British Government offered some money to buy the land for redistribution to the African peasants on a willing-seller, willing-buyer basis.[3] Traditionally a Zimbabwean man's wealth is composed of his land, his livestock and his children, particularly his daughters, for whom he expects some *roora* (bride price).

Since 1890 the land in Rhodesia had been divided on a racial basis with the colour of one's skin determining which part of the country one could live in and farm.[4] Under the Land Tenure Act of 1969, only 45 million acres of Zimbabwe's 96,4 million acres were allocated to Africans.[5] By 1976 the vast majority of the African population occupied the land communally in Tribal Trust Lands and Purchase Areas. Most of the farming was on a subsistence basis. The land allocated to Africans was generally poor and eroded and food production was static and even declining in some areas.[6] Moreover, between 1969 and 1976 the African population in the communal areas increased by almost 50 per cent.[7] It was this rapidly increasing African population pressure on the land and the resultant land hunger which made many rural Africans amenable to recruitment by the guerrillas.

Unemployment and accommodation problems
In 1976 over half of Rhodesia's population (6,6 million) was under the age of 15, yet only 846 260 of them were in primary school.[8] More than half of all children admitted to school dropped out after their primary education and only a tiny fraction (around 0,5 per cent) reached the sixth form (the top form of secondary school). Statistics for 1976 indicated that only 926000 Africans were employed in the cash economy (a mere 14,6 per cent of the total African population).[9] It was estimated that 131 000 men and women aged between 16 and 60 were unemployed in 1975, and that at least 54 000 new jobs would need to be created every year to absorb all those entering the job market. The plight of the unemployed school-leaver was reported by the Catholic Commission for Justice and Peace:

> These youngsters would be found walking in the streets of Salisbury [Harare] or Bulawayo, hungry and in search of work. But there was no work, even for many of those who had successfully completed their primary and secondary education: they were turned away by signs displayed everywhere in shop windows and at factory gates: *'Hapana Basa'* — 'No work'. Nevertheless, morning after morning, thousands of young Africans continue to walk from the townships to the industrial

sites where they gather around locked factory gates waiting patiently to take the place of a worker who has been sacked or of a group of employees who have been dismissed because they went on strike. In fact, it is not merely from the ranks of these frustrated penniless and hungry youngsters that most 'terrorists' are recruited, but also from among the privileged few. All fight from a sense of conviction. Many of those killed in action are very young; and some of those captured could not be sentenced to death because they were too young.[10]

In the towns unemployed loafers encountered food and accommodation shortages. The policy of the White government was to allow Africans to live in the urban areas on condition that they were employed. As the International Labour Office reported:

Numbers have grown rapidly, especially in Salisbury. Still, however, urban living conditions continue to reflect a divided character. Housing zones are still racially segregated (except for small 'multiracial zones') and no African may choose to purchase urban property in any White 'designated area'. This aspect of land tenure remains unaltered by the administration's recent acceptance of changes affecting White farm land.

Most freehold land and owner-occupied dwellings are probably held by Whites, Asians and Coloureds, though a small but growing class of Africans holds long-term leases to urban property in select areas of the townships and some additional provision has recently been made for home ownership. Most African dwellers in urban areas rent their accommodation, usually from municipal authorities. Others live in tied accommodation rented from employers. Many must lodge, legally or otherwise. Many thousands are squatters. Such persons face continuous harassment and constant threats of eviction.

The quality of accommodation can be broadly ascertained. In 1969, for example, it was estimated by the Central Statistical Office that there were 873 200 African dwellings, only 81 200 of which then had electricity. Of the 2.4 million rooms contained therein, over 55 per cent were of the 'traditional' type, i.e. they were made of pole and *dhaka*.[11]

Most African families lived in the townships and unmarried men lived in the hostels in Harari township. The municipality by-laws forbade any unemployed person to live in the townships. Night raids were carried out by municipality police to check on unemployed persons who might have been given shelter by relatives. If people were caught sheltering there illegally they received summary punishment at police camps (Matapi in Harare and Mzilikazi in Bulawayo). A fine of £1 and later $2 was imposed and if not paid the captive remained in police custody. As the fine was often paid by employed relatives, they would soon evict their lodging relative, who would then be forced to find accommodation in the squatter camps on the banks of the Mukuvisi River in Harare or go back to the rural areas. A woman could be forced to prostitute herself in order to find shelter.

If the unemployed person returned to the rural areas with his family they could not be allocated land automatically as it was very scarce. Even if land was available it was frequently too small in area and too poor for even subsistence farming. Such families also lacked the finance to acquire agricultural implements and fertilizers for worthwhile farming. This situation left the youngsters with no other option but to cross into Mozambique to join the ZANLA combatants (*vakomana*). On arrival in the refugee camps most recruits were screened according to age; the young ones were sent to schools such as Matenje, Toironga and Mejacaze in Mozambique or overseas, while the older boys and girls were sent to camps for military training.

Disruption of services because of the war
The intensification of the war from 1976 until 1979 meant some commercial farms and small mines were abandoned; clinics, business centres and rural schools were closed, and there was an exodus of refugees into Mozambique and Botswana from whom ZANLA could recruit its soldiers.

The following reports by the Secretary for African Education describe the effects of the war on education in 1977 and 1978, respectively.

> Curfews, closed schools and present terrorist danger militated against the smooth running of the normal Grade 7 testing programme. However, Field Testers were determined that the work would go on and that every primary school leaver would, as far as possible, be given the chance to prove his/her ability. At the same time, all concerned were assured that no secondary school applicant would be penalized because of unavoidable absence of a result. Out of 71 000 pupils in Grade 7 in 1977 only 63 600 sat for the examinations.[12]

> Tragedy continued to stalk our schools and the following statistics are indicative of the mounting toll of destruction and disruption although many of the children concerned were placed in over-crowded conditions or 'hot-seated' in other schools usually in urban areas.
> The problems of reaching rural schools multiplied. Inspectors, the administration of examinations (including scholastic aptitude tests), the holding of courses for teachers, the distribution of school materials, the receipt of statistical and other information were all severely intercepted or discontinued in many rural areas.

> The absence of male teachers on National Service disrupted many schools, but children reacted remarkably well to the stresses and strains imposed by a war situation, even when this meant, as it did for many of the remoter schools, travelling in armed convoys at week-ends to play organized sport.[13]

With the independence of Mozambique in 1975 the level of political consciousness among students along the eastern border increased. Some of these students had relatives who had fought with FRELIMO against Portuguese colonialism in Mozambique. FRELIMO's victory inspired many students and led to an exodus of students from schools such as St. Augustine's Mission, Old Umtali Teachers College, Mutambara, Sunnyside, Biriviri, Mount Selinda, Bonda and Mary Mount to Mozambique.

Internally, nearly all politicians were claiming leadership over the forces and recruits assembling in Mozambique and hence youths of different party affiliations flocked out hoping that they could be joined by their leaders there.

The resuscitation of the war in January 1976 caused a revolutionary fever to spread all over the country. This resulted in an exodus of recruits which alarmed the Rhodesian government, but, by the time they realised that something had to be done to check the 'go east' spree, thousands of youngsters had already crossed the border and were undergoing military training in Mozambique and Tanzania.

As the war intensified the Security Forces declared 'total war' against the 'terrorist collaborators', and this left the guerrillas with no other option but to drive the masses into the bushes for protection. Many of these people were forced to cross the border into Mozambique or Botswana to seek refuge.

RECRUITMENT

Press-ganging

Both ZANU and ZAPU started recruiting in the early 1960s, but in the period 1964–9 they relied on recruitment outside the country. By 1979, however, the recruitment process had gone through three phases: voluntary recruitment, press-ganging and voluntary recruitment again. When recruitment started, the officers tasked with recruitment used to identify Zimbabweans residing in the neighbouring countries by the languages they spoke, usually Shona or Ndebele, their places of employment and the location of their residences.[14] But as both ZANU and ZAPU had difficulties in getting sufficient recruits by this means they decided to employ a method once widely used by the British Navy; that of press-ganging.[15] Many young men originally from Rhodesia who were living in the Mumbwa rural area and in Lusaka were press-ganged into going for training. Inevitably desertions before, during and after training were common. Some of these conscripted guerrillas gave themselves up to the Rhodesian Security Forces at the first opportunity and made press statements accusing the parties of kidnapping them and exposing the Party's strategy and tactics.[16] Simbi Mubako, who at Independence became the Minister of Justice and Constitutional Affairs, explained that press-ganging was in part due to the pressure being exerted on ZANU and ZAPU by the OAU and host countries, particularly Zambia and Tanzania.[17] Funds tended to be allocated according to the number of recruits in the training camps so the rival parties vied with each other in their recruitment drives. For instance, Major General Vitalis Zvinavashe (then known as Sheba Gava) recalled that in 1967 when ZANLA was being pressed by the OAU to show evidence of recruits and when Tanzania was threatening to close the Intumbi ZANLA training camp in Chunya unless ZANU could demonstrate its commitment to the armed struggle by having an army under training, ZANLA recruiting officers launched an armed attack on a ZIPRA recruiting camp called Luthuli in the Mumbwa area in order to disperse their recruits.[18] (The Camp Commander Col. Tshinga Dube responded to the assault by returning fire from a 303 mm gun). ZANLA's objective was to scatter the ZIPRA recruits, pursue them and press-gang them for training with ZANLA.[19] At that time ZAPU had more recruits than ZANU because it had established itself in Zambia before ZANU was recognized by the OAU.

Forced recruitment was also carried out within Rhodesia by both ZIPRA and ZANLA liberation armies. In 1973 a ZANLA group operating in the north-east of Rhodesia under the command of Thomas Nhari (whose real name was Raphael Chinyanganya) abducted hundreds of students from the Roman Catholic Mission of St. Albert and drove them all the way to Zambia through Mozambique. The exercise was so clumsily conducted that when they reached Chifombo in Zambia only a handful of the schoolchildren still remained — the rest had managed to escape back to their homes. After this fiasco, which was frowned upon by other ZANLA commanders and the political leadership, ZANU stopped press-ganging altogether. Later the vast numbers of refugees who soon flooded ZANU camps in Mozambique and South Eastern Zambia made such methods unnecessary. ZAPU, however, continued to press-gang recruits until 1977, when the local parental and international outcry at the abduction of the Manama schoolchildren at the end of January 1977 was so great that ZAPU was obliged to stop forceful and violent recruiting techniques.[20] Soon ZAPU was also able to obtain voluntary recruits from refugees in Botswana and Zambia.

Influence of spirit mediums
In the north-east of the country voluntary recruitment was facilitated by the participation and support of the spirit mediums. For example, when ZANLA fighters arrived in the Dande area they discovered that the tradition of the spirit mediums Sekuru Kaguvi and Mbuya Nehanda, who had participated effectively in the first *Chimurenga* of 1896–7, was still alive in the 1970s and that the new generation of mediums was equally opposed to the oppressive system of the Rhodesian government.

Moreover, the peasants were shifting their loyalty from their chiefs, who were seen as puppets of the colonial rulers, to the mediums. ZANLA guerrillas, who always sought for long-term co-operation with the peasants, persuaded the mediums to support them. This was purely a tactical manoeuvre aimed at winning the hearts and minds of the Dande people. This was to some extent easily achieved because the guerrillas offered to return the land to its rightful owners — through the mediums to the peasants. With the help of the spirit mediums the guerrillas were able to carry out their instructions to politicize the masses, to cache arms and to recruit would-be fighters in the Dande area.[21] Thus in the Nehanda sector which covered Dande, Sipolilo, Mazoe and Centenary, spirit mediums such as Chipfeni, Chidyamauyu, Chiodzamamera, Mutota and Mbuya Nehanda, whose real name was Nyamita, played a major role in the recruitment of young men and women. For instance, as Sarudzai Chinyamaropa, who at Independence became the Superintendent at Ruwa Rehabilitation Centre, recalled, 'Sekuru Chipfeni gave us a guide from the Mozambique border (Mukumbura River), to Mavhuradonha along the Hoya River to look for routes and caves to hide our war materials in September 1972.'[22]

Before ZANLA combatants infiltrated Rhodesia in 1972 Chipfeni had already been in touch with Joa Binda, a FRELIMO Commander, who commanded the

Third Sector of Tete Province in Mozambique. Binda revealed to Chipfeni that 'sooner or later you shall have guerrillas from your country coming to fight the boers'.[23] In 1972 Chipfeni led the first party of ZANLA combatants to Chiodzamamera and Chidyamauyu, the latter was the youngest of the mediums and was possessed by the spirit of Mbuya Nehanda.[24] The mediums explained to the villagers that the guerrillas were not foreigners from Zambia and Mozambique as described in government propaganda. They told the *povo* why the guerrillas had come and assured them that they had their interests at heart. They went further to remind the *povo* that this was what Nehanda had meant when she had said, '*Mapfupa angu achamuka*' (my bones shall rise from the dead).[25]

In the Chaminuka Sector the spirit medium of Chaminuka (whose birth name was Resipina Gwerevende) worked with the combatants in the Chesa and Gwetera areas but was later captured at Gomo Village in 1973 and detained in prison until Independence. By January 1973, however, the build-up of guerrillas in the northeast and their relationship with the local spirit mediums and *povo* was known to the enemy. The Security Forces mounted a man-hunt for the spirit mediums so the guerrillas asked them to retreat for safety to Chifombo which was a FRELIMO camp and ZANU entry point at the Mozambique border with Zambia. Many young men and women saw that their religious leaders had joined the liberation war so they flocked out of Rhodesia to join ZANLA forces in Mozambique.

Pungwes *and ZANLA's media*
During 1974 and 1975 recruitment was disrupted by the détente exercise which had emerged after the South African Prime Minister, Dr Balthazar Johannes Vorster's failed attempt to initiate dialogue with Black Africa. However, the Independence of Mozambique in 1975 and the resumption and intensification of the war in 1976 facilitated ZANU recruitment. Moreover, as the dust of the détente exercise settled, countries such as Mozambique, Tanzania, Ethiopia, China, Yugoslavia and Romania began to offer more training facilities to ZANU. As the war spread into the greater part of the country recruitment became almost automatic. Young men and women became more politically conscious and voluntarily joined the *vakomana* (guerrillas). Through night-time political rallies called *mapungwe*, the guerrillas won more and more support every day. 'The Voice of Zimbabwe', a programme which was broadcast over Radio Mozambique at eight o'clock every evening, also encouraged people to rally behind their brothers and sisters in the bush who were fighting against the settler regime. *The Zimbabwe News*, an official organ of ZANU, was also very effective as an instrument of propaganda both in Rhodesia and overseas. The effectiveness of these means of recruitment was clearly seen in the number of refugees from Rhodesia who were willing, even eager to join ZANU. By December 1977 there were three major refugee camps in Mozambique. They were: Doroi with 17 000 refugees, Toronga with 12 000 and Mavudzi with 6000 — making a total of 35 000 refugees. It was from among these refugees that ZANLA recruited cadres for military training.

Characteristics of recruits
From the records of ZANU's Department of Personnel, 66 367 people were registered as recruits undergoing military training or trained combatants in 1979.[26]

Of this number about 51 868 were of school-going age, that is 19–24 years of age.[27] This age-group attended *pungwes* and listened to 'The Voice of Zimbabwe' on Radio Mozambique more than any other group — hence the strong youth movement during the war. Because of its revolutionary activities this group gained favour with the guerrillas and became the worst enemy of the Rhodesian Security Forces as they fed the guerrillas and collected information on the Rhodesian Security Forces' movements which resulted in their being either ambushed or attacked. The Security Forces subjected this group to harassment, arrest, torture and, later, 'call-up'. The youths were forced out of their homes at night, driven off in armoured vehicles or marched under heavy guard to camps where they were accused of being terrorist collaborators. They underwent severe punishments such as forced marches, electric shocks and beatings with *sjamboks*, were starved and submitted to other forms of torture. If suspected that they were '*mujibas*' they might be killed by firing squad and their corpses thrown into mine-pits (such as those found in Bindura) or in dug-out pits (in Rusape and at Zaka). Very few were brought before the courts of law. The imposition of martial law in rural areas enabled the Rhodesian forces to carry out summary trials and inflict punishment as they saw fit. From 1975 until the end of the war in 1979 most young people killed were shot as curfew breakers or were victims of crossfire. In 1977 this age-group was the most affected by the compulsory call-up for Africans. This meant they had two options: to fight with the liberation forces or with the Rhodesian Security Forces.

In contrast recruits above the age of 27 years constituted the smallest group (they only totalled 3 438).[28] Although they comprehended the political situation better than the youngsters, their family obligations seem to have prevented them from joining the war. They might also have feared Security Force retribution on their families as they themselves could be identified easily by means of *zvitupa* or identity cards which bore the names of their village heads and chiefs. In addition, some of them might have been prevented by debts incurred through the hire-purchase system which was becoming popular.

Selective recruitment
In 1978 it became necessary to recruit skilled manpower and professionals for the various party departments. According to its policy of self-reliance ZANU needed teachers to teach in schools such as Matenje in Tete, Doroi in Chimoio and Chibawawa in Sofala which were run under the leadership of Dzingai Mutumbuka, the Party's Secretary for Education, who became Minister of Education at Independence. Drivers and mechanics were also needed; they came under the directorship of Kumbirai Kangai, Secretary for Transport and Welfare, who became Minister of Labour and Social Welfare at Independence; doctors and nurses were needed to attend to patients at the Parirenyatwa Hospital in Chimoio, which was under the supervision of Herbert Ushewokunze, Secretary for Health, who became Minister of Health at Independence. The party also needed managers to run the Mudzingadzi farming project in Chimoio under the direction of Mandizvidza, Secretary for Production, who, after falling out of favour with the party during the war, was rehabilitated into ZANU at Independence. Secretaries were needed to run offices in Chimoio, Maputo, Chimurenga High Command Headquarters, the three provincial operational headquarters: Chimoio Operational Base in Manica, Tembwe Operational Base in Tete and Xai-Xai Operational Base in Gaza and to staff most of the military attaché

offices in Africa and overseas. Most of the recruits who remained in the country were trained to be *mujibas* and *chimbwidos*.

From 1978 onwards the selection of personnel for both military training and civilian tasks was carried out in the three refugee camps and was based on political background and qualifications. People were chosen and channelled for different types of training on the basis of their political consciousness, physical fitness, and discipline. Even though a large percentage of the refugees at this stage had just left school and were too young to have a criminal record, there was, however, a small percentage of refugees who were criminals who had evaded the courts and sought sanctuary in the refugee camps in Mozambique, Zambia and Botswana. Such elements were soon rehabilitated when, like everybody else, they underwent intensive political education and military training.

Recruitment by provinces

Between 1976 and 1979 ZANU embarked on a major recruitment drive in order to build up a large fighting force to carry out the objective which was outlined by its President R. G. Mugabe in his 1979 new year message, code-named '*Gore regukura hundi*' (The year of the people's storm). This drive produced the largest number of recruits. Moreover, recruits came from all parts of Rhodesia, including those areas which had not yet been directly affected by the war.[29]

During the liberation struggle ZANLA and ZIPRA contested for recruitment in the Midlands, Matabeleland South and Mashonaland West. Before the opening up of the north-east the main route to join the liberation forces was through Botswana. Most of the recruits from these provinces went through Botswana and almost all were sent to ZIPRA Camps by the Botswana authorities as ZAPU was supported by the Botswana Government. Only a very small number managed to escape to join ZANU. In the Records and Statistics from ZANLA's Department of Personnel, it appears that these provinces contributed very little to the liberation struggle, but ZAPU statistics show that the majority of the ZIPRA forces (who numbered 6 000 at the time of the ceasefire) were from these provinces.[30]

By the time of the ceasefire Manicaland, Masvingo, Mashonaland East and Mashonaland Central provinces had been subjected to military activity for many years. Each of these four provinces shares a border with Mozambique which was a refuge for ZANLA freedom fighters. With the exception of Mashonaland Central these provinces also had a greater population than the others, so naturally, the number of men and women of military age from these provinces was greater. Recruits had been drawn from Mashonaland Central since the beginning of the campaign in 1972 so that if the records had been taken from 1972 this province would have shown much greater recruitment figures than is shown by available statistics. By the end of the détente period and the resuscitation of the war in 1976, most of the young people of military age had left the province and joined the ZANLA combatants in Mozambique.

Security screening

Before entering the refugee camps the recruits passed through a security base where they were thoroughly screened by the Security and Intelligence Department headed by Major-General Vitalis Zvinavashe of the ZANLA High Command. The recruits were thoroughly searched and items such as weapons, money, radios, watches, registration cards, passports and literature were confiscated. All these items were sent to a special unit for processing. Documents were closely studied, letters analysed and radios and watches were tested, after which items such as watches would be returned to the recruit. The rest would be sent on to the Superior Authority (composed of Emmerson Mnangagwa, who was Special Assistant to the President and who became Minister of State for Security in the President's office at Independence, and Major-General Zvinavashe). It was during this period of screening that the Security and Intelligence officers were able to find out about Security Force agents and their methods of infiltrating into the ranks of ZANLA. Information leading to arrests of spies (operating under the Rhodesian 'Operation Capricorn') who had already infiltrated into the movement and those who were still coming was obtained during the screening process. When registering new arrivals the Intelligence department used a system codenamed 'The three check-ups' (see Appendix 1).

Chimurenga *names and their significance*
These were pseudonyms given to or taken by the recruits. These names were sometimes adopted by recruits before or immediately after they had crossed the border into Mozambique, Zambia or Botswana. In most cases, however, they were given to the recruits during the screening process before their being admitted into the camps. These names reflected their new political awareness and their new role in the armed struggle.[31] Combatants could not operate using their original names as that would have endangered their families who might have been victimized by the Rhodesian Security Forces, if it ever became known their father, son or daughter had joined the 'ters' (the Rhodesian short term for 'terrorists'). Appendix 2 lists some Chimurenga names and their meanings.

CONCLUSION

The study of records of the Zimbabwe Defence Forces after the integration exercise shows that all the administrative provinces of Zimbabwe contributed recruits to the liberation struggle although some, because of their proximity to neighbouring countries which gave sanctuary to the guerrillas, contributed more than others. The largest number of ZANLA combatants were born between 1953 and 1960 and were therefore in the 16–21 age bracket. The most usual educational qualifications were Grades 6 and 7.

APPENDIX I

ZIMBABWE AFRICAN NATIONAL UNION (ZANU)
H.Q. OF SECURITY & INTELLIGENCE DEPARTMENT

DATE: ....

NAME & RECORD ....

HOME NAME: ....

CHIMURENGA NAME ....

FATHER..

CHIEF ....

DISTRICT..

HEALTH ....

AGE ....

OCCUPATION ....

EDUCATION ....

PROFESSION ....

RECRUITER ....

AUTOBIOGRAPHY

DATE OF BIRTH...

EDUCATION ATTENDED ....

JOINED ZANU YEAR ....

ARMED STRUGGLE YEAR..

TRAINED YEAR ....

PLACE...

EMPLOYED: ....

PLACE...

LAST EMPLOYED ....

POLITICAL ACTIVITIES: ....

PLACE...

MARITAL STATUS ....

COUNTRIES VISITED ....

PURPOSES ....

....

PREVIOUS PARTIES ....

....

WERE YOU ARRESTED? ....

Security & Intelligence Department

APPENDIX II

TYPICAL CHIMURENGA NAMES

Name	Interpretation/meaning
Teurai Ropa:	Shed blood.
Ridzai Gidi:	Fire the gun.
Pfumo Reropa:	The spear of blood.
Mao Hurungudo:	Maoist tough fighter.
Tonderai Nyika:	Remember our country and dedicate yourself to its liberation.
Mationesa Nzira:	You have shown us the way to liberation.
Edzai Mabhunu:	Try you boers and you will suffer the wrath.
Tichaona Freedom:	We shall witness liberation.
Ticharwa Magorira:	Guerrillas shall fight.
Mabhunu Muchapera:	Boers your reign/kingdom shall be destroyed by the war.
Joseph Chimurenga:	Joseph committed to the war of liberation.
Sunungurai Nyika:	You must liberate your country.
Regedzai Zvamutswa:	Leave them alone for they have declared war on each other.
Patrick Mupunzarima:	Patrick who travels at night.
Mabhunu Muchabayiwa:	Boers shall be butchered.
Tichaona Hondoyakura:	To see the outcome as the war intensifies.
Chinangwa Rusununguko:	Our objective is freedom.
Tariro Tichazvipedza:	Looking forward to destroying oppression forever.
Ropafadzo Tichafiranyika:	Blessed are those who will die for liberating the country.
Togarepi Nyikayakapambwa:	Where do we live as the country has been colonized by settlers.

3

Daring to Storm the Heavens: The Military Strategy of ZAPU 1976 to 1979

Jeremy Brickhill

In the overall pattern of class struggle, guerrilla movements play the role of an auxiliary factor; they cannot of themselves achieve historic objectives, but can only contribute to the solution provided by another force.[1]

This chapter sets out evidence detailing the singularity of the military strategy of the Zimbabwe African People's Union (ZAPU) in the final years of the war of independence. In the first part of the chapter I describe the evolution of this strategy and analyze its key components. In the second part I examine the composition of ZAPU's armed forces, the Zimbabwe People's Revolutionary Army (ZIPRA),[2] and the means by which ZAPU was able to build a force which was capable of implementing their strategy.

PART ONE: MILITARY STRATEGY (1976-79)

Our Path to Liberation

In late 1976 ZAPU leaders in Zambia were engaged in preparations for two key conferences. The first was the Geneva Conference, convened by the British Government in an attempt to explore the possibility of a political settlement to the war then rapidly escalating in rural Rhodesia. The second conference was an internal affair, whose deliberations were destined to have a profound effect on ZAPU's strategy for the rest of the war.

By 1976 ZAPU had been at war with Rhodesia for well over a decade. The early campaigns of the 1960s had not been militarily successful, and they culminated in an internal party conflict which paralyzed ZAPU and was only resolved by a split in the party in 1970/71. Slowly ZAPU rebuilt its forces in the early 1970s and relaunched its guerrilla war. This time ZAPU avoided deploying the large self-contained guerrilla detachments which characterized many of its 1960s operations, and instead successfully developed a campaign of ambush and land-mine warfare along the Zambezi river. During this period ZANU also successfully opened a new guerrilla front (from Mozambique), and by 1974 the combined pressure of these military campaigns, and some arm-twisting from the South African government, forced the Rhodesian government to open negotiations with the nationalist movement. This resulted in the release from detention of the key ZAPU and ZANU leaders. But it also led to the de-escalation of the military efforts of the nationalist movement, and to the South African-inspired period of 'détente'.

The ZAPU Consultation Conference of 1976 was in part an attempt by the ZAPU Vice-President Jason Moyo and other ZAPU veterans of the 'détente' experience to limit the demobilizing effect of the negotiating process on the armed struggle. It was also for the benefit of the recently released ZAPU leadership, whose long period of incarceration had isolated them from the experiences and lessons of the armed struggle. But it was principally another step in the long and painful process of developing a successful political/military strategy for the party. Moyo oversaw the drafting of the key policy document presented to the conference in what was to be his last major contribution to the liberation war. He was killed by a parcel bomb a few weeks later.

Our Path to Liberation, as Moyo's strategy document was called, defined the framework which was to determine ZAPU strategy until the end of the war. It both extended the debate on military strategy within ZAPU and raised the central issue of what, precisely, was the objective of the nationalist movement.

Our Path to Liberation began by warning that the negotiations then under way were aimed at installing 'an interim African government acting as caretaker for imperialist interests' in an effort to 'prevent genuine independence and transfer of power to the people'.[3] The Party strategy, the document argued, should be geared to defeating this attempt to prevent 'genuine independence':

> The only way to ensure the independence of our country is to conquer state power . . . The objective is power to the people. This objective cannot be realized unless the liberation movement of Zimbabwe seizes state power.[4]

Our Path to Liberation went on to identify two strategic tasks whose achievement could enable the liberation movement to seize state power. The first of these committed ZAPU to build unity with all forces which shared a 'common desire to defeat colonialism'.[5] To a large extent this argument had already been won within ZAPU, and had resulted in the formation of the Patriotic Front alliance with ZANU a few weeks earlier.

The second strategic task the document identified was the 'intensification of the armed struggle' with the specific objective of 'seizing state power'. It was this task which posed a real challenge to the military commanders. If the objective was to seize state power by military force, what type of military forces would be required?

As Dumiso Dabengwa, who was a key figure in the military command and in the debate, recalls,

> We were talking about seizing power. When we looked at other guerrilla wars we could see that guerrilla warfare does not enable you to seize

power. It only creates the conditions for another force to settle the question. We wanted to take it a step further than that, and prepare ourselves to develop our military strategy and gear it to the final goal of a military victory. We felt that guerrilla warfare on its own could not achieve that. What is the next step?[6]

The experience of guerrilla warfare in Africa provided few answers to Dabengwa's question. Nationalist armed struggle in Africa has invariably been confined to two broad strategies: guerrilla warfare and urban insurrection. But one contemporary African experience of armed struggle did have an impact on the debate in ZAPU.

Angola's MPLA had fought a guerrilla war and, following the collapse of Portugal's pro-colonial government, it was poised to take power. But an invasion by conventional South African military forces, backed up by mercenaries, had come close to defeating the MPLA guerrillas who were unable to hold territory. MPLA were only saved by the arrival of conventional Cuban forces.

The example of Angola was very fresh in our minds . . . We had realized that if we had to go through and take (our) country, we needed military forces that could seize power and defend it.[7]

This experience, and the debate on military strategy provoked by *Our Path to Liberation*, led ZAPU to decide to divert some recruits into conventional military training courses. At this time there was still little strategic coherence to ZAPU's plans to upgrade their army. Apart from the introduction of heavier weapons into guerrilla units, there was no clear conception of how conventional military forces might actually be used in the war. But for the first time in Africa, a liberation movement began to prepare military forces which actually had the potential to achieve its stated political objective: to seize political power.

Towards the Turning Point

With the collapse of the Geneva Conference the war escalated. ZAPU's guerrilla campaign of mine warfare, raids and ambushes had driven the Rhodesian forces out of their small posts along the Zambezi, back over the escarpment and into more defensible garrisoned positions. This development had overcome the second major obstacle to ZAPU's infiltration from Zambia: the absence of settlements near the border whose inhabitants could feed and support the guerrillas. (The first obstacle was, of course, the river itself.) The ZAPU guerrillas could now reach the vital sanctuaries in the rural villages without having to fight every inch of the way.

In 1977 ZAPU continued to employ the same tactics: mine warfare, raids and ambushes as it consolidated its military gains in the north and north-western parts of the country. The political commissar for the units operating in Urungwe described their progress in the following terms:

The enemy was very much affected, especially by mine warfare. They could not move by truck. They had also to move on foot, and when they moved on foot it was easier for us . . . People were giving us information on the movement of the enemy. We asked them [for information about] the patrol routes and OPs (Observation Posts). Then maybe we would put a grenade on an OP. When they go to that OP it blasts them. Then they fear using their OPs.

We cut the enemy's supplies by ambushing supply trucks and mining the roads. By so doing we were starving the enemy soldiers. As a result they had to retreat, going to bigger camps and tarred roads. They would only come into our area for operations.[8]

From that time our troops started going deep into the country. Let's say the enemy was based here. We would then deploy another unit beyond, to start operating behind the enemy. That's when the enemy was disrupted. That made it easier again for us to move in. That's when the enemy started now retreating from the Tribal Trust Lands. That's when we were free in the Tribal Trust Lands.[9]

This penetration of the rural hinterland marked the real breakthrough for ZAPU forces, and during 1977 and 1978 they pressed home their advantage by infiltrating almost 2 000 guerrillas and rapidly extending their operational areas. The ZIPRA commander in the Zambezi/Wankie area opened the operations in that area in September 1977 with nine guerrillas.

Our unit grew so rapidly that within five months we were over 400 comrades in that area . . . We did a lot of sabotage work, especially derailment of goods trains. Once we derailed a train on the Matetsi Bridge. We made a lot of raids on bush camps . . . This was the most successful campaign I experienced in the whole of the struggle. We had very few casualties. We moved in small units unless we planned to hit bigger targets. We lost only 12 men, of which more than half were lost capsizing in the river crossing. In action we lost very few men . . . Enemy casualties counted were 32, but it should be more. We did a lot of mine warfare which is safe to our side and deadly to the enemy. They lost a lot of men.[10]

Operating at the other end of Lake Kariba, the regional commander of ZAPU's Northern Front described the spread of the war southwards towards the strategic commercial farms in the Lomagundi area.

By 1978 our forces [in Urungwe] had grown to a battalion. My general plan was to base two companies in Urungwe and operate southward. One company was to direct its efforts towards Karoi, Lions Den and Sinoia. The second company would concentrate its efforts towards Lomagundi, moving into Hartley, Gatooma and the African Purchase areas . . . Two of my platoons were left on resupply duties and crossing recruits and wounded comrades.
My orders from the ZIPRA High Command were to deploy forces into Urungwe and Lomagundi, to carry out guerrilla operations, to win the

confidence of the population and to recruit personnel . . . The campaign
had vigorously grown by mid-1978 due to the operations carried out by
these units.[11]

By the end of 1978, ZAPU guerrillas were operating in a wide arc — from
Sipolilo and Urungwe in the north, through Gokwe and Silobela in the centre of
the country, to Lupane, Nkai and Tsholotsho in the west. ZAPU forces had also
crossed the Salisbury–Bulawayo railway line south of Shangani and opened their
Southern Front towards Shabani, and further south towards Gwanda and
Beitbridge.

By mid-1978, according to Dabengwa, semi-liberated areas — which he defined
as 'areas where the Rhodesian forces had lost control' — existed in the ZIPRA
operational areas at Urungwe, Sipolilo North, Gokwe, Lupane and Tsholotsho.[12]

Behind the Turning Point

As the guerrilla war progressed, the debate which had been prompted by the
Consultation Conference of late 1976 continued. This debate increasingly focused
on the Vietnamese theories and practice of 'mobile warfare'. Other advice was also
on offer, notably from the Soviet Union and Cuba, but it was the Vietnamese —
whose successes were headline news — who seemed to provide answers to the
questions of strategy that faced the ZIPRA commanders.

The Vietnamese revolutionaries argued that guerrilla war was only a preparatory
stage in revolutionary war, and that it had to be developed into higher forms of
warfare to enable strategic victories to be won. According to the renowned
Vietnamese theorist and practitioner of revolutionary war, General Vo Nguyen
Giap:

> To keep itself in life and develop, guerrilla warfare has necessarily to
> develop into mobile warfare. This is a general law . . . If guerrilla warfare
> did not move to mobile warfare, not only the strategic task of annihilating
> the enemy manpower could not be carried out, but even guerrilla activities
> could not be maintained and extended.[13]

In the battlefield ZAPU's guerrilla forces were increasingly experiencing
problems which bore out the Vietnamese experience. According to Dabengwa, by
mid-1978 there was

> almost a sufficient presence of guerrilla forces in most ZIPRA operational
> areas. The danger in guerrilla warfare if you start having too many
> guerrilla units in an area, then you create confusion and lose the initiative
> . . . We did not think it wise just to pour in as many guerrilla units as
> possible without having specific objectives, just to have a presence in that
> area.[14]

A ZIPRA platoon commander operating in the Gokwe area at that time expressed
his view of the problems the guerrillas were experiencing:

By that time the unit which was operating on the northern side of the Khami river was in confusion. They were too many. They were conducting operations there, staying there. So the enemy located their positions and managed to see how they carried out their daily activities. Then they combed them.[15]

The introduction by the Rhodesian forces of airborne 'Fireforce' tactics against the lightly armed guerrillas, was also seriously disrupting guerrilla efforts in the north of the country, where ZIPRA forces had grown most spectacularly. At this time the units at this front were also facing difficulties in mounting attacks against the heavily defended garrisons into which most Rhodesian forces had retreated.[16]

These experiences persuaded ZAPU to deploy the first of their regular forces, in particular some of their artillery and anti-aircraft units. These forces were intended to provide defence against airborne attack and greater firepower in mounting attacks against garrisons.

Large artillery pieces, such as the 105 mm B10s and heavy 82 mm mortars greatly increased the guerrilla offensive capacity and were first used in attacks on garrisons and the towns of Kariba[17] and Chirundu during 1978. Anti-aircraft units equipped with ZGU anti-aircraft guns and SAM missiles were attached to the guerrilla units in the north of the country, and provided the guerrillas with their first real air defence capacity.

The introduction of these heavier weapons, however, posed new problems which exposed the weaknesses of guerrilla training and tactics. The guerrillas lacked the infantry training which would enable them to assault garrisons and press home the advantages which their weapons now gave them. There was a second weakness; the poor defensive character and capacity of guerrilla units, who were not trained to hold defensive positions. This prevented ZIPRA from consolidating its hold in areas which had been successfully cleared of Rhodesian forces, and developing strategic rear bases inside the country.

The earlier decision to begin training regular forces meant that ZAPU now had the capacity to qualitatively intensify the war. Specialized regular units had already been introduced into the guerrilla detachments on an experimental basis but this piecemeal reinforcement of the guerrilla forces was inadequate. What was now required was a clear strategy which could integrate the guerrilla and regular forces in a co-ordinated way.

The Rhodesian forces too were debating strategy at this time. By the end of 1978 it was estimated that there were 9 000 insurgents operating inside the country, with a further 21 000 trained ZIPRA and ZANLA personnel in rear bases. The guerrilla war had reached most rural areas, and had 'encircled the economic heartland' of the country. A classified Rhodesian Security Forces briefing of the time declared that, 'in classical COIN [counter-insurgency] terms, this is a no-win or rather, sure lose situation'.[18] The truth of this statement had been apparent to many of the commanders of the Rhodesian Security Forces for some time and they had been pressing for changes in military strategy. At the end of 1978 the strategy of mobile counter-offensive was finally abandoned, to be replaced by a strategy of area defence. In effect the Rhodesians decided not to contest most of the rural areas, but rather to concentrate on holding the key economic and strategic parts of the country.

This strategy implicitly conceded that the war could not be won by the Rhodesian forces. The Rhodesian government was pressurized to seek a political settlement. It was at this very moment that ZAPU convened a conference in Zambia to determine its own new military strategy.

Before dealing with this crucial conference, however, it is necessary to outline the structures which ZAPU had created to prosecute the war.

The Zimbabwe People's Revolutionary Army

Although ZAPU had initiated the armed struggle in the early 1960s, ZIPRA was in fact only formed in 1971, after the crisis and split in the party leadership-in-exile. The roots of this conflict lie outside the scope of this chapter, and here I shall simply assert that the formation of ZIPRA, as an independent organ of the party, was the culmination of an inner-party struggle which finally enabled military strategy to be developed by the military, though ZIPRA remained subordinate to the political control of the party.[19]

At the same time that ZIPRA was created, ZAPU also formed another important organ of the party-in-exile. This was the Revolutionary Council, whose membership comprised members of the National Executive Committee, heads of departments and military commanders. The Revolutionary Council enabled the party to broaden the leadership of the party-in-exile, and acted in effect as a provisional National Executive Committee.

Linking the Revolutionary Council to the party membership, soldiers and party workers, was the Congress of Militants, in effect an *ad hoc* party congress with limited powers and duties.

Too large to perform the centralized functions of elaborating and conducting the military struggle itself, the Revolutionary Council ceded these duties to another body, the War Council. The War Council, undoubtedly the most powerful and significant organ of the party during the war years, comprised only five permanent members. By 1978 these were:

- the President of ZAPU, Joshua Nkomo;
- the Party Commissar, Samuel Munodawafa;
- the Secretary for Defence, Akim Ndlovu;
- the ZIPRA Commander, Lookout Masuku;
- the head of ZAPU's National Security Organization (NSO), Dumiso Dabengwa (who served as War Council Secretary).

Occasionally various other people were co-opted into the Council.

The War Council had the responsibility to develop and implement the military strategy of the party, and issued the general policy directives which governed the conduct of the war. By agreement of the Revolutionary Council, its reports to that body were not to include any sensitive military details, and so it was empowered to take all strategic decisions.

Before dealing with ZIPRA itself, I will briefly mention the National Security Organization (NSO), the security and intelligence department of ZAPU. In addition to its security and intelligence functions, the NSO provided the War Council with research briefings and formulated strategic option proposals for the consideration of the War Council.

ZIPRA was represented in the War Council by the Secretary for Defence, who assumed overall responsibility for policy and administration, and the ZIPRA Commander, who carried out the command functions within the army. Other senior ZIPRA commanders frequently attended War Council meetings to brief its members on particular aspects of the war.

At the next level of command within ZIPRA was the High Command. This comprised:

- the ZIPRA commander and his deputies;
- the chiefs and deputies of departments in ZIPRA, including artillery, communications, engineering, logistics, medical services, operations, personnel and training, reconnaissance and transport;
- front commanders and their deputies (regional commanders);[20]
- rear camp commanders and their deputies; and
- NSO department heads and their deputies.

The High Command provided the link between the ZIPRA Commander and the army, ensuring that policies elaborated in the War Council were carried out. It also provided a forum at the command level for discussion and analysis of military strategy. Conferences of the High Command, or relevant sections of it, were frequently held, enabling the centralized command of the War Council to implement their policies over the range of military forces and formations within ZIPRA.[21]

It was to just such a conference that all members of the High Command were summoned in November 1978.

The Turning Point
Present at the conference were almost all the members of the High Command, including the Front and Regional Commanders who had travelled to Lusaka from the battlefield. They brought with them the high expectations and good morale of the ZIPRA forces in the field. But they also brought demands for greater logistical support, for more and better weapons, and above all else the call for deployment of ZIPRA's regular forces.

By the time of the conference, the training of ZIPRA's conventional military forces was far advanced. The precise nature of these forces and the numbers involved was a closely guarded secret, but most ZIPRA soldiers knew, or suspected, that regular infantry battalions were being trained, and rumours of the sophisticated weaponry they carried swept through jealous guerrilla ranks. Combat commanders and rank-and-file guerrillas alike were somewhat in awe of the firepower potential of their own regular troops, having experienced the capacity of equivalent Rhodesian units so often.

The debates of the past two years about guerrilla warfare and its efficacy, about mobile war and the prospects of 'seizing power' through military means, and about negotiations and 'selling out', peppered the reports presented to the conference.

Having heard the reports and proposals from the various departments and military fronts, and having analysed the development of the guerrilla war, the conference decided that, as the Rhodesian forces had lost sufficient control, ZAPU could now implement a new military strategy. This strategy was called 'The Turning Point Strategy'.

Dumiso Dabengwa, whose NSO had been instrumental in developing the new strategy, describes the strategy as 'marking a highly developed stage in the armed liberation struggle in Zimbabwe'; he explains the success of the conference as establishing a strategy to move on to the phase of 'mobile warfare'.[22] According to Dabengwa, the tasks set at the Turning Point Conference relied, in the first instance, on wresting full control from the Rhodesian forces of 'semi-liberated areas'.

> Those areas where the Rhodesian regime had lost control needed to be completely liberated from the regime. This meant that the liberation forces must be able to defend these areas. In order to do that we needed to make careful preparations. It meant that some guerrilla units should be transformed into regular units, and guerrilla tactics developed into regular tactics.[23]

The first element of the new strategy was based on consolidating the gains of the guerrilla war by enabling the insurgent forces to actually hold territory. This was to be achieved by the introduction of regular forces to defend these 'liberated' areas. This aspect of the strategy, creating in effect strategic rear bases inside the country, provided the basis for the second element:

> to regroup big armed forces in favourable conditions in order to achieve supremacy in attack, and at a given point and at a given time to annihilate the enemy.[24]

With the Rhodesian forces falling back into 'area defence', larger and better equipped ZIPRA units were now needed to assault the larger Rhodesian garrisons. This process had in fact already begun in localized operations, where guerrilla units were combined and reinforced for particular attacks. The new strategy was intended to generalize these occasional operational tactics into the basic military strategy of ZIPRA.

This did not mean that ZIPRA would no longer deploy guerrilla units or utilize guerrilla tactics. The 'Turning Point' was an attempt to develop conditions for the emergence of mobile warfare, which in the words of General Giap is 'a form of fighting in which principles of regular warfare appear and increasingly develop, but still bear a guerrilla character'.[25]

While guerrilla warfare is intended to attenuate and exhaust enemy forces, economic resources and morale, mobile warfare provides the conditions to concentrate the insurgent forces for the purpose of inflicting military defeats on the enemy forces. Hence, while it is a defensive strategy in one sense, it is principally aimed at preparing the conditions for a qualitative leap in offensive capacity.

ZAPU's 'Turning Point' embodied precisely these features, as can be ascertained from the instructions issued in the declaration which was prepared by the War Council summarizing the orders issued to ZIPRA:

All ZIPRA forces throughout the country have been ordered to act as follows:

- openly engage and drive any remaining enemy or its agents out of controlled areas;
- protect all citizens within the liberated areas, irrespective of race, colour or creed;
- organize and defend the masses of Zimbabwe;
- advance with gallantry on all those areas still in enemy hands, including all enemy military, economic and strategic installations.

The Turning Point Declaration also dealt with the creation of new administrative systems inside the country, and included instructions to members of the 'Revolutionary Council within the liberated and freed areas' to

- organize administrative units;
- run agricultural, educational and health services; and
- generally harmonize the consolidation of the liberated and controlled areas.[26]

This public declaration of the Turning Point Strategy was only issued in April 1979, several months after the High Command had received (and for the large part, implemented) its own military orders. These were not publicized, and are summarized as follows:

- new command structures to be established to enable better command and control of forces inside the country, and the transfer of almost half the High Command into the country;
- more communications equipment to be moved into the country to enable more efficient centralized command;
- many of the guerrilla units inside the country to be organized into detachments and brigades;
- regional offensive plans to be drawn up by the High Command inside the country;
- Large quantities of war materials, including heavy weapons, to be moved into the country and cached.[27]

The new strategy was enthusiastically endorsed by the High Command, and in particular, by the military commanders inside the country, for whom it meant far greater resources and command responsibilities. Members of the High Command immediately set forth from the conference to introduce the new policy to their forces. A veteran guerrilla commander sent into the north of Zimbabwe to implement the 'Turning Point' explained the re-organization of forces required by the new strategy:

The situation by this time demanded mobile warfare and the proper exercise of command and control. It was decided at Headquarters to form brigades inside the country to deal with this. We formed one brigade in Lomagundi, concentrating its efforts towards Hartley, Gatooma and Salisbury, and another brigade in Sipolilo, concentrating its efforts towards Umvukwes, Mount Darwin and Salisbury.

The brigades were formed to enable us to co-ordinate the troops and exercise effective command and control. The situation inside the country was that the Rhodesians were paralyzed, and remained guarding only big garrisons. This led us to the formation of brigades. There was now a need for company and battalion size attacks. So we had to organize brigades for efficient big attacks.

At the same time we were preparing for the arrival of our regular battalions from Zambia. We needed to prepare for co-ordinated efforts between the regular units and the guerrilla fighters.[28]

Another High Command member describes the exercise as follows,

We were sent to the front to organize the small guerrilla units into detachments and brigades. We appointed experienced guerrilla commanders and some regular officers who had been trained as company commanders and platoon commanders. It would be easier now to control larger units. We were centralizing command of the units so that it would be easier now to control larger units. We were centralizing command of the units so that they could support the regular units when they entered the country.[29]

These were precisely the features of the move into mobile warfare which the Vietnamese experience dealt with so knowledgeably. This shift into mobile warfare required, according to the Vietnamese, new systems of command and control, new logistical arrangements — in short its own particular strategy.

The move towards mobile warfare was not itself unique to ZAPU. Mobile warfare, in various tactical forms, has appeared in many African guerrilla conflicts. In Zimbabwe, the military forces of ZANU, the Zimbabwe African National Liberation Army (ZANLA), had also begun to concentrate guerrilla units into detachments for particular operations. ZANLA's attack on the Grand Reef Air Base in 1978 contained many of the features of the move into mobile warfare. Certainly ZAPU's decision to prepare regular forces made the move towards mobile warfare easier, and ZAPU's systematic preparation for mobile warfare reflected a strategic comprehension of the nature of guerrilla warfare. But this was not the real innovation.

The new ZAPU strategy was also, according to Dabengwa, the transitional phase to develop our war strategy and gear it to that final goal of a military victory. Hence it was necessary that we should prepare military forces, with all the necessary armament, to inflict a military defeat on the enemy.[30]

What was unique in ZAPU's 'Turning Point' Strategy was — as Dabengwa put it — that ZAPU was actually moving into mobile warfare in order to 'inflict a military defeat on the enemy'. Behind the 'Turning Point' strategy lay the issue which had emerged two years earlier in the debate on *Our Path to Liberation*. Apart from mobile warfare, ZAPU was preparing a plan to actually attempt to defeat the Rhodesian forces militarily and to seize power. Herein lies its singularity.

Immediately following the decisions of the 1978 High Command conference, a team of senior ZIPRA and NSO officers began making final preparations for a major military offensive, whose objective was to end the war by launching a major strategic offensive. The plan was called 'The Zero Hour Operation', and its details were the most closely guarded ZAPU secret of the war.

The ZAPU President, Joshua Nkomo, was talking about this plan when he wrote:

> ZAPU and ZIPRA, in the closest secrecy, had decided that the war could not be allowed to drag on. We had set in motion what we called the 'turning point' strategy, for a transformation of the war from a guerrilla operation into a full-scale conflict in which we could match the Smith regime's armour and air cover with our own.[31]

Before tackling this last element of ZAPU's military strategy however, I need to make a brief rebuttal of the hearsay and disinformation which until now has passed as scholarly or journalistic evidence of ZAPU's military plans for ending the war.

Truth is stranger than fiction

The little that has been written of ZAPU's military strategy in the latter part of the war has been grossly misleading, often deliberately so. In large measure this results from a very successful disinformation operation mounted by the Rhodesian Central Intelligence Organization during 1979, which depicted ZIPRA strategy as being 'Soviet inspired' and principally aimed, not at attacking the Rhodesian forces, but at seizing power from ZANU. This CIO operation was part of a last-ditch effort to depict the ZIPRA military build up as 'Soviet expansionism', in the hope of bringing the Western powers into an active alliance against the Patriotic Front. Its secondary aim was to augment an existing CIO operation aimed at encouraging division and conflict between ZAPU and ZANU.[32]

ZAPU was never able to offer its own account and thus the disinformation has gained credence. Even serious academic studies have presented caricature and unsourced generalizations as evidence of ZAPU's military strategy. Cilliers's account is typical:

> The planned ZIPRA operation was to be a concerted bid by Nkomo and his Soviet backing to forestall ZANU (i.e. Chinese) political or military victory . . . in a typical Warsaw Pact type operation . . .

> Early in 1979 a high-powered Soviet military delegation arrived in Lusaka
> to reorganize the ZIPRA strategy. They emphasized the need to go onto
> a conventional war footing . . . From then on ZIPRA was divided into a
> conventional and an insurgent force.[33]

Similarly false (and similarly unsourced) versions of the planning of the 'Zero
Hour Operation' are to be found littering most published accounts of ZAPU's
conduct of the last year of the war. In assessing ZAPU's military strategy in this
period therefore, it will be necessary to first purge the record of a decade's worth
of falsification of evidence.

As the evidence I have cited makes clear, the framework behind the Zero Hour
planning had been evolving at least since the latter part of 1976 — indeed it can be
argued that this issue lay behind the inner-party conflict of 1969-70. The decision
to train regular forces was taken shortly after the ZAPU consultation conference of
November 1976, and not in 1979. J. Z. Moyo's argument that the liberation
movement should develop a military strategy capable of achieving its political
objective: to seize power and not rely on negotiations, remained the key element
in the development of ZAPU's military strategy for the rest of the war.

Not everyone in the War Council, however, necessarily saw this aspect as
central to their endorsement of the strategy. The ZAPU President, for example,
was instrumental in developing the strategy, but emphasized the post-independence
requirements for the defence of Zimbabwe as justification for the development of
conventional military forces.[34]

The point is that it was the long-standing debate on military strategy within
ZAPU not the arrival of any Soviet delegation which led both to the 'Turning
Point' and the 'Zero Hour' plans.

Both Joshua Nkomo and Lookout Masuku, who dealt with the Soviet political
and military leadership, respectively, in requesting support for ZAPU, deny
emphatically that the Soviets had any role in determining ZIPRA strategy.[35]
Dabengwa says that

> the Turning Point was purely a ZAPU plan. It originated from ZAPU and
> was approved by the ZAPU Revolutionary Council. When it came to its
> application, it was at that stage that we requested assistance. Soviet
> advisers came in and we unveiled the plan to them, and showed them
> how we intended to go about it. All they could do was give their advice
> where they thought we might have difficulties.[36]

Dabengwa also adds a further interesting dimension, namely that the Soviet
military advisers actually expressed serious reservations about the Zero Hour
Plan, 'until we satisfied them about the practicability of its application'. It took
considerable effort, Dabengwa says, to persuade the Soviet officials working with
ZIPRA that the plan was both necessary and workable. Even after this was achieved,
Nkomo reports that the Soviet Central Committee remained wary of the plan.[37]

It should also be pointed out that ZIPRA was working closely with advisers
and seeking military support from several sources. In 1979 there were both Soviet
and Cuban advisers attached to ZIPRA and the NSO, and intelligence officers

from the German Democratic Republic also played an important role in assisting ZAPU. They by no means shared a common perspective on African guerrilla wars, and, together with the Vietnamese, offered widely differing advice.

Finally, I should address the commonplace account of ZIPRA's Zero Hour plans, as a central African combination of the '*blitzkrieg*' and 'an Ethiopian-type Warsaw Pact style invasion'. Such formulations are neither useful nor accurate, though they do illustrate how important the ideological tags were to the disinformation campaign being mounted against ZAPU at the time. ZAPU's own plans were far more inventive than has been supposed.

The Zero Hour Plan

The broad concept of the Zero Hour Plan involved launching a co-ordinated, all-round offensive on several fronts simultaneously. Five conventional battalions with artillery support were to seize bridgeheads in the Northern Front at Kanyemba, Chirundu and Kariba to enable the crossing of ZIPRA regular troops with armour and artillery. Simultaneous attacks were to be mounted on the airfields at Kariba, Victoria Falls and Wankie, which were to be secured to enable the transfer of ZIPRA's airforce from Angola. The airforce of MIG fighters was to provide air cover for the ground troops.

The principal objective of these attacks was to enable the regular troops to seize and hold the strategic rear bases along the border in support of the offensive to be launched from within the country. The Zero Hour Plan did not require (though it did make provision for) the regular troops to advance any further after seizing the bridgeheads.

The central offensives were to be launched by the newly reinforced guerrilla brigades already inside the country, along several simultaneous lines of advance. In the north they were to attack Karoi and Sinoia. In the midlands the guerrilla brigade based at Gokwe was to attack Que Que and Hartley, while the brigade based in Nkai was to assault Gwelo. The brigades based in Tsholotsho had the task of attacking Bulawayo. In the Southern Front there were three lines of advance: towards Plumtree, Kezi and Gwanda/Beitbridge.

In each case local strategic sites were to be attacked or captured. These included military garrisons and police posts, railway stations, fuel supplies and vehicle depots and the administration offices. The commander of the forces attacking Plumtree outlined the military targets in his battle plan as

> the police, the District Commissioner's office, the District Assistants, the RLI and RAR camps, and the Selous Scout camp and the post office.[38]

The local party branches had roles to play too, and details of efforts to stimulate local risings were an important aspect of the Zero Hour Plan. Regional ZIPRA commissars who had, as part of their normal military work, the task of co-ordinating with ZAPU structures, were responsible for organizing civilian support for the attacks.[39] Almost 50 000 AK and SKS rifles and ammunition were destined for arming local militias, and the ZIPRA Training Department (which was already carrying out training inside the country) had the responsibility to organize crash-course training programmes under the auspices of the Youth League.[40]

Finally guerrilla units and specialized intelligence, commando and sabotage units were to launch a simultaneous wave of ambushes and attacks in urban areas and behind enemy lines, aimed principally at disrupting efforts by the Rhodesian forces to reinforce and supply the troops facing the main offensive. Key targets included Rhodesian air bases and military garrisons in the strategic heartland of the country.

In the early months of 1979 members of the High Command inside the country were busy transporting large quantities of arms and ammunition and cacheing them in preparation for the offensive. The commanders in each region were preparing detailed plans to attack their designated targets.

In Zambia, High Command members were preparing for the conventional assault on the bridgeheads. Among the technical problems facing the Engineering Department was the river crossing itself, which had to be accomplished without relying on existing bridges. The Logistics Department was already handling thousands of tons of supplies. The Reconnaissance Department had to prepare crossing and routing details for more troops than they had deployed during the entire war.

At this time members of the High Command were crossing the Zambezi frequently, organizing the military forces. As one experienced guerrilla commander explained:

> At the rear we were busy re-organizing the regular units, that is during the first months of 1979. We were busy organizing various units — reconnaissance, engineers and so on — to support the regular units. I was working with the reconnaissance department. Then we returned into the country to make preparations for the guerrilla offensive that would support the regular offensive.[41]

Meanwhile, in Zambia, ZIPRA began moving its regular troops into the rocky gorges of the escarpment above the Zambezi. Each night convoys of heavy vehicles moved enormous quantities of war materials into the escarpment. It was during this exercise that the Rhodesian forces launched a series of attacks into Zambia aimed at disrupting the preparations.

In October 1979, in one of the only two conventional set-piece battles of the war, the élite Special Air Service and the Rhodesian Light Infantry attacked a half-strength ZIPRA regular battalion which was establishing a base in the escarpment. Cole's history of the Rhodesian SAS describes the battle from the SAS viewpoint:

> From the outset, it was very apparent that the Rhodesians were up against a vast assortment of military hardware — and an opposition whose discipline and determination were outstanding.[42]

Despite repeated air raids against the ZIPRA camp, the Rhodesian ground forces were unable to attempt an assault on the camp, and spent most of the day pinned down by ZIPRA fire and taking casualties.

Suddenly there was a roar from the heaviest smallarms fire the Rhodesians had heard for a long time — and trooper Andy Houghton went down fatally injured. Like the other group of RLI on the neighbouring ridge, Don Price and his men had been stopped dead in their tracks. They regrouped but were out of the battle.[43]

By nightfall the SAS concluded that 'the enemy had undoubtedly won that round'. Following a 'very accurate' artillery bombardment in the night, in which the Rhodesians took further casualties, the ZIPRA forces completed an orderly withdrawal, about which 'there were some extremely harsh words said' in Rhodesian ranks the following day.

When the Rhodesians entered the empty camp the following morning they walked straight into a series of booby traps, taking further casualties. They were helicoptered out of Zambia that morning. Cole concludes:

> The mission had been bad news for the Rhodesians. They had grossly underestimated the enemy and had the living daylights shot out of them. They had been outgunned and outranged and had been unable to take the position.[44]

The SAS had located a further nine ZIPRA bases on the escarpment at this time, but they never attempted another ground attack. Instead the Rhodesian Air Force launched the largest-ever series of concentrated air attacks of the war.

Mark Ndlovu was the camp commander at ZIPRA's Chinyunyu Camp, which contained 4 500 troops when it was first attacked by 18 aircraft in late October 1979. Ndlovu describes the attack:

> Before they launched their missiles I ordered the anti-air units on the northern side of the camp to fire . . . When they fired at the first echelon the jet fighters missed their formation and one of them was shot. The second echelon and the rear one also missed the formation and were scattered all over the garrison.
>
> The attack lasted for one hour and thirty minutes, but they could only do random bombing very fast . . . Moreover they were bombing outside the garrison because the firepower was too much . . . I even heard the commander of the jet fighters through our means of communication saying 'I want that target destroyed. Come on, get inside'. The pilot said 'I cannot get inside. The firepower is too much'.[45]

ZIPRA anti-air units brought three aircraft down in this battle, and hit several others.[46] Chinyunyu Camp was attacked by air again in early November. On this occasion two aircraft went down. A further attack took place on 30 November at the same camp, but on this occasion the Rhodesian pilots dropped their bombs well away from the camp, and no aircraft were hit by ground fire. In all ZIPRA lost fifteen men during the Chinyunyu air raids. The Rhodesian air force lost at least five aircraft.[47]

The Rhodesian ground and air attacks into Zambia in 1979 failed to halt the ZIPRA build-up, ironically, it was the guerrilla-type operations mounted by the Rhodesians at the time which caused most problems.

The regular forces that were supposed to go inside the country were already within the escarpment, and most of the supplies and materials had been moved there as well. The Rhodesians got to know about these preparations and they started bombing. In the escarpment they were completely repulsed.

> They did not really succeed in destroying our line of supply, but what they did succeed in doing in certain areas was to plant land mines which made it difficult for our transport system. We had minesweepers on all the supply roads trying to keep them clear.[48]

According to Dabengwa, the conventional ground and air attacks,

> were a godsend. They steeled our men and gave them experience of real regular battle. We had very few casualties, absolutely minimal. Our men were able to take it all in their stride and accounted very well for themselves. Later, after the ceasefire, the Rhodesian commanders told us they realized their mistake in carrying out those attacks.[49]

Zero Hour was planned for early in the 1979 rainy season, that is, in October or November. While the Rhodesian forces did manage to disrupt the movement of supplies, the basic ground preparations had been largely completed before the Rhodesian intervention, and this did not cause ZIPRA to delay its plans. The offensive was in fact delayed by ZIPRA's airforce whose preparations were incomplete. Pilots undergoing training in the Soviet Union had not completed their courses, and the Soviet Air Force was reluctant to release them despite increasingly urgent demands from ZAPU. An alternative option — to use Cuban pilots — was rejected by the War Council for political reasons.[50]

Meanwhile the Lancaster House talks were taking place in London. The War Council met there (after taking extensive precautions to avoid the widespread bugging of their hotel rooms) to discuss whether to launch the offensive without air cover. They decided to wait. Throughout the latter part of the negotiations at Lancaster House the War Council was on the brink of ordering the Zero Hour attacks.

According to Joshua Nkomo the British government became very concerned at the prospect of an imminent ZIPRA offensive at the very moment that the talks were threatening to break up over the land issue. At this point the British Prime Minister, Mrs Thatcher, approached Nkomo privately and warned him against launching any attacks across the Zambezi. Nkomo says he denied any such intentions, but

> she was right. She knew what was happening, because as the conference was about to break on the land issue we were moving our tanks towards the Zambezi. Although we didn't have the pilots, we would have crossed all the same. After that day with Thatcher we thought we would do it without the aircraft.[51]

Final preparations were stepped up and the ZIPRA High Command was ordered into full alert for the offensive. Meanwhile the Frontline States intensified pressure on ZAPU and ZANU to settle at the negotiating table. The ZAPU War Council hesitated, and the moment passed. A skilful manoeuvre by Britain sidestepped the land issue and an agreement between all parties was reached at Lancaster House.

ZIPRA's Zero Hour plan was never put to the test. Today its main significance is its part of the evolution of military strategy by ZAPU.

PART TWO: THE ARMY, THE PARTY AND MILITARY STRATEGY

The debates in the High Command and War Council on the need to develop conditions for 'mobile warfare' as the basis for 'seizing power and defending it', provide one perspective of the development of ZAPU's military strategy. But ZAPU's plans had to be based on the actual capacity of the party and the army to carry them through.

ZAPU's military strategy had to be based on the realistic prospects of upgrading the technical, organizational and command structures of a guerrilla army. The introduction of regular military tactics and heavy weaponry was itself ultimately dependant on the individual capacity of the soldier.

The Turning Point Strategy relied considerably on the organizational capacity, not only of the army, but of party structures in rural areas, which were required to assume administrative functions in 'liberated' territory. The Zero Hour Plan also envisaged a major role for the civilian population, which was expected to join the offensive under the auspices of local party-led risings.

I will now briefly examine the composition of ZAPU's army, the role of the party and the relationship between the two, and assess how these factors affected the development of military strategy.

The Army
Guerrilla armies are usually young armies. Often they are armies of teenagers. In Africa, guerrilla armies have been predominantly young, peasant armies. These young peasant troops have generally experienced little of the modernizing lessons of urban life and have had limited access to educational and training opportunities. These factors have undoubtedly restricted some of the organizational and military capabilities of nationalist struggles for independence in Africa.

Guerrilla warfare is the strategy of the poor and weak against the rich and strong. It is, therefore, the natural strategy of the nationalist liberation movement in its struggle to overthrow colonial rule. However, the strategic limitations of guerrilla warfare, in particular in relation to the contest for state power, have imposed real limits on the revolutionary potential of nationalist insurgency. Anti-colonial guerrilla wars in Africa have invariably succeeded only in bringing about conditions for negotiation over the transfer of power, with inevitable implications constraining nationalist objectives of social transformation.

ZAPU's military strategy attempted to address these limitations. But did ZAPU's armed forces have any real potential to achieve the strategic goals its commanders had set?

ZAPU established its armed forces in 1965 and for the following 15 years waged an insurgent war against the Rhodesian government. The number of soldiers in the army periodically rose and fell, but it was only after the first decade of war that their number could be counted in thousands. By the end of the war ZIPRA had over 20 000 soldiers in its ranks, the bulk of whom had been recruited and

trained between 1976 and 1978. Over 53 per cent of recruits entered ZIPRA training
or transit camps in 1977, the peak year of entry. Almost one third of ZIPRA
soldiers entered the army before this peak year, and they comprised the veteran
guerrillas.[52]

Ten per cent of ZIPRA soldiers were women, and they were largely incorporated
into one unit, the ZIPRA Women's Brigade. This was a conventionally trained
infantry brigade, complete with its own engineers, communications, other support
services and female commanders.[53]

ZAPU's military training was by and large conducted by ZIPRA's own
instructors, and usually took six to eight months. Thereafter selected members of
ZIPRA underwent specialist courses in a variety of countries including the Soviet
Union, Libya, Egypt, Cuba and the German Democratic Republic. Recruits in the
1970s were volunteers usually screened in refugee camps before being sent on to
transit camps to await training. Recruits had come from all parts of the country in
the 1960s but by the peak recruiting year the majority of recruits were Sindebele-
speaking youngsters from the south and west of the country.

ZIPRA was not a children's army. Regulations forbade the recruitment of
anyone under the age of 18, and only 7 per cent of recruits reported that they were
under that age when they joined. But ZIPRA was certainly a young army. Only 8
per cent of its members were over 26 years old when they joined and 84 per cent
of ZIPRA's members were between 18 and 25 years old when they were trained,
and, as I have already pointed out, most of them joined in the last three years of the
war.

Over half of the recruits had been employed before they joined ZIPRA. The
next largest group (43 per cent) described themselves as being scholars, peasant
farmers or unemployed before they joined the armed struggle. Over 53 per cent of
recruits had been engaged in urban wage employment prior to joining ZIPRA
which reflects the labour migration patterns of Matabeleland — although 50 per
cent came from peasant households and 32 per cent from urban working class
homes. Significantly, at least 10 per cent of ZIPRA members were recruited from
South Africa, where they were working as migrant labourers.

In educational terms, approximately three-quarters of the recruits could be
described as functionally literate, and just over 11 per cent had ten or more years
of education, providing the army with its core of skilled cadres.

From this brief statistical outline of the composition of ZIPRA, several features
can be ascertained.

Although the army was young, the bulk of the members were in their early
twenties, and most of them had not come straight from school. They had had some
experience of life outside school, and indeed, over half of them had been in urban
wage employment, many in South Africa. The majority of recruits had experience
of urban life and capitalist production.

Most had completed whatever education their families could afford well before
they joined the army, and generally speaking their educational standards provided
the army with sufficient suitable candidates for higher levels of (technical) military
training.

Of particular significance is the predominance of recruits with experience of modern urban capitalism. Although ZIPRA was certainly rooted in the peasantry, and many of its recruits were peasant boys, the evidence suggests ZIPRA was unusually urban and proletarian in nature. This is significant because it undoubtedly affected and suited ZIPRA's decision to develop more technologically advanced military skills and strategy. But it also raises the question of how such urban wage earners were recruited.

The mix of recruits to ZIPRA strongly suggests that this was an army that was actively recruited, rather than pushed into war by economic and geographical factors. Indeed many recruits reported that they were recruited straight from their jobs into the army. How this happened leads us into an examination of the role of the party in recruitment.

The Party

By the time that most recruits entered ZIPRA ranks, the party had been banned and hounded for almost a decade and a half. Nevertheless 60 per cent of ZIPRA's recruits reported that they had been members of functioning branches of the ZAPU Youth League before they left the country to join the armed struggle. The largest proportion of these were recruited in the towns and cities, and it was in these urban environments that the clandestine structures of the party survived most effectively. But many recruits were members of rural party branches too.

The survival of underground party branches and their significance in the war is a fascinating feature of ZAPU's history, but one which lies outside the scope of this chapter. For the present I can only assert that these structures *did* survive persecution and illegality, and played a major role in recruiting for the army.

Most of the recruits to ZIPRA, therefore, had experience of political organization in their illegal party branches before they went on to receive formal political education from army commissars. Many of them explain that they joined the army because they had to leave the country to avoid arrest for their political activities, while others explain that they were instructed by their party branches to leave and join ZIPRA. In addition to their experience in the party, many recruits were also active in trade unions. Recruiting for the armed struggle was, therefore, taking place as part of a wider process of political activism within the townships. Such recruits brought with them a level of experience and political maturity not commonly found in African guerrilla armies.

The role of parents and communities in moulding and developing the future recruits of ZIPRA further emphasizes the enormous significance of ZAPU. Over 66 per cent of recruits came from families in which one or both parents were members of the illegal party branches. The role of the older generation in introducing the youth to nationalism was clearly not simply the province of a few national figures. Local elders, including parents, provided the young with a rich source of their own historical mission, as the following comments illustrate:

- 'After school each day my parents were interested in teaching me about the party, ZAPU'.

- 'They are the ones who told me to go to the struggle . . . My parents told me I must follow others so that we will free Zimbabwe'.
- 'I (had) gone to work in South Africa as a garden-boy (where) I have been organized by my father, so I have contact with the ZAPU members'.[54]

The actual process of recruitment reinforces this evidence of the central role of communities and the party itself as a vehicle of the community. Only 15 per cent of ZIPRA recruits reported that they were directly recruited by other ZIPRA members. Thirty per cent of recruits were instructed to go for military training by party branches, and of the remaining 50 per cent who volunteered, many were taken out of the country by party recruiting structures.

It is apparent that it was the party structures which gave ZIPRA access to many communities, in particular in urban areas where guerrillas themselves could not easily recruit, and hence provided the army with many recruits who had experience of politics, trade unionism and the modernizing influence of urban capitalism.

The Party and the Army in the War
The party's role in supporting the army was not, however, limited simply to recruiting for ZIPRA, and the underground party branches were, as I have already outlined, expected to play a key role in the Zero Hour Plan. A detailed examination of the relationship between the party and the army lies outside the scope of this chapter, but the existence and influence of the party structures certainly played a role in the development of military strategy by ZAPU, and needs to be mentioned briefly.

ZIPRA guerrillas relied a great deal on party branches and party contacts for support during the war. Food, medical supplies, transport and intelligence was provided to the guerrillas by their local party contacts. When ZIPRA guerrillas were about to enter a new operational area, it was customary for the ZIPRA commissar to seek out the local party contacts before the guerrillas were deployed into that area. Where party branches already existed, contact was made through them. If no party branch existed, the commissar sought out individual party members and encouraged them to set up clandestine branches to prepare to receive the guerrillas. In many rural areas party branches which had become defunct were resuscitated by ZIPRA commissars. For example, when ZIPRA forces first moved into the Gokwe area, the unit commissar found that the local people were very cautious about the arrival of guerrillas and that the party was weak in the area. As one commissar explained

I first discovered there were very few political branches for ZAPU. Most were the UANC. So we started to show them and convince them politically until they started to pull up their socks.[55]

Two years later, when a new ZIPRA commissar entered the area for the first time he found a very different reception.

The situation here was different because the peasants were organized and interested in the war, and they were a bit mature . . . In Gokwe there was no problem. The peasants were very much interested and we were well supplied by them.[56]

ZIPRA guerrillas who moved into Lupane found the local party had collapsed at branch level, though the party district structure still existed. The ZIPRA commissars, therefore, worked with the district party leaders to re-establish the local party branches. Thereafter the party branches carried out a range of functions for the guerrillas, as the local ZIPRA commander explained:

They were collecting party donations for us . . . These branches had relatives working in town and they used to bring medicines with them from town. The commissars had a duty to organize with the party at branch and district level.[57]

In the same area the ZAPU District Chairman negotiated the surrender of 144 locally trained Security Force Auxiliaries in September 1978 to ZIPRA.

Those people organized themselves and contacted the chairman of ZAPU and told him, tell those ZIPRA forces we want to surrender and join them. They came in groups with all their weapons and equipment. We sent some to Zambia and we remained with some in the area.[58]

It is clear that the spread of the war and the approach of the ZIPRA guerrillas greatly facilitated the growth of the party branches. ZIPRA guerrillas related to the civilian population wherever possible through specific links to party branch structures. The commissars oversaw this relationship, but guerrilla logistics officers, security and intelligence officers and training instructors all sought to develop links with specific party officials responsible for a particular part of the relationship with civilians.

In addition to immediate local support, the network of party branches provided the guerrillas with vital links across territory controlled by the Rhodesians and even crossed borders, as Richard Chimba, intelligence officer in ZIPRA's Southern Front, explained:

The town people in Gwanda understood our position. They supplied us with food, clothing and even boots. They used to support us through the branches in the rural areas . . . We used to have party members moving even to Botswana to explain our problems and support us . . . The supplies (for the Southern Front) were routed through Botswana. It was taken inside the country through certain party contacts. Then the units came to collect the materials.[59]

The wider implications of this relationship are outside the scope of this chapter, but it is clear that this approach by ZAPU and ZIPRA was mutually beneficial and supportive in a wide variety of ways. Crucially, many of the organizing, mobilizing and logistical tasks of the war could be carried out by the party, leaving the guerrillas to concentrate on their military tasks.

Thus ZIPRA generally required smaller numbers of guerrillas to effectively cover an area, and in many ways imposed a lighter burden on the local population than ZANLA did.[60] As a rule, ZIPRA guerrillas did not need to build a new political support base or establish their legitimacy. They could simply say they were 'Nkomo's boys' and seek out the party members in the community. Where the party was weak, the arrival of the guerrillas rejuvenated the party and facilitated its expansion.

ZIPRA guerrillas held very few '*pungwes*' with the local population, and they regarded this method of politicization with distaste, viewing it as superficial and dangerous to the population. Similarly ZIPRA '*mujibas*' played little role in political mobilization — except where this was a party activity.

By operating through the party structures the guerrillas were able to avoid being drawn into too many local conflicts and divisions. As one regional commander put it, 'as far as controlling the local people and the party was concerned, we left that to civilians'.[61]

Party structures also provided ZIPRA with real prospects of operating in towns and cities. From the time of the Turning Point, concerted efforts were made to infiltrate intelligence and specialized urban commando units into the towns and cities. By the end of 1979 almost every urban centre, with the exception of the eastern part of the country, had been infiltrated by such units. The six ZIPRA units in Salisbury even had radio contact with their regional commander in Lomagundi, and through him were in radio contact with Lusaka. These urban units, which had been received and concealed by the party branches, were expected to play a decisive role in the Zero Hour Plan, as I have already outlined.

This clearly defined relationship between the party and the army was not without problems, but it did enable a concentration of effort in the political and military spheres. The existence and growth of party branches, and their role in support of the guerrilla war, enabled ZIPRA to take territory from the Rhodesian forces with far fewer guerrillas than was the case in the eastern ZANLA operational areas. By the end of the war ZIPRA operated over as much territory as ZANLA with less than half the number of guerrillas. Undoubtedly it was largely through the efforts and role of the party inside the country that ZIPRA was able to fight a guerrilla war and at the same time divert recruits into further training as regular soldiers.

In conclusion I will briefly examine the consequences and implications of ZAPU's military strategy, and complete my argument for the singularity of this strategy.

Military strategy and African nationalism
No African liberation movement has actually seized power from a colonial regime. As a rule African independence is preceded by negotiations in which the colonial power attempts to restrain African nationalism.

Zimbabwe was no exception. During the Lancaster House talks which brought the war to an end, and indeed for years after Independence itself, the nationalist leaders complained that they were forced to compromise their political programme to an unacceptable degree by Britain. While much attention has been focused on the problems of transformation after Independence, the strategies and conduct of the war itself have not been used to illuminate this debate.

ZAPU's military strategy in the late 1970s attempted to address this anticipated problem, and thereby represents an important contribution to the theory and practice of revolutionary war in Africa.

Without an appreciation of the Turning Point Strategy and the Zero Hour Plan, ZIPRA's military strategy in the latter part of the war makes little sense. The Zero Hour Plan itself arose from ZAPU's assessment that the Rhodesian rebellion was on the brink of collapse, and that the move into mobile warfare could provide them with the opportunity for a decisive strategic victory.

ZAPU's military strategy had, as I have shown, been formulated on precisely that premiss since early 1977. What ZAPU perhaps failed to appreciate fully, was the capacity of Rhodesia's (formal and clandestine) allies to force through a negotiated settlement at whatever cost.

The guerrilla war finally exhausted the capacity of Rhodesia to resist, and, while it did not enable the nationalist movement to take power, it paved the way for the final acceptance by the British government that it had to intervene. The alternative was, as intelligence sources must have made clear to Mrs Thatcher and Lord Carrington, the creation of a revolutionary situation in the country and the region.

ZAPU's military strategy attempted 'to storm the heavens' precisely in order to create conditions for a revolutionary transformation of the social order. ZIPRA's military commanders and strategists put into place a military strategy which faithfully reflected the political objectives of the nationalist leadership of both ZAPU and ZANU. Both parties frequently stated that they would seize power and 'liberate' the country without British decolonization if necessary. ZIPRA's strategy intended to do just that.

Today, as Zimbabwe struggles to implement structural adjustment policies determined by international bankers and, a full decade after Independence, still seeks a land reform programme to return land to the peasantry, the limitations of guerrilla warfare as a strategy for revolutionary transformation are more apparent than ever. ZIPRA's strategy, aimed at achieving a military victory, would certainly have created alternative options for transforming Zimbabwe after Independence.

The army required by such a military strategy, however, could not easily be created from peasant communities who are the typical recruits of African armed struggle. The urban African community is relatively privileged with its access to wage employment and the modernizing experiences of capitalist society. Its skills undoubtedly strengthen the insurgency. But in urban areas where colonial authority is strongest, guerrilla access is usually weakest. Recruiting in such communities, who are not literally pushed into the arms of the insurgents by geography and economy, is principally political and hence the central role of the political party in ZAPU's strategy.

Many factors need to be taken into account to explain the survival and indeed growth of ZAPU during the war years, but as the armed struggle was the principal form of struggle, the relationship between the political and military organizations was clearly crucial. Central to this relationship was the fact that ZAPU's armed struggle began through a mass-based campaign of simple sabotage and violence. This contrasts markedly with for example, the isolating and conspiratorial process by which South Africa's ANC took up arms.

Thereafter the party structures continued to play a major role in support of the armed struggle. Recruiting in particular took place largely in the Youth League branches, as part of the natural process of political activism — mobilizing resources for the guerrillas, organizing membership and discussing politics. This party activity in urban areas gave ZAPU access to young workers and intellectuals who could bring new skills and experience to the guerrilla army. The existence of the party branches in urban centres certainly profoundly influenced the social composition of ZIPRA.

It is difficult to ascertain the extent to which the arrival of the young urban recruits generated the debate and demand for the new strategy. But they certainly enthusiastically supported the upgrading of the army and accelerated the process. Undoubtedly their presence provided ZIPRA's commanders with a far more suitable basis for developing the more sophisticated military and organizational skills their new strategy required.

However, J. Z. Moyo's fear of negotiations finally proved well founded and ZAPU's efforts to create conditions in which the nationalist movement might actually determine its own post-Independence agenda failed. Nevertheless the development by ZAPU of a new type of military strategy, and the attempt to actually implement it, provides a new perspective from which the historical achievements of African nationalism may yet be viewed.

4

The Zimbabwe People's Army: Strategic Innovation or More of the Same?

DAVID MOORE

The question of 'strategy' in a guerrilla war is a broad one. It cannot be restricted to questions of military planning alone, as if that aspect of a war of national liberation was divorced from issues of politics and ideology. Indeed, the term 'guerrilla war' itself is a symbolically loaded one, full of all sorts of definitional problems. Many of these puzzles pertain to the relationship between the military cadres of an army and the people among whom they must operate — whose 'hearts' they wish to win. This is the stuff of politics. Perhaps ideology enters the picture when one considers the causes to which those hearts are to be won.

In the case of the Zimbabwe People's Army (ZIPA), the question of strategy goes even beyond matters of military planning, politics, and ideology. For the young men who made up the 'revolutionary' core of ZIPA, 'strategy' took on many different meanings.

Firstly, and at first most importantly, it took on the meaning that most conventional military analysts would ascribe to it. ZIPA wanted to win a war against the Rhodesian state, plain and simple. It wanted to perform a diplomatic task by forceful means, as Clausewitz would have put it, and in that respect ZIPA was not much different from any other liberation movement in Zimbabwe or in any other colonial war. This aspect of ZIPA's strategy will be studied to some extent in the following pages, and it will be discovered that ZIPA had some innovative approaches to this task. Even if we utilize the seemingly antiseptic perspective of analysts such as Cilliers,[1] it can be seen that ZIPA did represent something new on the scene of the 'struggle for Zimbabwe'. I will refer to this aspect of ZIPA's strategy as, prosaically enough, military strategy.

Secondly, it must be remembered that ZIPA's goals for Zimbabwe were revolutionary in the Marxist sense. The leaders of this group were committed 'ideological soldiers,' and thus their strategy was concerned with the matter of how to ensure the hegemony of Marxist principles within the liberation movement. This paper will argue that in this sense, too, ZIPA was a qualitatively new organization. ZIPA may not have been exactly what Gramsci had in mind when he wrote of a 'modern prince,' or revolutionary party composed of 'organic intellectuals', but given the circumstances, it came close to that ideal.[2] ZIPA's strategy for the unity of ZANU and ZAPU armed forces should also be considered under this rubric. Throughout the paper this strand of ZIPA's thinking shall be referred to as its ideological strategy.

Thirdly, it must be remembered that ZIPA did not exist for long. Within less than a year of its inauguration in November 1975, the ideologically committed leaders of the group were in peril. When the Kissinger initiative of mid-1976 took on momentum, resulting in the release of the 'old guard' ZANU High Command from the Zambian prisons (where they were incarcerated while accused of assassinating Chitepo) and the revitalization of the politicians, the ZIPA commanders were under a great deal of pressure to, at first, maintain their influence in the liberation process, and later, to save their lives. I will refer to these imperatives as survival strategies.

It will be shown that ZIPA did indeed bring innovation — and something approaching transformation — to the strategies of the Zimbabwean liberation war. In that sense, this work will be a departure from those which see the group as 'more of the same',[3] write it off as a group of 'ultra-leftists' and even 'counter-revolutionaries',[4] or, more benignly, claim that it was always simply a part of ZANLA.[5]

Before investigating ZIPA's strategies — as much as possible through the voices of the group's leaders — it is necessary to recount some background information about ZIPA.

ZIPA: A BRIEF HISTORY AND CONTEXT

A chronological narrative would start the days of ZIPA in November 1975 and end them in January 1977. Towards the end of the former month, a commanding group consisting of nine representations from each of ZAPU's and ZANU's armies was constituted in Maputo, and was heralded by the Frontline States as the progenitor of true unity within the Zimbabwean liberation movement. ZIPA reignited the liberation war (which had been in abeyance since the late 1974 Vorster-inspired détente), began its transformation into a political and ideological as well as military organization, and commenced diplomatic endeavours.

By the end of June 1976, however, violent eruptions had occurred between soldiers of both original armies in Mgagao and Morogoro training camps, and ZAPU pulled out of the arrangement. Following that, ZIPA's leaders attempted to get the political leaders of their parties together to forge unity 'from above', while ZIPA kept the revolution on track from below.

Henry Kissinger's shuttle to Southern Africa to save Rhodesia from the fate of Angola and Mozambique placed such plans in jeopardy. With the approach of the Geneva Conference of October 1976 and signs that a moderate group of politicians with control of the soldiers would be supported by international forces, the leaders of ZIPA were imperiled. By the beginning of 1977, those within the group who remained true to its stated principles were unceremoniously deposited in

Mozambican prison camps by a revived 'old guard' of ZANU leaders in collaboration with the Mozambican state, where they remained until early 1980.

If we are to take a view of history that is both more contextual and more detailed, however, ZIPA was much more than this. It represented an ideological, and perhaps generational, trend that began well before the conventional dates of demarcation and will end long after them. The challenge within that trend reached into the very core of the war of liberation's meaning, and extended into the totality of Southern Africa's social and political structures. ZIPA represented the culmination of the ideological contradictions which had been developing ever since the formative stages of the Zimbabwean 'ruling class-in-the-making.' The ideological trends ZIPA represented were not easily removed from the scene: in retrospect, it appears that it took the political, ideological, and economic forces of 'free-market capitalism' until 1990 and the enthusiastic embrace of the Zimbabwean state with 'structural adjustment' to fully eliminate what ZIPA stood for.

By the mid-1970s, the ideological struggles within ZANU had resulted in the official adoption of Marxism-Leninism as its corpus of principles. Détente and compromise with the settler regime had been discredited within the party, and its discourse — officially marked in 'Mwenje 2'[6] — was ostensibly that of a revolutionary and Marxist guerrilla movement. Yet such rhetoric masked a very uneven process. To some extent it was a matter of realpolitik: the support for the liberation armies was coming from the 'east' and radical groups in the west. But more importantly, ZANU's apparent ideological shift was complicated by the fact that the language of radicalism and guerrilla warfare made it difficult to separate 'authoritarian militarists' from 'militant transformationalists.'[7] The attraction to the lure of détente of such moderate nationalists as Abel Muzorewa of the United African National Council in Rhodesia and the recently released Ndabaningi Sithole served to draw a sharp line between potential 'sellouts' and those committed to furthering the armed struggle. The latter group, consisting of widely varying degrees of ideological preferences, shared commitment to the use of armed force, but not to socialist transformation. And as the Nhari rebellion and the Chitepo assassination demonstrated, the unevenness of such developments was complicated by traditionally nationalist forms of internecine rivalry.[8]

In many respects the ideological shift was the result of the rise of young intellectuals, returning from abroad to positions of some ideological power within the 'political' realms of the party. Yet within the armed forces, too, there were important, although as yet latent, changes in the works. The young commanders who would eventually form ZIPA were becoming militant transformationalists.

ZIPA's eventual leaders were part of a relatively new generation in the camps. They were part of a 'second wave' of guerrilla soldiers. The 'first wave' was made up mostly of press-ganged exiles in Zambia, led by the 'original' nationalists. The second wave was largely made up of young, relatively well-educated and urbanized Zimbabweans who had heard of the war in the late 1960s and early 1970s and crossed the borders into Zambia or Botswana (there were transit camps in the latter), or who had participated in the secondary school and university demonstrations of those days, experiencing firsthand the repression of the Smith regime. A 'third wave' consisted of younger and less educated recruits from the east, in the mid and late 1970s. Many of the second wave recruits were radicalized through their exposure to Soviet and Chinese military training, their own readings and discussions of the classical Marxist texts — carried on with considerable ingenuity against the wishes of their seniors — and their confrontations with superiors suspicious of forward young intellectuals.

From the earliest days of their interest in the liberation struggle, the young guerrilla leaders in the camps who would eventually form the core of ZIPA were not concerned with what nationalist party to join, but with how to join the struggle to liberate a nation. Their consciousness had transcended the level of ethnicity or political party — for many of them it was accidental which party they ended up joining upon exile from Rhodesia.[9]

The words of one ZIPRA member who later joined ZANLA, and then played a key role in ZIPA,[10] are indicative of the difficulty this view of unity often landed them in. While he was in ZIPRA, just returned from training in the Soviet Union,[11] he ran into trouble for advocating unity.

> I was talking about the need to unite in ZANU and ZAPU, I thought I was trying to write a book in which I was trying to argue my case that unity was imperative to secure our liberation. Then I was arrested by ZIPRA people on allegations that I was a ZANU agent. 'Why am I talking about unity?' And then they began to ask me, how did you come to ZAPU in the first place?[12]

Many 'Shona'[13] members of ZIPRA were unhappy with what they perceived as Ndebele dominance of the organization's command structures. For those Shona who were thinking of the idea of unity in any case, such practice was insufferable. 'The Ndebele were made commanders for almost every unit. The other tribes, like the Shona, could either be the deputies or commissars or whatever, but making sure that the senior commander is ZIPRA — I mean, is Ndebele.'[14] When Todlana returned from training in Bulgaria to Morogoro Camp in Tanzania, he was encountered with 'the height of the contradictions in ZAPU' which resulted in Chikerema's departure to form FROLIZI (the Front for the Liberation of Zimbabwe).[15] On arrival, the trainees learned

> that we could not proceed (to Lusaka) because the border between Zambia and Tanzania was sealed. So we waited in Tanzania for about five months in the camps. The information was filtering to us as to what was happening back in Zambia. We felt that it was unsafe for us and that we could not play any meaningful role as long as we remained in ZAPU. The best thing was to cross the floor.

> This transfer of manpower from ZIPRA to ZANLA included such actors as 'Rex Nhongo, myself, Thomas Nhari — that Nhari [who led the Badza / Nhari Revolt in 1974] . . . Robson Manyika, the deputy commander of ZIPRA, came to join ZANLA after us,' and thus represented a significant loss of ZIPRA personnel. It also constituted a large boost to ZANLA's fortunes: in early 1971 ZANU had less than one hundred soldiers.

Todlana's efforts to recruit more ZIPRA soldiers to the cause of unity via ZANU membership landed him in more difficulties.

> When I went back to ZIPRA to try to recruit others — the Shona people — to come and join us in ZANLA, I was captured by ZIPRA. I was imprisoned underground for a week or two. It was a pit. When we were taken out, we seized the opportunity [to escape].

On joining ZANLA, Todlana went to Dodoma camp — from where he was soon to be 'apprenticed' with FRELIMO — where he again aired his views on unity.

> It is that camp, at Dodoma, where I was quite outspoken about the need for this unity. Some people were wondering he has left ZAPU to come and join us, and now he is talking about unity with ZAPU, well what does he mean? 'You must be some ZAPU agent.' So I was put in prison again, but this time it was in a decent cell. I was there for some time. At the end, when the senior commanders came there, they asked for my release. But I never recanted. I still maintained that unity between ZANU and ZAPU was necessary and important.

Todlana's testimony is reflective of the 'attitude' of the ZIPA leaders as a whole — even though he does admit that he is more outspoken than most. It is clear that these young men were not amenable to following externally imposed party 'lines' and discipline: they were analogous to the youth of the 'sixties' in Europe and North America.

The militant transformationalists within ZIPA rose to prominence within ZANU's ideological contradictions, and a confluence of coincidence, circumstance and strategy. The political and military vacuum following Zambia's incarceration of ZANU's Dare (Command Council) for allegedly masterminding Chitepo's March 1975 murder, combined with détente's disaster, the *de facto* non-leadership of Ndabaningi Sithole, and Mugabe's enforced restraint in Mozambique while he tried to assert his as yet unsanctioned authority over ZANU, all contributed to a situation ripe for ZIPA's assumption of leadership and for the construction of the foundations necessary for the execution of a struggle based on the postulates of socialist transformation. In addition to ZANU's convolutions, leaders such as Muzorewa, Nkomo and FROLIZI's remnants were having little luck in forging their own unity: nor were they succeeding in the realm of negotiations or in gaining the allegiance of the essentially leaderless, but militarily powerful, ZANLA soldiers. As well, the failure of the 'moderate' groups to make détente work convinced the leaders of the Frontline States to look for an alternative mode of pressuring the powers that were to push Ian Smith out of Rhodesia.

It was more or less a coincidence that the media for this pressure was in the form of ideologically committed ZANLA commanders. That they had minds of their own proved somewhat troublesome for those who wanted the quickest settlement possible. To make matters worse, Mozambique — the country with the fronts most accessible to Zimbabwe — was barely able to cope with its early stages of independence, let alone with hosting a foreign liberation army.

The remaining pages will attempt to indicate the way in which ZIPA's innovations were implemented.

Most military analyses of the liberation war agreed that ZIPA's re-instigation of the struggle raised it to a qualitatively new plane, although few realize that ZIPA was not simply ZANLA with another name. From early in 1976 the Rhodesian forces were strained as never before, and it was apparent that the 'insurgents' were planning the war in a different way than ZANLA had in the past. Tamarkin summarizes the literature:

> It is absolutely clear that within a few months the guerrilla war scene had been dramatically transformed. Whereas at the end of 1975 there were barely a hundred guerrillas in the north-east, within six months many hundreds of them had infiltrated along most of Rhodesia's borders with black Africa. This quantitative change was also reflected in the volume and nature of the guerrilla war. Having gained the initiative the guerrillas began to pursue a more comprehensive and determined strategy. That this was aimed not merely at occasional harassment but rather at engulfing the whole of Rhodesia in guerrilla action reveals the new multi-faceted strategy. A major target of the guerrilla thrust was the disruption of the Rhodesian transport system. After the closure of the Mozambique border, the aim was primarily to hit Rhodesia's vital rail and road lifelines to the south. The guerrillas also concentrated their effort in disrupting the internal road communication system. This they achieved by laying ambushes and mines on roads in different parts of the country and in particular in the operational zones.[16]

In fact, ZIPA's plans were to establish fully liberated zones in Zimbabwe within the last six months of 1976. ZIPA intended to launch mobile warfare, described by Vo Nguyen Giap[17] (see pp. 52, 56). As the ZIPA commander in charge of military instruction put it,

> The first stage was to chase the enemy out of what would be the future base areas, so our main task there was to politicize the masses: you'd organize them, you'd chase out the enemy, you'd consolidate in this base area. What we are now in Tanzania or Mozambique should be in Zimbabwe, after we'd liberated some zones. That was the strategic thinking.[18]

Sources indicate that Soviet support for such plans was imminent, but that it was likely that American intelligence had intercepted this information through the Soviet offices in Maputo.[19]

The ZIPA High Command were well-versed in military strategy. Among them they had attended the military training programmes of both China and the Eastern Bloc. In this respect they were much more advanced than the members of the old ZANLA High Command, and were quite aware of this fact.

> Whether, for example, Tongogara himself understood exactly the difference between military strategies and tactics — he never. For example, the relationship between something of operational significance, tactical significance, or tactical-strategic significance, they never knew. There was no co-ordination: it was just fighting, defeating enemy tactics,

destroying . . . but not serving a given objective; for example a systematic blocking of roads so as to eventually cut off the enemy from . . . [distortion in tape] . . . Neither Tongogara nor any of the members of the High Command, we had just learned, could have helped. We knew their limitations.[20]

The ZIPA officers simply had more training than their previous commanders: while Tongogara and his cohorts were 'managing' the war and politicking before their imprisonment in 1975, their immediate underlings were taking advanced courses. Neither was ZIPA's ostensible commander and Tongogara's second-in-command, Rex Nhongo, as well-trained as the ZIPA leaders directly below him. Nhongo, considered by most ZIPA actors as a figurehead, was suspicious of those devising strategy for the war.

When we were discussing why we should attack this camp, and why we should exhaust the cadres from that province into this one that we are attacking . . . he would think that we were trying to build some plot within the base . . . [21]

That the ZIPA commanders felt they were better trained than their 'superiors' was not the result of youthful arrogance — it was simply a matter of fact.

I think I might add one significant point to do justice to them as well. The kind of training which they received, especially Tongogara, of course, that was basically mobilization . . .

. . . sabotage warfare, and these were the first groups. The Chinese wanted to start to see whether these people were serious, so they probably gave them less support then. They later opened up during our time [of training]. As I said, I belonged to the first group who were trained as military strategists. Then after that we were trained to train military instructors. So our level of military understanding was now higher. So they [the Chinese] opened up later. They [the members of the High Command] were never exposed to that.[22]

The ZIPA commanders were critical of the Mozambicans' approach to guerrilla war, too, although that disapproval was not based so much on theoretical grounds: 'it was their practice (laughter), their political practice, it was their commandist approach . . . That one never ceased . . . that one we never liked.'[23] It was felt that Tongogara was influenced to a great degree by this attitude: one of its manifestations was the manner in which women — both in the training camps and in 'the bush' — were treated. There was also evidence that FRELIMO was taking some of the supplies sent by the Chinese for ZIPA. Even before Samora Machel embraced the Kissinger vision of a settlement as 'victory', the ZIPA group held their supposed mentors with some degree of mistrust.

The success of the ZIPA strategy led to heavy Rhodesian counter-insurgency efforts, but for the ZIPA commanders the development of protected villages, hot-pursuit tactics, and even the devastating raids on camps such as Nyadzonia were indications of success. In an essay written after ZIPA's demise, one of its leaders reflected on the movement's military success:

> The liberation movement made great strides in a short period of time under the leadership of ZIPA and sent shock waves to the imperialist circles. By June 1976, evidence of the successes scored by ZIPA were manifest in the desperate manoeuvres of the Smith regime to thwart the revolutionary advance of the liberation struggle. It resorted to massive call ups, prolonged the period of national service, instituted convoy systems for all major transport services, introduced the curfew system and mobile martial courts, resorted to hot-pursuit operations and finally switched from a strategy of 'clear and hold' into one of general offensive. All this in a vain attempt to check the development of the people's war failed dismally.[24]

Less formally, it was put this way.

> No, actually, for us it was a victory. The enemy was now panicking. Our strategy was having an effect. The fact that the enemy was resorting to these measures was an act of desperation as far as we were concerned. This had happened in China, this had happened in Vietnam. So we did not panic at all.

> In fact, there were occasions when they would set up a protected village, abandon it, and then we would liberate that protected village.

> And also, there were occasions when we had actually destroyed some enemy camps close to the border, where we would set to combat 100 to 150 — normally we wouldn't overtake them, it was only guerrilla sections, but we were also gaining practice in some sort of semi-mobile warfare . . . [25]

As for Kissinger's diplomatic shuttle, 'we knew that the imperialists were at it again'. What ZIPA did not know was that Mozambique would soon let them down in order to facilitate the Geneva Conference and resuscitate the 'old guard.' By about April 1976 Machel was grooming ZIPA for more of a diplomatic role.

> Around this time, Machel made jokes . . . Machel said 'you are not well dressed . . . you must now learn to dress for things like big conferences because you may be called' . . . but we did not think far ahead at that time, we did not have much foresight.[26]

When it became obvious that the question of Geneva and the revival of the old guard were issues of importance, ZIPA's strategy had to turn to one of survival. Before those plans are investigated, however, a brief examination of some of ZIPA's ideological and political strategies will be examined.

Ideological and political strategy

When ZIPA's role in the Zimbabwean liberation war has been considered at all, its ideological stance has been given the most accord. Usually these assessments have rested with a judgement of whether or not the group was infected with the virus of 'infantile left-wing communism'[27] or not. The following words will not do justice to the intricacies necessary to refute such claims, but do indicate the complexities of an accurate assessment of this question.

In actuality, the essence of ZIPA's ideological strategy was not far from the 'orthodox' vision of Marxism-Leninism devised by the Comintern for colonial and 'backward' societies. This policy of the 'national democratic revolution' called for a definite 'bourgeois stage,' and a clear role for a national bourgeoisie, for an about-to-be-liberated country. But it called for a liberation war to be led by the proletariat — or its practical substitute, members of the revolutionary intelligentsia — who would take the bourgeoisie in stride and let it play its historical role. Presumably, after national liberation, bourgeois democracy would ensue and a proletarian-peasant alliance would win the day in free and fair elections.

Such a strategy is tricky to say the least. Emergent bourgeoisies in the 'third world' are notoriously undemocratic, and extremely suspicious of challengers of any stripe and of any degree of potentiality — especially Marxist ones. Yet in a battle against an external enemy, the unity of all 'progressive' forces was as essential for the bourgeoisie as for the subaltern classes and social groups. The crux of ZIPA's political and ideological strategy — and indeed of their survival — revolved around this dilemma. Their attempted solution was to press at all times for unity, and for the room within such unity to preserve and expand their 'ideological space.' Thus their stance was essentially one of unity and democracy.

It was not until half-way through ZIPA's tenure that its leaders really reflected seriously on their role within the liberation movement as a whole. Until then, they saw themselves as politically and ideologically conscious soldiers to be sure, and they tried to transform the military unity between ZANLA and ZIPRA into something approaching this, but it took until around June 1976 before they realized that they would have a primary role to play — after the battles at Mgagao and Morogoro between 'ZANLA' and 'ZIPRA' cadres resulted in ZIPRA giving up on military unity, and after they learned a little more about their predecessors.

> After ZIPRA had pulled out from Chimoio, from ZIPA, that's the time when we began to reflect. Because now the truth was coming out as to what task lay before us, and also the opportunities which were to arise out of the new situation. Now we came to grips with the reality that our leaders were arrested, and also from communicating with our forces we came to learn about the atrocities which they were committing within camps. Because Dzino, myself, and all these other members of the ZIPA High Command were mostly in East Africa, they did not know what was happening. So, that cruelty meted to the people by the ZANLA High Command was little known to the officers in East Africa. So, you see, from the people, these people who would tell us — so and so died through this way, and so forth, Tongogara did this and that, and so forth, all this. And we would also gage from people's responses that they were preferring us, they were appreciating that we were understanding,

compared with the previous regime. That was the time when we were beginning to reflect that we had a role to play. We could not accept only a secondary role, in which we played a junior role, leaving the whole determination of the liberation war to the High Command and to the party. We were now convinced that we had to put some inputs.[28]

The ZIPA leaders were not yet concerned with the possibility of their usurpation by a returning old guard: they were beginning to realize that they might have to lead the liberation movement. Furthermore, the tragedies in the joint training camps which resulted in the departure of ZIPRA convinced them that without serious ideological training, the cadres were prey to the vicissitudes of all the old nationalist contradictions — including the divisions inspired by the differences between the Soviet Union and China. Some of the latter contradictions had festered within ZIPA itself, until the protagonists discerned the folly of it all. Occasionally they were

> literally quarrelling, at times getting to the level of almost fighting. Well, it was also immaturity on our part. I had been in the Soviet Union, I had been given some inclination of what they said about Marxism and so forth, what they said about the Chinese. Dzino was also with the Chinese, he had gone to China, and at the camp where we were, the Chinese were the instructors. He had so much Chinese influence. I had so much Soviet influence. The Chinese were talking evil about the Soviet Union, the Soviets were talking ill about the Chinese. So now the two unfortunate Zimbabweans meet [laughter] . . . if the truth should be said . . . we quarrelled on many occasions on ideological . . . differences between China and the Soviet Union. We were rather — parrots of these two giants. We could not articulate exactly as to what was the issue of difference between these two powers, except what they were telling us. Then we were still very immature, we were not yet in a position to analyze on our own, or even, better still, to ignore [the 'lines' of the Soviet Union and China].[29]

With the recognition that such arguments were part of the problem rather than the solution, the ZIPA ideologues began to comprehend

> that there is a vast difference between understanding what a theory says and applying it — there is a vast difference. I had read Marxism-Leninism, I had read about the history of the Communist Party, I had read also about the Comintern, about the international revolutionary movement and so forth, I had read about that. But to apply it to the Zimbabwean situation, it was not possible, maybe because I was within the lower ranks, possibly, but that's a lame excuse . . . this immaturity ended, I would say, around '76 when we had opened up ZIPA and when ZIPRA ended.[30]

One of the results of this perception was the founding of Wampoa College, an institute meant to develop leadership covenants with Marxist principles and able to lead a national democratic revolution. Todlana was made the director of the college, and indeed it may well have been he who broached the idea.

We discussed. I don't want to say that I was instrumental, but I used to talk to Dzino and many others that it would have been a good thing if we established a college. Then, because of Dzino's influence . . . (Nhongo, who was the ZIPA commander . . . was not very powerful — he was more or less a figure-head) . . . I don't want to gain credit that I was instrumental in the establishment of Wampoa, but I am saying, just in our talk, talking about the importance of such an institution to serve the army . . . ZIPA made the decision, but I know for sure that it was Dzino's decision, because he knew how to win his day in the camp.[31]

The college — named quite consciously after Chiang Kai Shek's college for the Chinese Nationalist Army, which Stalin had instigated in the 1920s — was to serve 100 students at a time, four month courses on ideology, politics, economics, history and military strategy. ZANU orthodoxy ridicules the college as a breeding ground for those who wanted to contemplate 'space and time', and 'the negation of the negation',[32] but it actually spawned quite rigorous and concrete debate on the contemporary political situation — indeed, the students' vigour forced some of the ZIPA teachers to 'come down to earth' in discussions about the political and ideological nature of the Zimbabwean political leaders. The sessions on 'The National Democratic Revolution' in particular generated interest, and the works of such African theorists as Amilcar Cabral were inserted in the curriculum on student demand. As Todlana remarked, 'they had so much interest. But we had not ourselves read much. We were not very well read. We were more or less giving the general directions.'[33] No matter how the institute started, it became a democratic one.

Wampoa also held short courses

which we were calling *chimbichimbi*, that is, as quickly as possible. This was especially for people who were required to go into the country, not necessarily to go to fight, but to go and mobilize the people, to establish communications, so they would need orientation and also a little bit of training . . . They would be there for three weeks, unlike the others who were selected on the basis of their academic attainment, and who would stay there until they had finished their course, for four months.[34]

The fact that Wampoa was considered by the returning old guard to be the centre of the 'coup' they felt ZIPA was instigating indicates how much these actors feared ideological education. Machingura may have been referring to the Wampoa experience when he later wrote that 'all revolutionary political literature is anathema to the nationalist leadership and is considered subversive as it might incite the fighters into rebellion against the authority'.[35] But the college served as the beginnings of the institutionalization of democracy within the armed forces themselves. Machingura's reflections on the nature of the relationship between the political leadership of the struggle and the soldiers indicate the core of ZIPA's approach. In the course of a critique of the organizational relationship between the external leadership of the party and the local organizations in Zimbabwe (which in itself is a clarion call for deep democracy) he continued to outline the problems within the military.

> The organizational weaknesses that are peculiar to the nationalist movement find their expression within the nationalist armies as well. It will be recalled that the nationalist armies emerged in the course of the development of armed struggle to become the principal form of struggle in the national liberation struggle. Though the nationalist armies are organizationally dove-tailed into their respective nationalist organizations at the political level, they are regarded as being organizationally distinct from the nationalist organizations themselves.[36]

Machingura is referring here to the fact that in 1973 Tongogara managed to ensure that at the bi-annual elections to the Dare (executive) meetings the military High Command could run. Yet rather than ensure that the military as a whole had a democratic structure, this only meant that the general commander of the army was part of the political élite.

> The nationalist armies are considered merely as instrumental in the service of their respective nationalist organizations and not regarded as the political extension of the nationalist organization. In contradistinction to revolutionary armies elsewhere, the nationalist leaders have not extended the nationalist organization into the army through the setting up of organizational branches and political committees within the army. Consequently, the broad masses of the fighters are in reality not politically interred into nationalist organizations; they have no say in the political affairs of the nationalist organizations; they are only members of the army. This reduces them to the level of the bourgeois armies which are nationalist organizations because they have a say in the political affairs of the organization unlike the broad masses of the fighters who are never consulted and are regarded as military instruments. In a revolutionary situation, such political relations between the army and political organization, can only be counter-productive; the denial of democracy to the fighting forces reduces their combativeness and sows seeds of discord within the nationalist organizations which eventually give rise to political instability.[37]

Machingura then goes on to hint, in suitably abstract terms, just what happened to ZIPA in the absence of such democracy. After noting the fact that reliance on the socialist countries forced the leadership to allow Marxist ideas to filter into the camps ('this is the price the nationalists pay for getting military assistance from the Socialist countries'), Machingura accounted for the contradictions.

> From that time the seeds of the revolutionary ideology were sown into the ranks of the nationalist fighting forces, all that was left was the germination of the seeds . . . the best they can do is progressively weed out the revolutionary elements who become a direct threat to their authority. Consequently, though the fighting forces are under the political and organizational leadership and influence of the nationalist leadership,

ideologically the fighting forces pursue a line opposed to that of the leadership. In the course of time, this ideological outlook develops to the point of influencing the organization and political views of the fighting forces. This sets the fighting forces on a collision course with the petty bourgeois nationalist leadership, who, lacking a correct political line and the requisite military know-how, will eventually develop to hamper the development of the struggle. Furthermore, restriction of internal democracy within the nationalist armies will also eventually develop to become the hotbed of tension within the nationalist organization: the stringent internal organization within the nationalist ranks limits the combativeness of the army and arrests the initiative of the broad masses of the fighters . . . Waging the struggle without a sound organizational base will only serve to complicate the path to victory and thereby protract the people's liberation struggle.[38]

If one remembers what happened to ZIPA, this section of the treatise rings true. ZIPA was the result of some of the fighters taking the discourse of the Soviet Union and China seriously, and thus mounting a serious challenge to the nationalist leadership. When the presence of ZIPA served to restrict the nationalists' possibilities of making a deal with the Kissingers of the world, ZIPA was eliminated, and it took almost three more years for the nationalists to build up to the same position they were in mid-to-late 1976. It may be entering the world of 'what-ifs' to speculate on what would have happened had the returning old guard agreed to work hand-in-hand with ZIPA's contention that a firm united front among the political forces, with ZIPA as a united army, would have presented Smith and the diplomats at Geneva with a much stronger enemy. That degree of co-operation was not forthcoming, however, so ZIPA's strategy became one of survival — both in the physical sense and in the sense of preserving some of its ideological gains.

Survival strategies
With the advent of the Geneva Conference, the release of the original High Command, and the rise of Mugabe to international recognition as ZANU's leader, the ZIPA core had to come to some quick conclusions. In early September 1976, at the instigation of the leaders of the Frontline States, they met with all the nationalist leaders in Dar-es-Salaam. Before that, they had come to an agreement on the best strategy — but ZIPA was split.

There were some differences between the rest of ZIPA and Rex, and then Gwauya. These two were the only ones who took a different position. The rest, we were united. We were united in the sense that we had now come to the realization that while it was now difficult for us to oppose completely the coming back, the reunion with the old guard, we'd have to do something at least to contain them. We now realized we had to really play a role, if not an important role, to reshape the direction, the understanding, the theoretical understanding, of the party. It was becoming unavoidable. We were in a situation where we could not have our own way, but this time it was 'how do we do it'. At least we were convinced that we did not want these people to come back, the old guard

— particularly the High Command people. As for the Central Committee members, it was not really a very serious problem because we knew we could easily contain them. It was these people who would come in to overlord over us and for all we knew, their orientation was anything but bad.

So we were trying to find the best way in which we could keep a distance away from them. Now, Rex and Gwauya did not really see what the whole thing was about. They were ZANU people, they had not seen any reason for change, 'now that the leaders have been released, we must unite! ZIPA had played its role while its leaders were in prison. So what's the trouble about?' They couldn't understand us. They had no ambitions, you see. I don't know whether we had any ambitions but I think we were concerned with the survival of the revolution, more than personal or whatever ambitions. But these had none of these ambitions, so these were the differences, these were saying, no, lets go to Geneva![39]

ZIPA's solution to the problem was to propose a united front at the political level, consisting of three leaders from each of the nationalist groups — ZANU, ZAPU and the ANC. Another nine members of this executive council would be from ZIPA — it would be a separate, but united, army.

We were proposing a united front as a precondition. You see we were giving a condition that for anybody to claim that he'd be over-arching over us, he could only do it within the framework of a united front. No single political party could claim that we belonged to them. That applied to ZANU, that applied to ANC, that applied to ZAPU, to everybody. 'We would only accept your leadership if you kept us as one group.'[40]

Most of the literature suggests that Nkomo refused such a suggestion, because he saw ZIPA as a ZANU creation, and he remembered all too well the results of the battles in the camps. There is as yet no released information on how Mugabe reacted to such a proposal, but it is certain that Tongogara did not agree with it. In the end, Mugabe followed Nkomo's lead and did not pursue the notion of uniting the armies, and he co-operated with Tongogara in eliminating ZIPA. Machel's turning against ZIPA was the final nail in their coffin. When they were forced to go to Geneva by Machel, they attempted to maintain their own identity — but Mugabe seemed to be able to convince the rest of the world that they were under ZANU's control.

This chapter is based on a paper delivered to the Uppsala conference on Religion and War in Zimbabwe in March 1992. It will appear in revised form in Dan O'Meara, ed., *The Politics of Change in Southern Africa*, Canadian Research Consortium on Southern Africa, Montreal, forthcoming.

5

The Rhodesian Security and Intelligence Community 1960–1980: A Brief Overview of the Structure and Operational Role of the Military, Civilian and Police Security and Intelligence Organizations which Served the Rhodesia Government during the Zimbabwean Liberation War

Henrick Ellert

INTRODUCTION

The Rhodesian Security and Intelligence organizations came into being slowly but developed quickly in the early 1960s in response to the growing security threat posed by the rise of African nationalism. The Central Intelligence Organization (CIO) was formed in 1963 when the Rhodesian Prime Minister, Winston Field, agreed that an independent security and intelligence organization would be in the best interests of Southern Rhodesia. Until the formation of this apparatus, security and intelligence had been provided by the Federal Intelligence and Security Bureau (FISBY) which served the joint needs of the Rhodesias and Nyasaland. While FISBY concentrated on external issues the XB, later called Special Branch (SB), of the British South Africa Police (BSAP) was responsible for internal operations. The Northern Rhodesia Police and Nyasaland Police also established a Security and Intelligence division closely modelled on the British Special Branch system.

This chapter will examine the various components of the Rhodesian Intelligence community from a participatory and strictly non-academic perspective. I strongly believe that sufficient time has elapsed for the dust to settle and now a sense of urgency prevails upon those of us who participated in the Zimbabwe Liberation War, from whichever side, to contribute to a better understanding of that war and its legacy — to clear a path through what is fast becoming a minefield of fact and fiction.[1]

THE CENTRAL INTELLIGENCE ORGANIZATION

The activities of the CIO were largely unknown to the Rhodesian public. It was better known within the fraternity as the Department of the Prime Minister located at 'Red Bricks' (a contemporary nickname for Coghlan Buildings). The organization was funded by the Prime Minister's secret vote. The CIO was divided into two major departments. The first was the Internal Division headed by the Officer Commanding Special Branch who was known as the Director Internal (DIN). This division was also known as Branch I of the CIO. The second directorate dealt exclusively with external matters and was headed by the Director External (DEX) and was commonly known as Branch II. Both these directors were responsible in the hierarchy to the Deputy Director-General (DDG) and in turn to the Director-General (DG). Each major Directorate was supported by Sections and Desks with specific responsibilities which will be examined in greater detail. The Director-General was responsible for the Intelligence Co-ordinating Committee (ICC) which advised the Prime Minister. The Director-General was also a member of the decision-making Combined Operations (COMOPS) formed in the late 1970s.

In later years the Rhodesian Air Force, and Army Intelligence Directorates were incorporated into the Directorate Air Intelligence (DAI) and Directorate Military Intelligence (DMI), respectively. The latter also included the Rhodesia Intelligence Corps (RIC) which had specific responsibilities for topographical intelligence. Extremely close liaison was established with 'C' Squadron Special Air Services and the Selous Scouts as these organizations provided the executive muscle for the CIO.

BRANCH I: SPECIAL BRANCH

The Officer Commanding Special Branch at Salisbury Headquarters was known as DIN and was responsible to both the Director-General of the CIO and to the Commissioner of Police (COMPOL) through the Deputy Commissioner Crime and Security for all matters pertaining to internal security and intelligence. The Officer Commanding Special Branch (OCSB) was kept informed by his Provincial Special Branch Officers (PSBOs) and District Special Branch Officers (DSBOs) in the provinces and districts. The most important commands were those of Salisbury and Mashonaland and of Matabeleland. These stations, with their respective headquarters in Salisbury and Bulawayo were divided into sections known as Desks. Each Desk was headed by a Detective Inspector or Detective Chief Inspector with a staff of inspectors, section officers, patrol officers and woman patrol officers and an African police team led by a Detective Sergeant Major, Detective Sergeant and Detective Constables. The Salisbury and Mashonaland command was originally located within the main BSAP central station complex in Railway Avenue but later the European desk moved into Daventry House and the Projects Section moved into an old house within the Braeside Police Camp. Each morning, at 0800 hours, Desk officers would attend the PSBO's 'morning prayers' for briefing on major developments within the last 24 hours. Weekly or, when the security situation warranted it, daily briefings were prepared by the PSBO and sent to the OCSB under secret cover by courier. These reports were used by the OCSB to prepare his submissions to COMPOL and the DG CIO who prepared the Weekly, Monthly and Quarterly Intelligence Co-ordinating Committee Assessments of the Threat to Rhodesia for the Prime Minister and his close Cabinet colleagues.

PSBO Salisbury and Mashonaland also maintained a number of outstations at Chirundu and Salisbury Airport. These stations had the responsibility of monitoring incoming and outgoing security suspects, conducting overt and clandestine searches of baggage or 'facilitating' the arrival of special visitors such as foreign intelligence officers, Branch II officers and sanctions busters. (This meant that these persons were able to enter or leave the country without going through standard customs and immigration formalities).

The European Desk
The European Desk had a specific brief to report on all aspects of the security threat from Europeans, to obtain intelligence on a wide range of subjects including the activities and workings of neighbouring police forces, security and intelligence organs, armies and air forces, economic intelligence, the University, religious targets and both left- and right-wing organizations. The brief was so wide-ranging that often European Desk officers found themselves crossing paths with Branch II personnel. On one occasion surveillance operations were mounted — only to discover that the suspected premises were being used as a 'safe house' by Branch II. Again, while the Special Branch brief was generally internal, operations regularly took officers outside the country to meet sources.

Primary targets on the left included individuals or subjects active in political and religious organizations perceived as being in support of or sympathetic towards African nationalist aspirations. These included the Christian Action Group, Cold Comfort Farm, the Catholic Commission for Justice and Peace in Rhodesia, The Centre Party (CP), the Rhodesia Party (RP), the National Unifying Force (NUF), and Ranche House College. *The Central African Examiner*, founded in the early 1960s by veteran journalist, Theo Bull, and later edited by Eileen Haddon, was reckoned to be extremely anti-Government. Worse still, Eileen Haddon had links with the Black Sash movement of South Africa. After the Unilateral Declaration of Independence (UDI) the Government imposed censorship and the *Central African Examiner* appeared with more blank spaces than text. The publication of these blank spaces irritated Rhodesian officialdom who saw it as an act of defiance in itself and these too were banned. Before long the journal was proscribed and the Haddons abandoned the country for Zambia. The press corps were specifically targeted as a threat and an opportunity.

The account of White dissent in Zimbabwe's history is poorly documented and the only contribution with which the author is familiar is Ian Hancock's *White*

Liberals, Moderates and Radicals in Rhodesia 1953–1980.[2] One of the earliest voices of protest was that of Doris Lessing. Her marriage to Peter Lessing and apparent links with Communism were recorded by Special Branch in her Personal File. Her collection of short stories highlighted many of the racial and social injustices in contemporary White society. There is a special poignancy and bitterness in her writing which most Rhodesians did not like to read. In 1956 she returned to Southern Rhodesia and travelled extensively and spoke to listed Communists and liberals. Her visit produced Going Home,[3] a bitter, prophetic and often bleakly funny account of White society and its victims. She was declared a Prohibited Immigrant by the authorities acting on the advice of FISBY and XB who judged her to be a threat to internal security. Her return in 1982 left her dismayed that attitudes had not altered and the mentality so adroitly described those years ago still deeply embedded in the 'Rhodie' psyche. The left of Lessing's circle was involved in the International Club, the Capricorn Society, the Black Sash Movement and a string of organizations which were targeted as a threat to security.

Whites who stood up against the Rhodesian establishment were vilified and often the XB and later the SB were instructed to target them. Reports including even the minutiae of their daily activities were demanded. Recognizing that Garfield Todd was a threat, the SB instigated a smear campaign by circulating rumours that Todd was a defrocked Minister of Religion who had a penchant for smacking the naked bottoms of girls at Dadaya school. In the wake of the ill-fated Pearce Commission which sat to determine African opinion on the acceptability of the proposed settlement and the violence which ensued throughout the country on 18 January 1972, an SB team raided Todd's ranch at Hokomui arresting both the former Southern Rhodesian Prime Minister and his daughter Judith. Both were detained.

Right-wing political organizations spotlighted by the SB included the Rhodesian Republican Army (RRA) which began in the early 1960s. This was a group which had its roots in the Enkeldoorn (Chivhu) Afrikaans farming community and enjoyed some urban White support in Salisbury. The RRA initiated a crude urban bombing and pamphleteering campaign in support of their policy of closer ties with the apartheid policy of South Africa. The SB penetrated the group and when its leader, John Avery was convicted under the Public Order Maintenance Act on 2 November 1960, the organization died. The Republican Alliance (RA) formed in the late 1960s attracted Len Idensohn and Ernest Konschell (the designer of the ill-fated anti-landmine vehicle called the Leopard). Surveillance of the Right-wing continued when Idensohn formed the Rhodesia National Party (RNP) in 1968. This was supported by a dissident Rhodesia Front (RF) Member of Parliament, Christopher Wordsworth Phillip, who formed his own Democratic Party (DP) on 8 May 1972 with the principle that the White man and his civilization in Rhodesia should be preserved for all time.

The Rhodesia Action Party (RAP) was formed on 5 July 1977 by 12 renegade RF parliamentarians led by Des Frost who had resigned the Chairmanship of the RF as he was disgruntled with Smith's leadership. The RAP under Ian Sandeman, stood for total separate development and opposed Smith's settlement talks as a sell-out. These organizations were routinely penetrated by extremely well-placed sources who handed over minutes of meetings or tape recordings of meetings. Trusted agents were equipped with special briefcases fitted with concealed microphones and tape recorders. In extreme cases, political parties were so thoroughly penetrated that the SB directed their affairs through its agents.

So accurate were these SB reports that Smith was able to call a general election on 31 August 1977 and effectively destroy the credibility of the RAP. The existence of fringe right-wing organizations proved a continual embarrassment to the Rhodesian Government. These included the Candour League under the stewardship of Betty Wemyss who kept in touch with like-minded organizations and pro-Rhodesia lobby groups throughout the world. These included the Liberty Lobby in the United States, the John Birch Society, and the Herstichte Nasionale Partie (HNP) of South Africa. Betty Wemyss was also active in the Southern African Solidarity Congress (SASCON), an organization which stood for the White man in a united front against Communism. The SASCON was strongly supported by the right-wing journal, *Rhodesian Property and Finance*.

Following Smith's visit to Pretoria in September 1976 for his meeting with the United States Secretary of State, Henry Kissinger, SASCON met to organize a protest demonstration at the South African Prime Minister's official residence in Pretoria. Details of this plan were obtained by the SB and the Rhodesian contingent travelling to South Africa to participate in this bizarre affair where rounded up by the South African Police Security Branch and deported. Not since the days of the Ossewabrandwag in 1938–40 had the SAP been called upon to take action against their own kind. The SB later congratulated themselves when they sat down to watch an 8 mm home movie shot by their agent depicting scenes from this strange episode.

The University was a major target of the European Desk which focused on personalities within the student and academic population. Societies and organizations were targeted and routinely reported upon. The mid-1970s, 1973 in particular, were characterized by massive campus unrest. The student body was extremely militant and Black frustration expressed itself in violence. Political scientists such as Ashley Dixon were identified with the growing militancy within the Students Representative Council (SRC) and the Union Administrative Council (UAC). The monthly campus magazine *Grope* which was a popular medium for articles critical of the Rhodesian Government, was subsequently banned by government decree although the SB had argued that it acted as a safety valve.

Not for the first time, the Rhodesian government made decisions which ignored Security and Intelligence advice and succeeded only in aggravating the situation. Riots which lasted a week devastated the campus. In an unprecedented move, uniformed Police patrolled the University grounds for two weeks. In the aftermath of the university unrest many students fled the country for Botswana or overseas. Official scapegoats were found in the form of left-wing expatriate academics such as Dixon and were quickly deported.

Information on personalities and organizations was gathered by various means. It was collected from overt sources but largely through covert means in the form of source reports, from technical means, surveillance and clandestine searches of offices and residences. Text-book security and intelligence craftwork based on British MI5 procedures were employed with varying degrees of efficiency. Although the intelligence gathering was based on MI5 techniques, very little formal training was provided for new entrants into the SB and tradecraft was essentially learned on the job. However, some SB officers had a real knack for the work and very successful operations were mounted by them into Zambia during the late 1960s. When Air Rhodesia was still flying to Lusaka, pilots were recruited to act as couriers and agents. One successful and resourceful agent regularly burgled the ZAPU offices in Lusaka removing documents for his SB runner. Agents were later recruited within the Zambian Intelligence Service (ZIS) and from the Zambian Police (ZP), the Zambian Army and Air Force. The SB even succeeded in recruiting a 'Registry Queen' who worked at ZIS Headquarters in Lusaka and who handed over highly classified information to her runner for several months. Most of these sources, agents or couriers were ideologically motivated and pecuniary reward was not a major consideration. A personal file was later opened on one of these agents when he emerged as a right winger opposed to Smith's alleged 'sell-out' of the Whites in the 1970s.

Periodic, two-week 'advanced training courses' were held at Salisbury Headquarters for Detective Inspectors when they were introduced to the broader intelligence community including the external activities of Branch II, technical operations and administration. Special Branch manpower was drawn from the Criminal Investigation Department and therefore remained on Police payroll. Officers were often transferred back and forth because of promotion and it often happened that the Officer-in-Charge of a CID district or provincial station had at one time served in the Special Branch and retained his SB identity. To facilitate their duties, SB officers occasionally posed as Immigration and/or Customs Officials and carried suitable identity documents to support these personas. Security Reports were graded according to the known reliability of the source and the probability of accuracy and then classified either CONFIDENTIAL, SECRET or TOP SECRET. These reports were sent to Salisbury Headquarters where the appropriate Desk marked them up for indexing, processing into Intelligence briefings or for executive action. Reports concerning the peccadillos or human foibles of security subjects were routinely passed through to OPS for use in their Disinformation section.

The European Press also had the task of co-ordinating the security of the Rhodesian Prime Minister. A number of Section Officers and Inspectors were seconded from the Uniformed Branch of the BSAP to the SB for this work. On external trips, the Prime Minister was always accompanied by a Detective Inspector from the Special Branch whose job it was to liaise with the security and intelligence service of the host country for his security.

Because of the highly sensitive nature of Rhodesian sanctions-busting activities, the European Desk had the additional brief to monitor and report on any organizations or individuals suspected of being inimical to Rhodesian interests. Particularly threatening were visiting journalists who asked too many questions about this sensitive issue. Keeping a tight lid on sanctions-busting secrets also involved the Office of the Government Protective Security Officer (GPSO) which was placed in charge of physical security to prevent unauthorized access to factories and government offices. The GPSO was headed by a former colonial civil servant Colonel 'Buggy' Romily and his offices were located in Milton Buildings adjacent to the Prime Minister's rooms. Romily's brief was to supervise all aspects of physical security but he found the job of checking padlocks boring and came into conflict with the Special Branch who spent considerable time spying on both Romily and his Department. This was necessary because Romily's second in command, a South African named Jan Erasmus, who was suspected of having ties with the Bureau of State Security (BOSS), was busy running agents in Zambia. One of these unfortunate individuals was arrested by the Zambian Intelligence Service (ZIS) and later deported. The incident soured relations between the GPSO and the Special Branch and Romily was told to 'wind his neck in'. However, Romily's endeavours were recognized by the Rhodesian Government which decorated him for services to the Government.

Special Branch liaised closely with the Customs and General Advisor to the Prime Minister (a sanctions-busting section within the Department of Customs and Excise) providing them with information on suspects, assisting with forged travel documents, stationery and other requirements to beat the economic embargo — although most of this work was co-ordinated by Salisbury Headquarters there was considerable liaison between the two structures at provincial level.

A general brief for the European Desk was to report upon and identify illegal foreign intelligence activity within the country. There were a number of successes in this regard, the most notable of these being the arrest of Roger Nicholson and Trevor Gallagher who were working for the Central Intelligence Agency (CIA). The link between the two agents and the CIA resident was picked up during routine surveillance on US Embassy personnel. The Special Branch maintained a surveillance team comprising both mobile units and footmen who were deployed against security suspects.

Vehicles were equipped with false registration plates to prevent any official link. The non-availability of vehicles — often the Special Branch operated with dilapidated and conspicuous vehicles — was of continual concern and frequently a surveillance exercise was terminated because an operation had been blown when the subject took evasive action or behaved in a suspicious manner.

Terrorist Desk
This was an extremely important section responsible for reporting on the activities of ZAPU and ZANU. The most important Desks were at Bulawayo (chiefly occupied with ZAPU) and Salisbury and Mashonaland (largely concerned with ZANU) and their Salisbury Headquarters co-ordinators. These Desks maintained important clandestine links within the movements through a network of agents and sources who had been planted during the 1960s and early 1970s. The Terrorist Desk also ran agents in Botswana, Zambia and Malawi who provided information on ZAPU and ZANU. The formation of the Terrorist Desk had its origins in the Sabotage Squad formed in the 1960s by the CID before it was disbanded and all records transferred to the Special Branch. The Terrorist Desk reported on all activities relating to nationalist guerrilla activities in Botswana, Zambia, Tanzania and later Mozambique. This was done by infiltrating agents and sources into the organizations, by recruiting agents within the Security or Military Services of countries which provided training or transit camp facilities and by interrogation of captured guerrillas.

During the 1960s and early 1970s great achievements were scored by the Terrorist Desk agents, many of whom successfully returned from training in the USSR and China — to the glee of their runners. Incredibly detailed interrogation reports were regularly submitted by the Terrorist Desk and, depending upon the calibre of the capture, Sectorial, Detachment and Section names, Chimurenga code names, the serial numbers of weapons issued, the rank structures within Sectors and the

Rear, details on training camps, and so on were documented. Lists of known or suspected guerrillas were carefully scrutinized and every endeavour made to provide accurate identifications. Photographs collected from friends and relatives brought in for interrogation were also used. This was the procedure until the mid-1970s when the sheer volume of information dictated otherwise.

At Salisbury Headquarters level, interrogation and source reports were correlated against radio intercepts from countries hosting ZANU and ZAPU trainees and material made available by Branch II liaison with foreign Intelligence Services, to produce intelligence which by the late 1970s painted a very bleak picture indeed.

Although the Terrorist Desk had lists of thousands of recruits under training in Tanzania, Angola and Mozambique plus details of specialist courses at Nanking in the Chinese People's Republic, at Odessa in the USSR and other obscure locations, could talk authoritatively about at least four different models of the SKS 7,62 mm SimonovSl semi-automatic rifle (Chinese model 56, Chinese Sanitized model 56, North Vietnamese model, North Korean model 63), at least twelve different models of the Avtomat Kalashnikow 7,62 mm AK-47 Assault Rifle (Russian, Chinese type 56, Chinese type 56-1 folding butt, Bulgarian, Rumanian with front grip, North Korean, AKM East German, AKM USSR folding butt, M-64 Yugoslav), precious little of this extremely interesting yet highly academic intelligence resulted in actual kills for the Rhodesian Security Forces who became increasingly frustrated.

Technical information relative to Soviet, Eastern European, Chinese or Korean manufactured weapons, land mines, radio equipment, code-books and ammunition was routinely 'traded' with friendly foreign Intelligence Services. The Terrorist Desk established excellent liaison with the 'Military Attaché' of an Embassy in a neighbouring country and regularly handed over information on Soviet and Chinese training camps, samples of captured weapons, radio equipment and other data. This liaison was extremely valuable for the Rhodesians who received their *quid pro quo*. Even Eastern European Intelligence Services occasionally condoned this type of 'liaison' with the Rhodesians and on at least one occasion a Lusaka-based Czechoslovakian Intelligence Service Officer was 'facilitated' into the country for liaison.

In the beginning all this information had been collected and submitted for filing, but, increasingly, imaginative use was made of field captures for immediate deployment and the Terrorist Desk started to work in close liaison with the Selous Scouts. Other aspects of the Terrorist Desk reports were used by OPS of Branch II in their planning for external operations. By the late 1970s there was extremely close co-operation between Terrorist Desk, the Selous Scouts at both 'Fort' and 'Headquarters' (Bindura and Inkomo) levels, and OPS as the accent switched to hard utilization of intelligence. Initiatives undertaken by the Terrorist Desk in this regard included the use of sophisticated explosive devices installed in radios and the use of poisoned clothing which was then delivered to guerrilla units by informers and agents employed by their SB runners.

In the late 1960s and the early 1970s before the *Chimurenga* war started with a vengeance in the north-eastern theatre, the Terrorist Desk success stories focused on identifying and intercepting individuals and groups sent into the country by ZANU and ZAPU on intelligence-gathering, reconnaissance or sabotage missions.

Rhodesian ability to neutralize these early endeavours was one of the major contributing factors for ZANU's switch in tactics in the early 1970s.

Projects Section
The formation of the Projects Section came when the Terrorist Desk decided to make quicker and more efficient use of operational intelligence gleaned from interrogation reports. The section was formed by Detective Inspector Vic Opperman and accommodated in an old residence at the Braeside Police Camp. Regular SB officers were augmented by Police Reservists on national service plus a team of African Detectives. A field operational Headquarters was established on Retreat Farm north of Bindura in the Operation Hurricane area and it served to accommodate a team of Special Branch officers and Police Reservists ready to deploy in response to *hotint* or information of immediate operational value. After deployments, which occasionally resulted in kills or captures of genuine or suspected guerrillas or *mujibas*, the team would return to base for a de-briefing and R & R (rest and recreation). The Projects Section motto was *pachedu*, a Shona word meaning 'together' and a special beer mug was commissioned and issued to the section members.

The old-style farm house at Retreat provided the offices and sleeping accommodation for the command structure while the disused tobacco barns were converted into barracks for the *mujibas* who were paid a kill bonus of $1 000 per head after a successful hit. The Projects Section was the forerunner of the Operation Favour Programme which provided full-scale training of Security Force auxiliaries in support of the internal settlement initiative of 1978–79. The switch to Operation Favour was relatively easy because the facilities to accommodate and train large numbers of men were now in existence. Two additional farms, Buckridge and Champagne, were opened as training centres to accommodate between 200 and 400 men on thirty-day training cycles before their deployment into the so-called proscribed areas as supporters of the UANC. This concept was soon extended in support of Ndabaningi Sithole's ZANU elements and extra training camps mushroomed as the concept was taken on board. The Special Branch were increasingly involved in Operation Favour until the *Phumo re Vanhu* (Spear of the People) force was finally disbanded in early 1980.

As Projects was drawn into the training aspect of Operation Favour so was the European Desk. Two Detective Inspectors were delegated to liaise with the UANC and ZANU (SITHOLE) respectively to co-ordinate the gathering of intelligence, channel cash for recruitment of urban unemployed for the training programmes and generally administer operations. While recruits for the UANC side were relatively easy to find in the townships, the Special Branch had to fly to Uganda to collect a ragged band of Sithole's men who later masqueraded as ZANLA guerrillas who had switched sides. A horrifying sequel to this operation was the killing of nearly 200 of Sithole's auxiliaries at Nembudziya in the Gokwe district in April 1979. The men had become an embarrassment and had to be eliminated.

Nationalist Desk
This Desk served to gather information on all Zimbabwean African Nationalist Movements locally and externally until it was amalgamated with the Terrorist Desk in the late 1970s. It also reported on the activities of Zambian and Malawian

political parties, that is, the United National Independence Party (UNIP), the Malawi Congress Party (MCP) and allied organizations. An important function of the Nationalist Desk was to report upon and recommend the detention or restriction of Zimbabwean nationalists. These recommendations were submitted to Salisbury Headquarters where the appropriate paperwork recommending the detention or restriction of an individual was prepared for signature by the Minister of Law and Order. Appeals were heard by the Review Tribunal at Salisbury Headquarters which would recommend to the Minister of Law and Order whether or not a particular individual could be released from detention or restriction.

Administration, Finance, Training and Liaison
In addition to the Headquarters Desk structures which were generally commanded by a Detective Chief Inspector or Inspector plus a team of 'Research Officers' responsible for receiving and processing station reports into useable intelligence, there were additional sections at Salisbury Headquarters level. These included Finance and Training, Personnel Administration and Liaison with the South Africa Police Security Branch in Pretoria. The Finance and Training Officer handled the reimbursement of the station impress accounts for source and operational payments, provision of foreign currency, passports and periodic advanced training programmes.

Personnel took care of staff films, leave, transfers and identity documents. As noted earlier, all manpower was held against the BSAP establishment for reasons of pay and promotions; costs were debited to the annual budgeted Police vote. Branch II resources were held against the Department of the Prime Minister, the Department of External Affairs and from 1975 onwards the annual 'official' expenditure of the Prime Minister's Office was Z$6 million with additional funding being provided by the South Africans for specific operations. Liaison was conducted by an officer seconded to the Rhodesian mission in Pretoria. The links with the South African Police Security Branch was considered extremely important and operated independently of the liaison which Branch II had with the Bureau of State Security (BSS) and later National Intelligence Service (NIS) which was largely eclipsed by the aggressive SADF Directorate of Military Intelligence (DMI).

Both Branch I and II were served by a Registry for confidential and secret matters and a special Top Secret Registry. The Registries were generally overseen by awful peroxided or blue-tinted harridans who knew all the gossip about Salisbury Headquarters staff. The Salisbury and Mashonaland Special Branch Registry with its thousands of dusty files on persons, organizations and subjects — some dating back to the earliest days of the SB — was overseen by a 'Registry Queen' with a vicious tongue who was reputed to be on a bottle of gin a day. The monotonous work of indexing and filing secret papers appears to attract a particular kind of person. These members of staff took care of all incoming and outgoing paperwork, card indexing and filing. Every Friday night the See Eye Oh bar at Salisbury Headquarters was open for drinks and here assorted security and intelligence officers and invited guests mingled and swopped yarns.

Ground coverage scheme
This section was located at Salisbury Headquarters where the Officer Commanding (OCGC) received ground coverage (GC) reports from his stations throughout the country. Regular, uniformed branch officers were seconded to the scheme to

supplement a need for grassroots intelligence. In reality, the GC scheme generated even more paperwork and their only effective contribution was to provide the SB with additional manpower. It can be argued that the formation of this new intelligence-gathering organization came about because of inter-service jostling; the Uniformed Branch did not want to be left out of the fast-developing and 'sexy' intelligence game. Every Police station throughout the country had a GC Section Officer or Patrol Officer and a number of Sergeants and Constables. Their expenses were funded from a special cash float established by the SB. The GC reports, frequently based on rumour, local beerhall gossip and petty feuds, were channelled to the SB for comment: many of these reports were consigned to File 13 — the waste bin.

The post of OCGC was a comfortable sinecure for the early incumbents but as the pace quickened the scheme was distorted and the manpower swallowed up by the operational maw. The Ministry of Internal Affairs (INTAF) established a similar scheme based at District Commissioner level in the provinces and this structure proved similarly ineffective in the fast-changing context of providing operational intelligence. Indeed there were a number of successes but these were an exception to a standard ineptitude.

BRANCH II: EXTERNAL SECURITY AND INTELLIGENCE

Branch II was commanded by the Director External (DEX). DEX was served by a central evaluation division which comprised a number of Desks or Regions. These were:

- Portugal and Lusophone Africa
- South Africa, South West Africa and Lesotho
- Zambia, Malawi and Botswana
- Africa (Francophone)
- Europe and International Organizations, UN etc.
- Communism
- General (the rest of the world).

The most important Desk was the one dealing with Communism; its brief included just about anything and everything. It provided for absolute liaison with all friendly intelligence services on matters relating to the Soviets, Eastern Europe and China. Excellent bilateral liaison was established with foreign intelligence services interested in bartering this type of intelligence.

Desk Officers submitted their requirements to the field intelligence gathering division, Production (PROD), which was later re-named Collection (COL) whose task it was to meet these demands by overt or covert means. Desk Officers needed a regular supply of newspapers, Government Gazettes, Legislation and Government reports. Desk Officers would prepare detailed requirements on target countries, organizations or personalities and present these to COL. Based on this raw intelligence, the Desk Officers prepared evaluations or hard intelligence reports were channelled up the line to DEX, the DDG and DG for the ICC briefing papers.

Most Branch II Desk Officers were experienced men with a background in the old FISBY, British MI5, Northern Rhodesia Police (NRP) Special Branch, Kenya Police Special Branch or retired officers from the BSAP SB or CID. Many were multi-lingual which facilitated liaison with both the French internal and external security and intelligence services and the Portuguese. The diverse backgrounds of these officers gave rise to a popular misconception within certain Branch I circles that Branch II was riddled with MI5 and MI6 agents and may even explain the post-independence rumours within the exiled Rhodesian community in South Africa that Ken Flower himself was a British agent.

If any routine reports submitted by COL contained 'dirt' or information considered to be of value to OPS division, it was channelled to them for disinformation purposes. No questions were ever asked. During the Internal Settlement manoeuvres of the late 1970s OPS instigated a smear campaign against leading ZANU personalities. Information was leaked to press contacts or supplied anonymously. The authoritative newsletter, *Africa Confidential*, was a convenient medium for channelling information.

Collection was supported by the radio and telecommunications monitoring division. Cryptographers employed by the CIO monitoring division and supported by national servicemen in liaison with DMI successfully intercepted radio traffic in neighbouring countries. Most countries were extremely lax or employed outdated codes which were readily broken. The Zambian Intelligence Service (ZIS) code was broken as was that of the Kenya Special Branch. The Zaïre code was also deciphered. After Mocambique and Angola became independent the local codes presented no problems. This source of intelligence provided important corroboration for human intelligence or *humint*. Interestingly, the CIO tried to crack the South African networks but this proved impossible because of their superior technology including the use of one-time pads.

Collection division officers travelled regularly throughout the world in persuance of their assignments. The regular routing took them through the Pretoria station for a change of passport and identity or on an Affretair sanctions-busting flight to Libreville in Gabon where the Foreign Affairs representative provided them with fresh travel documents and identity papers. Not all the information obtained by Collection was authentic and on more than one occasion, officers tasked with a particularly difficult question, would manufacture information based on their own intuition or after a general thumb-sucking session with friendly intelligence officers or field agents. The Collection division enjoyed considerable operational independence and a high degree of integrity was expected. For example, financial accountability was not always desirable because of the clandestine nature of the work. Unfortunately for one senior operative, the temptation proved too much, and thousands of dollars of operational expenses were misappropriated before the officer concerned was discovered and dealt with.

Branch II posted officers to foreign stations which were established with the consent of the host country's intelligence service. These were:

- Athens
- Paris
- Lisbon

- Pretoria
- Washington
- Libreville
- Lourenco Marques

In addition to these intelligence stations, the department of Foreign Affairs established posts in Madrid and Rome. A key player in this regard was the Rhodesian Minister of Foreign Affairs, P. K. Van der Byl, who ordered his men to liaise with the Spanish Royal Family, Otto Von Hapsburg, the exiled ruler of Albania, King Zog, and his South African wife, the Bourbon pretender to the French throne, Henri Sitx, plus a score of obscure personages. The CIO made good use of the Foreign Affairs connection and officers were posted to the Ministry where they worked covertly on intelligence-gathering operations.

The South Africans posted permanent intelligence officers on a reciprocal basis. The SADF stationed a Military Attaché at their Trade Mission and so did the civilian intelligence service. Other friendly services made regular liaison visits to exchange intelligence or communicate particular messages. Intelligence services belong to a sort of brotherhood; they provide an important conduit by which hostile Governments can communicate in secret. The Rhodesian CIO was not excluded from this fraternity of the twilight world.

OPS

This division enjoyed an executive function including clandestine military style operations abroad, disinformation plus intelligence gathering from friendly services and organizations. OPS worked in very close liaison with 'O' Squadron, Special Air Services who provided them with operational muscle and training facilities such as the case of the Biafrans who sent a contigent to Rhodesia for military training preparatory to armed insurrection against the Federal Nigerian Government.

The section came into being soon after the formation of the CIO itself. Evidence of its earliest operations came on 12 October 1966 when Colour Sergeant Cahill and Warrant Officer Bouch of the SAS and a Police Superintendent died in an explosion while trying to enter Zambia across the Zambezi. In a similar operation, Corporal Eggleston of the Rhodesia Light Infantry (RLI) died on 15 February 1966 when crossing the Zambezi river into Zambia. In the mid-1970s, OPS activities were massively upscaled and retired Assistant Commissioner E. J. May was appointed to head its activities on 1 January 1975. May was known as 'C' and under his direction OPS were in regular contact with French intelligence in both Libreville and Abidjan and several African intelligence services who found it convenient to 'liaise' with the Rhodesians for one reason or the other. Contact was also made with Col. Bod Denard in the Comores and other former or still active mercenary elements. OPS grew into a powerful division and towards the end of the 1970s represented the most conservative and radical element within the Rhodesian intelligence community. OPS were involved in a series of letter bombings which targeted external nationalist leaders and one of their successful operations caused the death of J. Z. Moyo on 18 February 1977.

OPS were responsible for setting up the MNR operations in Mozambique. The training camp was established at Rusape with Peter Burt, a former Branch II liaison officer in Lisbon, in charge of operations. OPS were similarly involved in the ill-fated Angolan escapades of 1975–76 in support of the FNLA. The details of these foreign adventures are covered in my *Rhodesian Front War*.[4]

The division was responsible for the planning and execution of several external operations including those against Joshua Nkomo's ZAPU in Lusaka, Zambia. OPS established good working relations with the SADF DMI with whom they enjoyed a common hawkish philosophy. During the final hours before Zimbabwe's independence, OPS sought to escalate the war externally and on more than one occasion when asked why they had selected a particular target for sabotage answered by saying 'because it's there!' Often, they had no valid reason at all. OPS recruited a team of former SAS men and a network of hard-bitten agents for field operations in neighbouring countries. One of their agents, Michael Borlace, was subsequently arrested in Zambia which gave rise to the suspicion that OPS activities were being compromised from within.

Department Z
The planning and intelligence aspects of the Selous Scouts were co-ordinated at Salisbury Headquarters level under Department 'Z' while field operations HQ was located first at Bindura and then at Inkomo barracks. Provincial and district 'forts' were established throughout the country adjacent to Joint Operational Command posts (JOCs).

The Directorate of Military Intelligence (DMI)
The Directorate of Military Intelligence reported to the Director-General on all matters of military intelligence. The Rhodesian Intelligence Corps (RIC) was responsible for the production of topographical intelligence and they produced 1: 250 000 maps covering the whole of Zimbabwe and neighbouring target countries. These maps were marked RESTRICTED indicating that they were for military use only and reflected useful items of ground intelligence such as water points, villages and even caves which could be exploited by Security Forces during ground operations. The RIC posted men to all Joint Operational Commands (JOCs), sub-JOCs and other military locations to carry out this work in close liaison with SB stations where they were physically accommodated.

JOCs and Operational Intelligence
Each operational command or JOC comprised Army, Airforce, Police and INTAF personnel (in Security Force jargon, the Browns, Blues, Bailiffs and INTAF) at various levels of seniority depending upon whether it was a main JOC or a sub-JOC. Those uniformed services which jointly provided the bayonettes and air support were briefed by the Bailiff Acorn or Special Branch representative on the JOC. At some JOCs, the Bailiff Acorn was supported by the local Selous Scouts' representative and they would provide operational intelligence based on the interrogation of captured guerrillas and source reports from external operations. This was supplemented by Observation Point reports radioed in from fixed observation points established on hill features overlooking known infiltration routes or suspected guerrilla rendezvous or feeding points. It was also the role of the SB representative to the JOCs to prepare the daily intelligence report which accompanied the daily 'sitrep' telexed through to COMOPS every night. SB also

accompanied SF units on field operations where there was a chance of capturing and interrogating guerrillas in the field.

As the tide turned against the Rhodesian Security Forces the most effective operational intelligence was increasingly supplied by captured guerrillas who could be quickly de-briefed and 'turned' for field deployment with the Selous Scouts. This tactic brought the SB into conflict with some conservative CID officers who wanted to prosecute guerrillas in terms of the Law and Order (Maintenance) Act. They perceived the war as they had done in the 1960s when bands of armed insurgents had come into the country and been quickly dealt with. The task of translating SB INT to operational intelligence was carried out by the G3 INT officer at every JOC. G3 INT officers worked in liaison with the SB, RIC or the Selous Scouts where appropriate.

DAI

The Directorate of Air Intelligence held against Air Force establishments also reported to the Director-General on all aspects of air and naval intelligence. In addition to their primary function of providing aerial photography of external training camps or possible targets for sabotage operations they also provided naval intelligence on the port of Beira and inland water traffic on Lake Kariba. DAI provided efficient photographic interpretation which was of great assistance in planning external operations such as in the case of the raids against Chimoio, Tembue and Nyadzonia. Not only did DAI map outside the country but they also had instructions to map Zimbabwe: their aerial photographs are a valuable legacy.

During the internal settlement initiatives of the 1970s, the US Ambassador in South Africa and Lusaka made frequent visits. On one occasion DAI learned that the US Government aircraft was equipped with aerial photographic equipment so, to teach the Americans a lesson, OPS were tasked to blow-up the nose-cone of the aircraft where the camera equipment was installed. The SAS were deployed and the dual mission of destroying the equipment and telling the Americans that they should have asked for permission first was duly accomplished.

SUMMARY

Towards the end of the 1970s a marked difference of opinion emerged within the CIO and this manifested itself particularly in the viewpoint represented in the briefing papers prepared by OPS, COL and individual Desks. As noted earlier, OPS took a more aggressive and militant stance. During the crucial period just before Independence, the Director-General Ken Flower, argued repeatedly that the best way to serve the interests of the country and ensure stability was by continuing to provide intelligence needs in the most professional manner. Senior Branch II officers knew which way the wind was blowing in late 1979 and early 1980. Liaison with the South Africans and US intelligence services underscored the British resolve to respect the outcome of the Zimbabwean general elections come what may. COMOPS were fully aware of the bleak, no-win situation which now prevailed in the operational areas. In terms of manpower alone, the Rhodesian Security Forces were heavily outnumbered on the ground. Large tracts of countryside were no-go areas for all but the Selous Scouts on their clandestine missions. Exactly how forcibly this message was communicated to Smith is a matter for conjecture.

Ken Flower was also badly advised by the Director of Psychological Operations (PSYOPS), who argued that large-scale intimidation by ZANLA and ZIPRA guerrillas would influence the outcome of the elections. His view was, of course, echoed by the hysterical Ministry of Internal Affairs with their proven track record of knowing the 'African mind'. Smith's Internal Affairs 'wormtongues' got it completely wrong back in 1972 during the Pearce Commission Test of Acceptability. There were also a number of hawks within COMOPS who had to be pacified. Ken Flower's task was to make Smith realize that, irrespective of the truth of these assertions, the British were absolutely serious — the message had been received *Strength Five* from liaison sources. Smith and his immediate colleagues had always been difficult to convince. That Flower was now able to do this and dissuade the Rhodesian leader from listening to the hardliners must be considered a major turning point. Early warning signs of the inevitable had come from the Special Branch in mid-1972 who submitted A1 reports on the extent of guerrilla recruitment, the caching of weapons and munitions and the ZANU-FRELIMO co-operation in the Tete province of Mozambique.

The SB later established that porterage groups, one hundred strong, were busy ferrying equipment into the mountains of the north-east. Whether or not these reports had been accurately presented to Smith cannot be established but it certainly came as no surprise to some members of the Special Branch when the ZANLA *gukurahundi* swept down on the Centenary and Mount Darwin districts and Operation Hurricane was launched in early 1973. The successful outcomes of earlier counter-insurgency operations may have convinced Smith that a swift military solution could again be employed. He was distrustful of the alarmist reports now being presented to him in support of a political solution.

Worse still, Flower had to contend with the conservative and hardline views presented by OPS, PSYOPS and INTAF and balance these against the more pragmatic and realistic argument from the moderates within the CIO, which included the Special Branch.

There is no doubt that both Branch I and II were very efficient at gathering information and preparing assessments and briefing papers for the politicians and hard operational intelligence for Security Forces in the Field. Yet, the die was cast in late 1972 and early 1973 with the opening by ZANLA of the Nehanda and Chaminuka sectors in north-eastern Zimbabwe. No amount of information or intelligence could reverse the tide and as the chaps settled down to have a *good war* with plenty of cold 'chimboolies' (beers) to wash away the dust after 'foot slogging it' in the bush, the war raged on to its final conclusion. In the event the records of thousands of guerrilla names; weapon numbers; details on how many times the Mugagao camp commander went to the toilet in a twenty-four hour period; how many men had been executed during the ZIPA or third-force internecine political struggle in the Mocambique camps; and the extra-marital affairs of a particular left-wing suspect known to be a ZANU sympathizer were all very interesting but irrelevant. It mattered not that the SB could report in lavish detail about the Birmingham-based Zimbabwe Medical Aid (ZIMA) and their endeavours to raise funds and purchase medical supplies for Zimbabwean guerrillas. The comfortable days of the 1960s when mass incursions of SAANC and ZAPU and isolated ZANU insurgents were speedily eliminated in fire-force operations were long gone. The bottom-line effect of all this efficiency was to prolong the agony of the war. There were some successful operations — the assassination of Herbert Chitepo, Alfred Nikita Mangena, J. Z. Moyo, Ethan Dube and others set back ZANLA and ZIPRA plans for large-scale external raids but they only helped stave off the final day of reckoning.

The paucity of valid, published contributions by former participants towards a better understanding of our recent history is disappointing. This International Conference on the Zimbabwe Liberation War may now provide an opportunity to enhance our comprehension — myth must not take the place of facts.

6

The Metamorphosis of the 'Unorthodox': The Integration and Early Development of the Zimbabwean National Army

ABIODUN ALAO

INTRODUCTION

The Independence of Zimbabwe in April 1980 marked the end of an era in the country's history. It also marked the beginning of the Zimbabwe National Army. The three contesting military forces, ZANLA, ZIPRA and the Rhodesian Security Forces amalgamated to form a new national army with a common loyalty and a single allegiance.

In this chapter I discuss the creation of the Zimbabwe National Army (ZNA), paying particular attention to the political and military problems encountered during the integration exercise. I then proceed to examine the development of the force during its early years and examine how the new army, which was largely composed of former guerrillas, adapted itself to conventional tactics. I also consider the extent to which the army coped with the political differences that characterized the pre-Independence relations of the three armed forces. I do not discuss the formation of the Air Force of Zimbabwe or the demobilization exercise in any detail.

The discussion may be divided into four sections. The first section introduces the issues; the second focuses on the integration exercise, the third presents an overview of the ZNA between 1980 and 1990 and the fourth discusses the role of the ZNA in the future.

The background to the integration exercise
The integration exercise was undertaken amid considerable difficulties. Firstly, the Lancaster House Agreement imposed certain restrictions on the new leaders.[1]

Secondly, the political situation in the country was unstable: the ZANU/ZAPU coalition born immediately after Independence had not been tested and its cohesion against the stress and strain of the military integration exercise could not be relied upon. Thirdly, social and economic conditions were difficult: divided allegiances created by the liberation war made inter-group relations potentially explosive; and the cost of fighting a potracted war had left the national treasury virtually empty. Thus, at the time the Zimbabwean government had to start the military integration exercise, the new country was politically, economically and socially fragmented.[2]

There were three military and political considerations in the post-Independence military reorganization exercise. Firstly, the two guerrilla forces, ZANLA and ZIPRA, had to adapt to conventional tactics. Secondly, it was necessary that the armed forces should reflect the national character of the new state and representing all its ethnic and racial groups and, thirdly, a demobilization exercise was necessary.

The integration exercise in Zimbabwe is unique in military history. While examples abound of opposing armies being brought together in a reconstituted or reorganized national army once the conflict is over,[3] the Zimbabwean case is worth noting for four reasons. Firstly, the war produced no clear victor or vanquished which made it difficult for any of the contending parties to claim authority over the others. Secondly, there were three opposing forces in Zimbabwe whereas in other cases there had been only two. Thirdly, it was a problem Zimbabwe had to contend with from the very beginning of its existence, along with other problems equally demanding of government's attention. Finally, the Zimbabwean exercise involved more than bringing the former combatants together into one fighting force, it also involved the conversion of guerrillas into conventional soldiers.

The units that were integrated to form the new ZNA were a motley collection of military formations with considerable military and political differences. I will not describe these differences in detail as they have been addressed by others far better qualified than myself. However, before considering the technicalities of post-Independence re-organization, two issues must be considered. The first is to discover how the military fared during the brief Internal Settlement period under the administration of Bishop Abel Muzorewa, and the second is to investigate how the political parties controlling the armies viewed the issue of post-Independence military integration.

A consideration of the place of the military during the Internal Settlement period is essential for two reasons. Firstly, as the Internal Settlement was meant to be a transition period between the 'extremes' of White conservatism and Black radicalism, which came together after Independence to form the new national army, the role of the military during the period is very important. Secondly, a number of defence and security problems were created during the Internal Settlement period which the ZNA had to address in later years.

The Internal Settlement period clearly showed the extent to which the White settlers wanted to retain their control of the military. Before the agreement was signed Prime Minister Ian Smith had, in fact, made it clear that the Rhodesian Security Forces would not be involved in concessions made in the Internal Settlement deal. While speaking at the passing-out parade at the Gwelo School of Infantry in February 1978, he declared 'we can discuss and talk about other subjects and countenance some give and take [but] when we are dealing with security . . . this is an area in which there can be no lowering of standards, no bargaining'.[4] Many constitutional constraints were imposed to prevent Black members of the administration from having any impact on security considerations.[5]

It is interesting to discover that the Internal Settlement Government envisaged — at least at one point — a scheme of military integration. During the negotiations preceeding the agreement, a Rhodesia Front spokesman declared that those former guerrillas considered 'suitable' would be admitted to the Security Forces for 'retraining'.[6] However, the criteria of suitability, the content of the re-training, and the position the 're-trained suitable' would occupy in the command and control structure of the army were not made known. A new military force — the Security Force Auxiliaries — was created to assist the Rhodesian Security Forces. The activities of the Auxiliaries in later years were to become a major security consideration for the new nation.

The view of the political parties controlling the three military units of a post-Independence military integration was to play an important part in the integration and early development of the ZNA. All the parties had divergent positions on how to constitute the new national army. The Rhodesia Front believed that any peace-time settlement that included the incorporation of guerrillas into the army would not work. Ian Smith stated that 'there is no such a thing as guerrilla armies . . . they are a bunch of people who have very little training, who do not acknowledge commands and operate as individual units'.[7] He concluded that the guerrillas would have to lay down their arms, return to civilian life and only then, if they wanted to, might they enlist as raw recruits and be considered as such.[8] ZANU believed that the new army should be made up exclusively of guerrilla forces and the Rhodesian Security Forces should be disbanded.[9] ZAPU appears to have supported some form of merger between the two forces although how they envisaged this was to be done is not known.[10] This was the state of affairs when the three parties met at Lancaster House for the talks that brought Independence to Zimbabwe. At these talks the three parties agreed that the three military units — ZANLA, ZIPRA and the Rhodesian Security Forces — should be brought together to form the new national army.

THE INTEGRATION EXERCISE

Any analysis of Zimbabwe's military integration exercise should be prefaced with the comment that much about the exercise is as yet unknown. It is only natural that some time will need to elapse before all the ramifications of such a significant event can be discussed in a single study. All I seek to do, therefore, is to present the available information as a contribution to our understanding of an exercise which, in due course, will attract intense academic attention. In this attempt I divide the analysis of the integration process into three parts: the military aspect, the political aspect, and the involvement of foreign countries in the exercise. In this way I hope to indicate as much as possible the multi-dimensional intricacies of the exercise.

The military aspect
The military integration exercise commenced after the cease-fire when all the three forces were in their respective camps. The first steps towards creating a new national army were taken shortly after the cease-fire, when a ZIPRA battalion at

the Madlabuzi Assembly Point started training under the Commonwealth Monitoring Force.[11] Initially ZANLA refused to participate in this arrangement but later, its forces at the Foxtrot Assembly Point near Buhera were permitted to start re-training under the Commonwealth Monitoring Force and the Rhodesian Security Forces.[12] As will be discussed later, this pre-Independence retraining exercise created a controversy, as the creation of the army was supposed to be the prerogative of the new, elected national leader. Although all that was done at this time was an informal re-training of the guerrillas by the Commonwealth Monitoring Force Team, it has been argued that this re-training exercise forced the new government into making some decisions which it would have preferred not have made at all, or would have made differently.

Immediately after Independence the new government took over the training initiated by the Commonwealth Monitoring Force and began the task of reorganizing the military. To handle the exercise a Joint High Command (JHC) was set up under Lt.-Gen. Peter Walls, the Commander of the Combined Operations of the Rhodesian Security Forces. Other members of the JHC were: the Commander of the Rhodesian Security Forces, Lt.-Gen. Sandy Maclean, the Commander of the Rhodesian Air Force, Air Vice-Marshal Frank Mussell; the Field Commanders of ZANLA and ZIPRA, Rex Nhongo and Lookout Masuku, respectively, and the Secretary of Defence, Alan Page.[13] Apart from the integration exercise, the JHC was also charged with other issues pertaining to the standardization and development of the army. It was to work along with the British Military Advisory and Training Team (BMATT) which was specifically invited to assist in the exercise.

Although the composition of the JHC was in itself a most unpromising combination, the government's decision to make Peter Walls the chairman seems to have heightened the controversy, as many people thought that it would be difficult for him to forget his loyalty to the former regime. Although subsequent events were to justify this suspicion, the government's appointment can be explained by one or all of three considerations. Firstly, it might have been an acceptance of the significant role which the Rhodesian Security Forces (which Walls had led since 1972) could play in any military reorganization effort in the country. Secondly, it might have been a conciliatory measure meant to reassure the Whites of their continued safety under the new dispensation and, thirdly, it might have been a manifestation of the government's intention to respect military professionalism.

Before embarking on the integration exercise itself, the government disbanded some units of the Rhodesian Security Forces which were not considered eligible for integration. These units were the Selous Scouts and the Guard Force. Muzorewa's Auxiliary Force was also disbanded. This decision raised some controversy as the Lancaster House Agreement had recognized all three forces (ZANLA, ZIPRA, and the Rhodesian Security Forces), as having legitimate claims for incorporation into the ZNA and disbanding any of their units could be seen as contravening the agreement. The government justified its action through a technical clause; arguing that the disbanded units were *ad-hoc* forces, 'established for a specific purpose [and] never meant to be of a permanent nature'.[14] Thus, since the 'specific purpose' for which they were established was completed, they could be disbanded.[15] It is probable, however, that this was an ostensible reason, as the ruling party's dislike for some of these units was public knowledge.

The integration of the army was achieved in two phases. The first involved the gathering of the guerrillas in the assembly points and the second was the merging of the guerrilla forces with the Rhodesian Security Forces. All those members of the Rhodesian Security Forces who were considered acceptable and who wanted to remain in the army were retained and were allowed to retain their old rank while all guerrillas were relegated to the rank of private. This was a concession made to the experience in conventional warfare of the Rhodesian Security Forces,[16] but, as will be shown later in the chapter, it was deeply resented by the guerrillas. Later the guerrilla troops were divided into two groups depending on their level of education. Those whose educational level was considered adequate and who possessed potential for the officer cadre were separated from the rank and file. These potential officers underwent a training programme designed by BMATT to convert them into conventional soldiers. The conversion programme lasted for four months, during which time they were taught drill, signals, map reading, weapon training and unit administration. At the end of the course, those who proved themselves worthy were given a rank equivalent to their performance. The rank and file from the two guerrilla units were integrated and divided into battalions. The entire exercise was code-named Operation Sausage Machine.[17]

Shortly after Operation Sausage Machine began, the ZNA attempted an experiment called Operation SEED that was unique in Southern Africa. This is what it was. SEED stood for 'Soldiers Employed in Economic Development', and it was modelled on the Chinese scheme of employing soldiers in agricultural and other related ventures during peace time.[18] The SEED idea did not come out of the blue, as the Zimbabwean government had always wanted its army to take on extra-military duties.[19] Operation SEED can also be seen as an attempt by the government to defuse a volatile situation. Most of the guerrillas had been kept idle for months at the assembly points and the lack of activity had led to boredom, low morale and indiscipline. It was necessary, therefore, to engage the soldiers in some form of activity. In order to forestall possible clashes between the forces, ZANLA and ZIPRA units worked separately on different projects.[20] The government realized the necessity for tact in presenting Operation SEED to the guerrillas, as many of them might have seen it as a means of removing them from the army. It was, therefore, presented to them as another phase of the 'continued struggle'. This time, however, the struggle was for 'national prosperity'. ZIPRA and ZANLA representatives toured the assembly points marketing this idea to the guerrillas. However, the exercise was not successful and the government was forced to abandon it.

The promotion of Blacks into the officer cadre of the ZNA started in August 1981. Apart from the fact that there was a need to extend the spirit of majority rule to the post-independence army, many White army officers had left for South Africa after Independence. It was, therefore, necessary to create Black officers quickly. Hence some guerrilla leaders who had played dominant roles during the liberation war were exempted from Operation Sausage Machine. Among these 'political appointees' were the Field Commanders of ZANLA and ZIPRA, Solomon Mujuru and Lookout Masuku respectively, who were both promoted to the ranks of Lieutenant-General.[21]

The political aspect
The political aspect of the integration exercise was far more complex than the military, as it was characterized by three interconnected political conflicts — all

taking place simultaneously. The first was between the two former guerrilla armies on the one side and the former Rhodesian Security Forces on the other; the second was between ZANLA and ZIPRA; and the third was between ZANLA and former Rhodesian Security Forces on the one side against ZIPRA on the other.

The confrontation of the two guerrilla forces against the former Rhodesian Security Forces arose out of the guerrillas' objections to the initial advantages enjoyed by former members of the Rhodesian Security Forces in the ZNA. These advantages were the result of several factors. Firstly, soldiers of the former Rhodesian Security Forces had been practising conventional warfare (which the guerrillas were about to learn) and, secondly, the entire infrastructure of the Rhodesian Security Forces was based inside the country, which made it the nucleus around which the new army had to be built. However, the fact that former Rhodesian Security Forces soldiers were allowed to retain their rank while the guerrillas were lumped together as recruits, placed the former in an advantageous position which was compounded by the fact that former Rhodesian Security Forces soldiers were initially responsible for the re-training of the guerrillas.[22] All these factors virtually created a superior–inferior relationship between the two groups.

Other subtle disadvantages arose out of the 'conventional inexperience' of the guerrillas. They had to adapt to unfamiliar customs such as a disparity in salary scale, the use of the officers' mess and so on. The fact that the guerrillas had to ask members of the former Rhodesian Security Forces for assistance on such issues gave the latter an inestimable advantage. All these points were exploited to the disadvantage of the former guerrillas, many of whom had, by that time, begun to wonder whether their sacrifice had been worth the effort.[23] Against this background ZANLA and ZIPRA allied together to express their objection to the dominant position assumed by the former Rhodesian Security Forces. However, it must be mentioned that the tension voiced in these complaints did not become explosive, and, as time went by, and the former guerrillas grasped the intricacies involved in the new system, the balance of power was redressed, if not reversed.

The second political battleground, that between ZANLA and ZIPRA, was an extension of their pre-independence rivalry and that of their sponsoring political parties. In the immediate post-independence period there were a number of clashes between these groups, to the detriment of efforts to build a united national army. This animosity reached its peak in the unrest in Matabeleland and in the mass desertions that preceded it. In the clash in February 1981 in Entumbane, White-led troops were used to quell the uprising.

Some of these clashes were, in a way, inevitable. By the end of 1980, only 15 000 of the estimated 65 000 guerrillas had been retrained. The remainder were still in the assembly points — and they still had their weapons. Towards the end of 1980 the JHC decided to transfer them from the assembly points to low-cost housing schemes near Harare and Bulawayo. This transfer of armed men into already over-crowded townships where pre-independence ethnic and political differences had not been completely resolved increased the possibility of violence. What ignited the tension in Entumbane was that ZANLA and ZIPRA troops were obliged to live next to each other. These clashes were to have a fundamental impact on the early development of the ZNA. Firstly, some ZIPRA soldiers deserted the army after the Entumbane insurrection in February 1981 and joined the dissidents. Secondly, the suppression of the revolt showed those ZIPRA soldiers who remained in the army the consequence of seeking redress through revolt.[24]

Another problem arose from the discovery of an arms cache in February 1982. The story of the discovery of the arms cache is already well known, so I will only consider those aspects that are relevant to the development of the ZNA. The discovery of the cache resulted in the dismissal of Nkomo, Chinamano and Msika from government, and the arrest and detention of Masuku and Dabengwa. ZAPU property was also confiscated. To many former ZIPRA combatants remaining in the army, the dismissed politicians were their main representatives in parliament, while Masuku (Deputy Commander of the army before his arrest) was considered their main representative in the ZNA. Dabengwa was a former officer for whom many former ZIPRA combatants had tremendous admiration and respect. Furthermore, many of the confiscated properties were ventures in which they had invested time and money. The punishment the government meted out was such as gave ex-ZIPRA combatants the impression that their future in the new army, indeed the new nation, was bleak. This, together with a deep-seated fear of persecution, made many former ZIPRA combatants feel unsafe in the army and resulted in their deserting it to join the dissident forces in Matabeleland.

The role of the unrest in Matabeleland in the development of the ZNA will be treated later in the chapter. At this stage, however, I will consider why former ZIPRA combatants felt that desertion was the best option open to them. Many former ZIPRA guerrillas believed, rightly or wrongly, that they would not get justice in any conflict with former ZANLA troops, since appealing to government for arbitration was almost out of the question. Secondly, the suppression of the riots at Connemara and Entumbane had shown them that revolt from within the army was counter-productive. Thus, they felt that desertion from the army and joining the dissident operation was the only option left. This choice became all the more attractive as the dismissals and detentions of prominent ZAPU leaders after the discovery of the arms cache had provided an operational base for the disenchanted in Matabeleland.

The third political conflict within the ZNA was the alleged 'ganging-up' by the former Rhodesian Security Forces and ZANLA against ZIPRA. Although this discrimination was largely imaginary, there was sufficient evidence to support ZIPRA's fears that the Rhodesian Security Forces and ZANLA were co-operating at the expense of ZIPRA. ZIPRA believed that the government relied more on the former Rhodesian Security Forces than on ZIPRA, and that the officers of the former Rhodesian Security Forces had a direct access to the Prime Minister — an access which ZIPRA alleged was used to influence the Prime Minister against ZIPRA.

The former ZIPRA combatants in the army felt that they had sufficient reasons to suspect a conspiracy. Firstly, although it was seldom mentioned, the ZIPRA Air Force and their Intelligence unit had been considered ineligible for the integration exercise and had been disbanded. There had been in effect two 'air forces' in the country at Independence, the Rhodesian Air Force and ZIPRA's air force. Although ZIPRA agreed that the Rhodesian Air Force was more sophisticated than theirs, and as such, should form the nucleus of the new force, its members believed that ZIPRA should have been involved in the formation of the air force. In the end ZIPRA troops left their air force out of frustration. The intelligence wing of ZIPRA was also alleged to have suffered a similar fate. All this was seen by ZIPRA as a conspiracy between ZANLA and the former Rhodesian Security Forces.[25] In addition, ZIPRA believed that the order Prime Minister Mugabe issued to the former Rhodesian Security Forces officers to quell the insurrection at Entumbane and the ease and enthusiasm with which this instruction was carried out was a clear indication of an anti-ZIPRA solidarity between ZANLA and the former Rhodesian Security Forces.

Another political crisis arose as a result of the expulsion of Lt.-Gen. Peter Walls from the army. Before the re-organization exercise was completed, the government expelled Walls from the army and deported him from the country for making disparaging remarks about Black rule.[26] The most significant outcome of this expulsion was the resignation of many Whites from the ZNA. As might be expected, many of them took up employment in South Africa which increased the already tense relationship between Zimbabwe and South Africa.

These, then, were the major military and political issues that arose from the military integration exercise in Zimbabwe. However, the structure of the ZNA was not determined only by internal military and political considerations. Equally important was the role of foreign countries which were invited by the government to assist in shaping the army.

FOREIGN COUNTRIES' INVOLVEMENT IN THE CREATION OF THE ZNA

Five countries played a significant role in the development of the ZNA in the first decade of its existence. These were: Britain, North Korea, and, to a lesser extent, China, Pakistan and Nigeria. Britain was invited largely because of the offer she made during the Lancaster House negotiations that, should the request be made, she would be willing to assist in the re-organization of the army. Apart from this, the military integration exercise was a potentially explosive issue, and the possibility of South Africa's exploitation of the situation to destabilize Zimbabwe was considered quite likely. It was thought expedient, therefore, that a country with some form of authority over South Africa should be in charge of the exercise. It is possible that North Korea and China were chosen because of their assistance to ZANU during the liberation war. It is not certain, however, why Pakistan and Nigeria were chosen, but perhaps it was because the Zimbabwean government thought that the cost of their assistance would not damage the recovering economy.

The British (through BMATT) were the first foreign team to assist in the development of the ZNA. Twenty-four of the officers who had come as part of the Commonwealth Monitoring Force remained after Independence and formed the core of what later became BMATT. Their number was later increased. Their first assignment was to assist in the integration exercise. This accomplished, they assisted in the standardization of the army into a conventional fighting force. These tasks were accomplished to the satisfaction of the Zimbabwean government and marked the beginning of a new role for the British Military in Africa — that of converting guerrilla units into conventional armies.[27]

In 1982 BMATT became involved in the establishment of the Basic Training Centre for the ZNA at Inkomo Barracks. This centre was responsible for the training of ZNA officers and senior NCOs, who in turn were to form the nucleus of the training organization at unit level. By August 1983 the Centre had trained 12 400 ZNA members.[28] In 1985 a BMATT team also trained Tank and Armoured Car

Regiments. BMATT's recent assistance falls into three categories: training ZNA officers at the Zimbabwe Military Academy in Gweru and the Zimbabwe Staff College in Harare; infantry brigade and battalion training at the Battalion School in Nyanga; and advising the ZNA in training logistics and any other area that the ZNA seeks assistance.

Britain's role in the creation of the ZNA — commendable as it was — also created a controversy which is worth noting. It has been alleged that after the cease-fire (when legally Rhodesia came under British control), Britain made certain decisions concerning the national army which were opposed to the intentions of the Patriotic Front. For example the decision to start re-training the guerrilla forces before Independence, hijacked some of the Patriotic Front's plans regarding the numerical strength of the army.[29] It was because of this and to regain the initiative from the Commonwealth team that the government created the JHC immediately after Independence.

Zimbabwe's reliance on Britain for training its defence force seems to be in line with precedents established by other Commonwealth countries. Although there is no British equivalent to the intricate defence arrangement between France and its former colonies, a heavy reliance on Britain is a basic feature of the early defence policies of Anglophone African countries. Nigeria's dependence resulted in the unpopular Anglo-Nigerian Defence Pact which was abandoned not long after Independence. The Ghanaian Army — despite the incendiary radicalism of Kwame Nkrumah — was commanded by a British Army General after Independence. Kenya signed a Defence Pact with Britain in 1964. Even Zambia, which had reason to be anti-British, still relied on that country after Independence.[30]

The second country with whom Zimbabwe had substantial military relations was North Korea. This relationship turned out to be one of the most controversial defence policies made by the government. The reason for the controversy was not the training team itself — even though it was not totally satisfactory — but rather the activities of the brigade they trained.

A North Korean military team was invited by the government to assist in the training of a special brigade of the ZNA. This brigade (known as the Fifth Brigade) was composed almost exclusively of former ZANLA guerrillas. Even before the activities of the North Koreans and the Brigade became known, there had been considerable objections to the arrangement. The objections, which were voiced largely by opposition members of parliament, were based on two grounds. Firstly, the exclusivity of the membership of the brigade was questioned. It was argued that the membership of the Fifth Brigade should be mixed as was the case in the other brigades. Secondly, many members of parliament argued that the North Koreans had no history of successful operations to warrant their invitation to train the army.

The government argued that the Brigade was composed of exclusively ZANLA guerrillas because, after the formation of the first four brigades, there were only ZANLA guerrillas left and there was no alternative but to put them all in the same brigade.[31] As for the North Koreans, the government claimed that it had the right to seek military assistance from any country it deemed suitable. The adequacy of these explanations depends on one's personal opinion.

The deal with the North Koreans initially seemed most satisfactory from a military point of view. The training team arrived with a great deal of equipment, including seven T54 tanks and armoured personnel carriers and artillery to a total value of Z$12,5 million as unconditional gifts to Zimbabwe. It became clear, however, that after almost a year of training, the Fifth Brigade fell short of expectation and that the ability of the North Korean instructors had been over-estimated. What imprinted the name of North Korea into the minds of Zimbabweans, however, was the activities of the Fifth Brigade in Matabeleland.

China's military link with Zimbabwe was comparatively weak. This is rather surprising, especially when one considers the close pre-Independence relationship between ZANU and China. This could be part of the government's determination to attain uniformity with other Commonwealth armies. The most important post-Independence link between the two countries was the purchase of thirty-nine T59 tanks from China in 1981, and the invitation extended to China to assist in training the ZNA's artillery.

Pakistan's assistance was initially confined to the Air Force, but was extended to the army when the ZNA Commander, Solomon Mujuru, and his deputy, Lookout Masuku, went to Pakistan in 1981 for six months training. Nigeria's involvement was restricted to the training of officers. Many ZNA officers were sent for training at military institutions in Nigeria, especially at the Command and Staff College at Jaji.

OVERVIEW OF THE ZNA

By 1983 both the integration and the demobilization exercises had been completed and the ZNA had begun to take shape. Two forces appear to have affected the creation and early development of the army. The first was the way in which the country's war of liberation was resolved, while the second — which played a greater role in the *development* rather than the *creation* of the army — was the political, economic and military policies of the post-Independence government.

The process of transition to majority rule in Zimbabwe was performed in such a way as to enable the country to escape some of the problems that confronted Angola and Mozambique at independence. The transition process in Zimbabwe gave the new government unquestioned legitimacy, which made the integration exercise easier than it would otherwise have been. It also attracted external support. Apart from this, the outcome of the election clearly showed that ZANU had sufficient support to enable it to weather any political storm that might arise and gave the government the confidence to take some decisive — if sometimes controversial — defence policies.

The second factor that shaped the development of the ZNA was the post-Independence policy of the government towards the military. Throughout the first decade of Independence the government's desire to have an efficient, combat-ready conventional fighting force was vigorously pursued. Despite the country's slender budget, the military was not allowed to suffer any serious financial problem. Many steps were taken to ensure the rapid transition to a conventional army. The JHC was dissolved in August 1981 to be replaced by a Defence Force Headquarters and a Defence Council. The ZNA Staff College was established the same year; in 1982 it commenced with junior and intermediate staff training and by 1986 it undertook a full command and staff course. In 1984 the government created the

Zimbabwe Defence Industries (ZDI) as a private limited company owned by the government.

The army suffered a series of major losses in the early years of Independence which impeded the growth of a strong national army. The first occurred shortly after Independence when weapons worth thousands of dollars were stolen from Cranborné Barracks near Harare. Later an explosion at Inkomo Barracks resulted in the loss of weapons worth about £10 million. The Air Force lost a great deal in the July 1982 explosion at its Thornhill base near Gweru. By 1986, however, the army had recovered these losses and had established itself in a place of primacy in the sub-region.

The twin preoccupations of the ZNA are internal security and external defence. The army has engaged in two major operations since its creation. The first was the unrest in Matabeleland between 1982 and 1987 and the second was containing RENAMO incursions on the eastern border with Mozambique.

In the Matabeleland campaign the role of the ZNA proved most controversial. The activities of the North-Korean-trained, ZANLA-dominated Fifth Brigade gave the ZNA a poor image and brought Zimbabwe into disfavour with international opinion. It was alleged that the Fifth Brigade soldiers carried out their assignment in ways that bordered on genocide. The activities of the Brigade have been attributed to boredom, indiscipline and poor training. The military performance against the dissidents they went to control was not impressive. Instead, many civilians became casualties. People in Matabeleland have not forgotten, nor are they ready to forget, their suffering during that period. The Fifth Brigade was eventually withdrawn from Matabeleland and sent for re-training.

The involvement of the ZNA in the war in Mozambique alongside FRELIMO forces against RENAMO is also controversial although the involvement has considerable military advantages for the ZNA, for Zimbabwe and for Mozambique. This campaign has assisted in establishing cohesion in the ZNA as this is the only engagement in which all units of the integrated forces have operated together. The experience has also assisted in assessing the combat preparedness of the army and has shown areas of weakness to be corrected. The ZNA's activities have given FRELIMO the upper hand over RENAMO. Some of the towns that had fallen under RENAMO control were recaptured and returned to central control. One of the most successful operations in this regard was the raid on the RENAMO headquarters at Casa Banana. Similarly, in February 1987 the ZNA forces in Mozambique launched a successful assault on Mutarara and four other towns previously held by RENAMO in the Tete and Sofala provinces. This gave FRELIMO control over the lower Zambezi valley for the first time in two years.[32] The joint operation has also succeeded — to a large extent — in protecting the oil pipeline from Beira to Mutare and the railway from Maputo to Chikualakuala. Apart from these military gains, however, there are considerable political issues which should be considered in this context. There have been calls for a reduction, if not a total withdrawal, of Zimbabwean military involvement in Mozambique.

Since its creation, the ZNA has been troubled by two major factors that have affected professionalism in the army. These are: the political differences of the three armed forces that were combined to form the army; and the impact of the foreign countries who trained the army. The fact that the ZNA has surmounted these difficulties is as much a credit to the government as to the members of the

ZNA itself. The Fifth Brigade, however, presented a major threat to military professionalism in the ZNA. Firstly, the creation of the Brigade affected the evolution of a uniform standard in the army and, secondly, it created division among the members of the army.

The training the Fifth Brigade received from the North Koreans was different to that of other units who were trained by BMATT. They were issued with different weapons, AK 47 assault rifles, instead of the standard NATO assault rifles used by units trained by the BMATT. The negative impact of this special treatment becomes obvious when one realizes that the essence of the integration exercise was to eliminate those problems that had arisen from different military training. Secondly, the creation of the Fifth Brigade introduced dissension into the ZNA, as members of the other brigades looked at them with jealousy (because of their 'preferential treatment'), or with hatred (because of their 'pride').[33]

Although the government tried to minimize the role of politics in the development of the ZNA, this was not particularly easy and past political affiliations remained important — at least for the first few years of Independence. This could hardly have been otherwise, as the ZNA is different from most African armies where the defence force was inherited more-or-less intact from the colonial power. Instead, the ZNA had evolved out of a national struggle, a struggle in which the distinction between politicians and soldiers — if there was actually any — was blurred. In addition, all the three units that had been integrated into the ZNA had fought the war expecting certain political rewards but instead had to make do with a compromise.

The creation of a completely apolitical army anywhere in the world appears somewhat unrealistic, and particularly so in Africa, where the military is seen as an integral part of the political system, and whose position as a part of the ruling élite should not be underestimated. Sam Sarkesian points out the unrealistic nature of the desire for an apolitical army when he argues:

> Even in most developed western armies, political awareness and sensitivity create a political environment susceptible to manipulation and political gamesmanship by both military and political élites. Similarly it would be naive to believe that the military in the new states are apolitical. Even if there is no real propensity for intervention, the character of the military institution, its competence and loyalty are a matter of political concern. The fact that the military is in command of the instrument of violence gave it a political potential.[34]

The military and political élites in Zimbabwe are divided on the issue of an apolitical army. The Commander of the ZNA, Lt.-Gen. Solomon Mujuru, has said that the main goal of the army is to achieve a 'highly efficient, well disciplined and *effective, apolitical army*'.[35] However, former Defence Minister Emmerson Mnangagwa, described the idea of an apolitical army as leading to 'undesirable and total confusion'.[36] The most realistic assessment of the feasibility of an apolitical army in Zimbabwe was provided by the Commander of the Air Force, Air Marshal Josiah Tungamirai. While he agreed that such a creation was desirable he said that the peculiar history of Zimbabwe makes it difficult to achieve and the creation of an apolitical army may have to wait until the generation who shared the 'bush life' have died or retired. But while those in parliament, in the military, and in the executive are those who shared the 'bush life', the possibility of an apolitical army is remote.[37] While the controversy over the necessity of an apolitical army continues, it may be said that the ZNA has, by and large, resolved the ZAPU/ZANU divisions that characterized the army at the time of the Entumbane insurrection. This should be seen as a significant achievement. By 1987 these pre-Independence allegiances and divisions had been considerably reduced.

Although the remarkable achievement of the government in amalgamating all the pre-Independence units should be acknowledged, it would be inaccurate to say that there are no longer conflicts along the divisions of the past. As in most military organizations, there are many complaints from inside the army. Some members of the former Rhodesian Security Forces complain that military professionalism has taken a second place to ethnic and political considerations in the promotion of officers.[38] However, former ZANLA combatants (who believe that this comment is directed against them) disagree, and argue that these critics are motivated by desires less estimable than that of professional advancement. Those former ZANLA combatants who operate alongside these former Rhodesian Security Forces members argue that there is an inverse relationship between the criticisms voiced by these former Rhodesian Security Forces members and the depth of their professional knowledge.[39]

The former ZIPRA guerrillas also have their complaints. Some argue that army promotions favour former ZANLA troops and that former ZANLA members dominate the officer cadre of the army. According to the ZIPRA complainants, this was achieved through what one of them called 'tactical elimination' of ZIPRA officers through dismissal, retirement, tempting with political offices and the elimination of those offices that should have been occupied by former ZIPRA guerrillas.[40] The validity of these allegations is somewhat questionable. The first criticism that ZANLA dominates the officer cadre is valid but, as there were more ZANLA guerrillas than ZIPRA, that is only to be expected. The second criticism that promotions favour former ZANLA members is not easy to prove or refute. Promotions in the ZNA, as in all military organizations, have established procedures but, as in most armies in Africa, there are ways in which these procedures can be adapted to suit political ends. Whether this is being done in the ZNA, and if so, to what degree, is not known.[41]

FUTURE PROSPECTS FOR THE ZNA

The future coherence, development and relevance of the ZNA will depend on a variety of interconnecting factors, among which internal stability and political changes in the sub-region will play the most important parts. The signing of the Unity Accord appears to have stabilized the internal situation, but the benefit of the Accord will only be realized if it can launch Zimbabwe on a sustained course of development. The spirit of the Accord should be extended to all facets of Zimbabwean society. This would ensure internal stability and at the same time eliminate the remnants of pre-Independence allegiances that still remain in the army. Once this is achieved the ZNA could develop undisturbed. The end of political divisions, however, would not mean the end of rivalry within the ZNA. There would continue to be normal intra-service rivalries such as between academy and non-academy graduates; staff-college and non-staff-college graduates; combatants and support units, and so on, which are found in all military establishments.[42] Furthermore, as is so often the case, the effectiveness and development of the military depends, to a large extent, on the amount of money made available to train staff and procure modern weapons. It is not known whether defence will continue to occupy the important place it has enjoyed during the first decade of Independence.

The second factor that may determine the development and relevance of the army in the foreseeable future is the changing politics in the sub-region, particularly developments in South Africa and the war in Mozambique. Since the election of F. W. de Klerk and the introduction of his own version of *perestroika*, there have been fundamental changes in South Africa and it appears that the South African threat is considerably reduced. If this trend continues the then ZNA may have to change its focus away from the 'South African threat', a change which would significantly affect Zimbabwe's military doctrine.

With Zimbabwe's involvement in the war against RENAMO now entering its sixth year, the outcome of the war in Mozambique will affect the future of the ZNA. While I do not wish to comment on the political merits or demerits of Zimbabwe's involvement, it is hoped that the present peace initiatives sweeping Southern Africa will bring peace to Mozambique and allow Zimbabwean troops to return home. If, however, peace does not materialize, the government must ensure that public support for its involvement in Mozambique is encouraged. No military formation operates in a vacuum and it is very likely that, in the not too distant future, public opinion will affect the continued involvement of the ZNA in Mozambique.

7

The Heroes' Struggle: Life after the Liberation War for Four Ex-combatants in Zimbabwe

Teresa A. Barnes

'I can be a bus driver if I want, I can be a pilot if I want. Now I can be anything I want' (Ex-combatant 1980).[1]

'Perhaps I can still succeed if I work hard. But I don't know how much harder I can work; I thought I was working hard in the armed struggle for Independence — but only to find that I have gained completely nothing!' (Ex-combatant 1991).[2]

INTRODUCTION

The war which freed the people of Zimbabwe from the shackles of colonialism and the racist oppression of the Rhodesian regime is almost universally acknowledged to have been a 'just war'.[3] But how do we judge the outcome of a just war? Whose opinions matter? As displayed in the two quotations above, the passage of time can radically change peoples' perspectives on a war. How can we take these changes into account?

A further complexity is the common historiographical treatment of war. Wars are often summed up as the decisions of leaders and the movements of armies. It is often forgotten that these depend on ordinary soldiers, who make personal sacrifices to achieve advances and victories, and who suffer the consequences of retreats and defeats physically. But their experiences are usually obliterated in the manufacture of histories and may even be lost to popular memory. The result is the propagation of an official mythology of war, with heavy emphasis on its abstract and 'glorious' aspects.[4]

The purpose of this chapter is to bring the voices of four ex-combatants into the discourse on the aftermath of Zimbabwe's war of liberation.[5] These people were ordinary guerrillas in the war. They have not received any official designation as 'heroes' and they will not be buried in a 'Heroes Acre' when they die. Nonetheless, because of their contributions to the liberation of their country, they, like many thousands of their colleagues, are, simply, heroes; thus the title of this chapter.

This chapter is not meant to be a comprehensive study of the history or of the current situations of ex-combatants in Zimbabwe today. The interviews were carried out in Harare, and in English, between September 1990 and January 1991.[6] The people who were interviewed were known personally to the author. Each interviewee has achieved at least an 'O' level education, and all are currently employed. In terms of their language skills, urban residence, education and employment status these men are not currently representative of the majority of ex-combatants in Zimbabwe today. However, it is hoped that their ideas and experiences will be recognized as valid and at least as strongly indicative of those of other ex-combatants.

The people interviewed for this study were: Josephat Zenda, Mbuso Madonko, Endy Mhlanga and Edmund Manyange. Because of the sensitive nature of some of their comments, they are identified in the study only by their Chimurenga names.[7] These names are: Christopher Matema (CM), Tarzan Muparadzi (TM), Freddy Nyika (FN) and X (these two lists are not in the same order). Some background information on these men is displayed below.

Name	Date of birth	Home area	Joined struggle	Level of education in 1975
X	1956	Gwanda	1975	'O' level
TM	1962	Chipinge	1975	Grade 6
CM	1959	Honde Valley	1975	Grade 7
FN	1954	Marondera	1975	Grade 6

The statements which form the body of the chapter are edited excerpts from verbatim transcriptions. In a few cases sentences have been shifted from one part of an interview to another in the interests of the logical progression of the narratives.

WHY DID YOU JOIN THE STRUGGLE?

X: In 1973 I took a temporary job with the Ministry of Education, teaching primary school. I taught in Masvingo [province] near the Mozambique border. There was quite a lot of political activity going on. It was near Gonakudzingwa, where a lot of our nationalist leaders were detained for quite a long time. Also at the time, the ANC led by Muzorewa[8] was mobilizing people in the country. So I got involved in setting up branches [of ZAPU][9] with three other teachers at the school.

I was actively involved. I remember recruiting so many people to join the armed struggle. We actually had a network whereby somebody would drive up to that place and then collect the people and drive them straight out to the Botswana border and take them across. The border to Mozambique was about 10 kilometres away, but we were recruiting people to join

ZIPRA.[10] It was a very long drive to Botswana. But it was very successful, because the people who drove were very co-operative and it was a well-organized thing. They were not picking up so many people. One could count three people for a trip. Because if you take ten, it looks funny. But if you take three, there's no suspicion.

Our activities were clandestine, the government was not supposed to know that we were busy organizing. Then what happened was, the president of our district was arrested. It was at that time that we thought, 'Well, this man is going to reveal all the people he has been working with. So possibly to save our lives, we have to leave this country and join the struggle.' That is the main thing that forced me out of the country.

TM: I joined the struggle in 1975, that was on the 14th July. I was very young then. In fact we were close to the border [with Mozambique], and I even attended the Mozambican independence [celebrations]. That was on 25 June 1975. I was very interested in the way the FRELIMO soldiers were behaving, when they were holding their guns. Even I could see young people like myself, of which I was glued by their behaviour. The FRELIMO soldiers were also encouraging us to do the same as they did, that is to dismantle the Smith regime and replace it with the peoples' government. Since I was very young I didn't [know] much about why I was to join the struggle, but that was through the excitement of wanting to hold a gun. And I just crossed the border. That was that. Even being so young; and there were even younger people than myself.

CM: I joined the struggle, I think it was childish excitement. We live near to the border [with Mozambique]. It's about 15 kilometres away. We used to go and buy domestic needs in Mozambique. So this is when we used to see the FRELIMO guys, fooling round near the border. So we just developed an interest. We used to hear the elders talk about freeing our country, so we just developed that sort of interest. They used to talk politics in the evenings, about all the troubles they had. So we thought, suppose we join the struggle, join these FRELIMO people. We never knew we were going to be with ZANU(PF) or anything at all. We just knew we were going to join FRELIMO, which would help us fight. It was the interest of holding a gun, that sort of thing.

I think we were about five who started talking about trying to join FRELIMO. Join, that was the word of the day. So we just agreed, 'Let's go, let's go!' And we packed up and just crossed the border. We went in, we saw these FRELIMO guys and told them, 'We have come to join you, we have come to fight for our country.'

FN: In 1969 I finished my Standard 6 and joined the Ministry of Roads as a maintenance clerk. I worked for three years, up to 1974. This was the time when most of the Zimbabwean youth were all joining in the Zimbabwean struggle because they had heard that Mozambique was becoming independent. I waited until the beginning of 1975. I also had my reasons for joining the struggle: I had seen my family moved from one of the most fertile lands, in Headlands, to some rocky areas. I had always had this feeling (although I was very young at the time) like, how could we be moved from such an area? So when this exodus started from Zimbabwe, with many of the youth going into Mozambique, I thought that, 'Well, if this is what it means, that when we join the war, when we come back and fight the regime and start all over again, I think it would give us a chance to go back to our fertile lands where we were getting better yields.' So I just left my office and took my keys and started walking into the road.

WHERE DID YOU FIGHT DURING THE WAR?

X: I completed my training in 1977 and came back from the Soviet Union to Zambia. I only stayed in Zambia for about a week, and was deployed and came into the country, to Zimbabwe, to fight as a regional artillery commander. So from mid-1977 up to the cease-fire, I never went back to Zambia, I was here fighting. I started off in Feira in the north-eastern part of the country. I was operating in Sipolilo, Chirundu, Mana Pools area, then eventually we advanced to Karoi and Hurungwe. And Zvimba, I operated in that place. And later on, I was transferred to Gokwe, so I operated in Gokwe and parts of Midlands, Zhombe, some other places. So that was from late 1978 to the cease-fire at the end of 1979.

TM: I finished my training in Tanzania in 1976. I was sent to the front in 1977. I started in Zimunya, then Buhera, Charter, Mhondoro. We were advancing towards Harare, with the mission of blowing up the Harare–Bulawayo railway line. We had been given this task by Tongogara.[11]
There was a combination now of FRELIMO soldiers. They even fought here physically. By that time I was a detachment commander. I was leading a number of sections. Some of the sections were composed of a combination of the FRELIMO soldiers and the ZANLA forces. They couldn't even speak Shona! But military language, we could speak a bit, so as to understand each other.

CM: After completion of my training course, I was told plainly I was still very young to come into the front, but I sneaked! I just jumped into the truck which was carrying some people to the front, and that's when I came into the Mtoko area. That's where I started off fighting; that was early 1977.

FN: In 1976, I finished training in Tanzania and went to the front in Zimbabwe. My group came through Tete. And from Tete I got into Zimbabwe; Mtoko, Mount Darwin, I was operating in all those areas. In Murewa, Musana, Chikwaka and finally Goromonzi.

WERE YOU INJURED?

X: I wasn't injured. I only had a very minor injury; I was just scratched by a bullet on my knee. After about two weeks, I was OK.

TM: [From 1975 to 1980] I was not injured. I only had a scratch, at Tembwe
         Military Training Base, when we had an attack.

CM: Unfortunately in 1977, that was October 1, I got injured and I was captured.
         The most injured part was my right hand. But I know I received injuries
         almost all over my body. [This resulted in a permanent disability.] I have
         some 60 per cent disability.
         I was given very poor medical treatment when I was captured. I was
         treated in a camp hospital by a camp doctor. And on the other hand,
         during my treatment I was also receiving, well, I was also being investigated.
         This resulted in my recovery sort of, being — one cannot recover under
         such strange circumstances. And you know, the enmity between the two
         sides. I was a guerrilla, the person who was treating me was a Rhodesian,
         so you know . . . It's obvious he did not put all his effort on my treatment.

FN: Unfortunately in 1979 I was injured. I was with four comrades when we
         were passing through a certain school in Chikwaka, just near the Goromonzi
         area. And then it was at night, I think it was about 9 o'clock, and I'm sure
         the enemy had known that we were going to pass through that place. Then
         we were passing in the middle of the football ground, through the school,
         and they started firing. I was the only one who was shot, shot near the
         pelvis. Three of my fellow comrades ran away, they managed to grab my
         mortar. But I remained with my pistol.
         I had one bullet in my right arm, one bullet in my lower abdomen, I
         actually wanted to shoot myself. We didn't like to be captured by the
         enemy, we knew what would happen. We would be tortured and then
         probably end up showing the bases to the enemy. So I was ready to shoot
         myself, I had this pistol. But fortunately enough, I couldn't lift my hand to
         trigger the pistol. So I just lay down there unconscious. I didn't know what
         happened next, but I remember, I think after the second day, that I was in
         a clean, nice little room in a hospital. And I knew I was captured.

HOW DID THE WAR END FOR YOU?

X: At cease-fire, I went to St Paul's assembly point, that is in Lupane, at St.
         Paul's Mission. I stayed there for quite some time. Then in late 1980 we
         were transferred to Entumbane, in Bulawayo. So there, that's where we
         started this fighting between ZANLA and ZIPRA.
         The fighting at Entumbane — well, the whole thing was provoked by
         politicians. I wouldn't say it was provoked by the comrades themselves.
         Because I remember on the day when the first incident occurred, there was
         a rally which was organized by Enos Nkala at White City Stadium,[12] where
         he actually made some very bad remarks about ZAPU and ZIPRA. And
         then after that rally, some ex-ZANLA combatants came back to the camp.
         They visited a local beerhall at Entumbane where civilians were drinking.
         They started beating up the civilians. So these civilians ran away and came
         to our camp, that is the ZIPRA camp. And they said, 'No, these people are
         at Entumbane, they are beating us.' Some were bleeding. So when we went

to that beerhall to actually check what was happening, that's when the shooting started. People still had their weapons. The fighting only lasted for a day and a half.

Our leaders managed to separate us, flying over in helicopters, pleading with us to stop fighting. Both ZIPRA and ZANLA commanders actually came to Entumbane there and addressed us and told us, 'No you have to stop fighting.' That's how the fighting stopped. So we went back to our camps. So many people died, and so many people were wounded. Because in a township, that's a high-density suburb, so many people were victims, and property was destroyed. Some civilians were killed.

TM: We had much help of the masses, that made us to succeed, or to help lessen attacks from the enemy. We relied on the information from the masses at that time. And it was just a surprise to us, to me personally, at the end of 1979, when we heard about the cease-fire. We thought the war was still on. We didn't even think of ending at that time. Because we had gathered a lot of weaponry, and a lot of targets were on the books. And only to hear that we should stop fighting.

On the way to the assembly points, that's where the bus we were riding in detonated a land mine. And there was also an ambush. And there was not much resistance from our side. That's when I got injured. We were put in hospital in Chivhu, at that time it was called Chivhu African Hospital. Two of our men died. After I had been treated — the treatment was nice, anyway — I healed up quickly, and I joined the others at the assembly point, Foxtrot, in Buhera.

[From Foxtrot assembly point, in 1980] I decided to quit the army and not to join the [new, national] army. Not because I was injured. In fact I wasn't interested in the way the integration was taking place, whereby the ZANLA forces were to be trained by the Rhodesian forces, as having not achieved enough military training. They said that we were guerrillas and not soldiers. Yet I knew I could do as much, the same as they did. This made me not to be interested in the Zimbabwe National Army. So by that time, that's when I decided to go back to school.

CM: [From the camp hospital] I was taken by Special Branch to Bindura for some investigations. Finally I was dumped into prison. That was in 1978. And I was finally tried on the 11th, if I'm not mistaken, on 11 November 1978. I was sentenced to life in prison, in Harare Central Prison. Until 1980, on 1 February I was released on amnesty.

FN: [In 1979, after being captured] I was taken to that famous, notorious Selous Scout [camp] in Bindura. There was a lot of interrogation. I remember very well that they wanted me to tell them where most of my friends were, where their bases were, where the ammunition was hidden. And I refused totally to answer all those questions. I said [their threats were] useless because I didn't know anything, I never even went for training outside the country. But I think that they definitely knew I was lying. Because the head of the camp said that, from all I had said, it was all lies so they had to put me on the death list, for the firing squad. They were going to try and kill me; first they would make sure I was able to stand, and then I could go to the firing squad! They told me every day and I knew it was happening because we had some comrades who were also taken from the same hospital room; and they were shot. They would be brought back to the hospital to show us what they had done to someone we knew.

I recuperated, and they said that I was going to be next, and it was going to be the same thing because I had never released any information to them. I was feeling quite well, and I thought it was better for me to be shot while running away from the camp than be shot when I'm just taken out of that place and off to a firing squad. I thought it was better for me to be shot whilst running. If it was just waiting to be shot, I couldn't bear it.

So one night, I just walked out. You see, they thought, especially with my type of injury, I had a calliper, I could only walk very, very slowly. So at the gate, the security guards were only concerned about those who were strong. But to the very injured, they thought, 'No [such a] one could never go anywhere.' So that night they just allowed me out of the gate. I said, 'Well, I just want to go buy some cigarettes.' There was a police camp nearby. It was sort of like, we were all in a police camp, having this Selous Scout unit on its own but fenced in within the police camp. So I got out. They never knew that I could manage to run away. Then I was sort of going very slowly from the gate, and straight to the main gate. When I got to the main gate the guard who opened the gate said, 'where are you going?' I said, 'Um, you know I've just come to see someone, I'm a visitor.' I was just wearing ordinary clothing. So he couldn't notice; he just let me out. And when I was out, I started increasing my speed! And then I quickly got into the bush and started limping my way to freedom.

I limped my way into the bush and I think for a whole night I was walking. I remember my whole leg was swollen, I couldn't walk any longer. The following morning there was a follow-up operation, there were some helicopters looking for me, and some ground troops also following me in the bush. They almost got me, but I was lucky. I ducked myself in some mud, somewhere between Musana and Masingura. They passed through and they kept on going, thinking that I must have covered a long distance. Fortunately enough, when they had passed me, one old man riding his bicycle came by and I saw him. Then I waved him down and he stopped and I told him everything. In fact he knew me; I was the commissariat in that area. So he said, 'It's you, Nyika!' And then he carried me on his bicycle. He pedalled as far as his legs would carry him, I think for nearly 20 kilometres, close to the Mumurwi mountains in Musana. He took me to some of my comrades I was working with. In fact I'd gotten straight to my section.

My section commander was there, they were all very happy that I'd come back. And then they said it wasn't safe for me with a swollen leg to move around, so they took me to a cave in Musana. I stayed in that cave for six weeks. They had to give me some *mujibas*,[13] guys who were helping me all the time. They gave me food at night.

My wound became worse, it became infected. I think I would have died if the war had gone on much longer than it did. I think I was lucky, because when these people started talking at Lancaster, they started saying that the comrades must go into the assembly points. And I was one of the first persons to come into Harare, into Harare Hospital.

WHAT WERE YOUR EXPECTATIONS FOR ZIMBABWE IN 1980?

X: My expectations were that after liberation the major political parties were going to be united, because we had actually started some moves already, by this Patriotic Front.[14] So the first thing that actually demoralized me was that when we went for elections in 1980, ZANU(PF) decided to go for the elections alone, and ZAPU alone. Which I thought was very dangerous, and there were signs that at some point there would be a lot of fighting between the two parties.

One other thing that I expected was the line that we wanted to follow, the socialist ideology. [I expected that] the government was going to nationalize some of the major industries, bring the economy to the people, especially the land. That was one of the most important things I was anxious to see: how the new government was going to deal with the land question. The whole fighting that had occurred for all these years between the Whites and the Blacks — the thing that was at the top of the agenda was the land question.

TM: My expectations were that the ZANLA forces were supposed to be put in their own camps with their own military structure, and that we would be attested into the army without facing any difficulties in undergoing further military training. And I thought that as trained soldiers we were going to start earning salaries for being soldiers. I also expected ZANLA and ZIPRA forces to be regarded as the super-army for the country: those who would be called when things were very tough. I didn't expect the kind of integration which took place.

And I thought there was supposed to be a refer-back to the masses. By refer-back I mean a big rally by the authorities, or the Prime Minister (which he was at that time). A big rally whereby the masses would be briefed about the struggle for Independence, and how we came to have Independence. And to tell them all the names of those who had died. I don't think, if my memory can serve me, that there was that brief to the masses. And I also expected the handling of the ex-combatants to be nice: which is not as it is now. By 'handling' I mean cognizance that there were supposed to be special arrangements for ex-combatants to improve their lives.

CM: As liberators of the people I expected us [ex-combatants] to acquire a moderate kind of life, not like we are today. We were made to believe that after liberating the country we would be the forces of the people, the defense forces of the people. And I also expected some of our disabled combatants to be taken care of in institutions, to be taken care of by the state. Care should be taken of such people. I definitely feel that they contributed. Their main aim was not to suffer after liberating the country. I also expected a change in the living conditions of the people. We have always been crying for land, and that was the people's hope from our fighting. And I thought people could be given better pieces of land, not like the areas where people are dumped now. Because the lands are no longer viable, you see? And we really expected a bettering of conditions for those who were working — in terms of pay — and bettering of conditions for those living in towns, to have accommodation. Well, a government of the people, I thought, should do it.

FN: When we came back we expected to be led, just like we were led in the war. We would expect our leaders to come back to us and say, 'OK, gentlemen, we are going to start from here. We are going to do this or that. You are going to be fitted into the society in some way.' But then I'm sure when we came back, there was very little attention given to the ex-combatants. The ideology and the politics we had been given were sort of like hidden somewhere, kept in a bag, kept quiet. And we actually started looking for our own ways through it. I [also] had fairly high expectations in terms of land. I expected my family to go into better land. And I thought the government was going to have a very strong educational drive for those ex-combatants who could manage to go back to school, or some technical training for those who couldn't manage to go back to school.

HOW WERE YOU REGARDED BY MOST PEOPLE AT THE TIME OF INDEPENDENCE?

X: Well, there are two kinds of people and attitudes I will talk about. Immediately after Independence when we came home, we were accepted by everybody; 'these are the liberators', and everybody accepted us. And then as time went on, up to possibly 1983–4, when the ex-combatants started feeling the pinch of the neglect of government — most of them were suffering and could not find jobs anywhere — some people actually then had that contemptuous attitude towards ex-combatants. It changed quickly. I remember on several occasions I would hear people say, 'Ah, these people worked to liberate this country, now they are suffering, what did they suffer for? They are useless. They thought they were clever by joining the struggle but we who didn't go there, we kept our jobs and continued with our education so we had nothing to lose. But they just wasted their time because they were stupid.' Things like that.
Some people have that attitude, even up to now. As a result, you find that there are very few people who want it to be known that they are former combatants. Just because they have been victimized by this attitude that some of our people have. But there are some people who have sympathies for ex-combatants. There are some people.

TM: Just after Independence, people were very, very happy when seeing us back from war. And they thought that we were going to be of great significance to their development. They thought we were going to be fully integrated in the development project, so as to assist them to develop also. Because we had been with many people during the struggle. So they thought that those ideas we used to tell them, if we were to continue like that, we would all be better off than before. But to their surprise, they saw different people coming to them. And they never saw one of the ex-combatants going back to them, telling them about Independence.

CM: We were made to understand that after the war we would build bridges, roads and all the developmental projects in all these places. For the people. And this is what we told the people during our time of war. We expected to turn our guns into ploughshares! For the development of our country, that's what we want. Nothing else.
   After having told the people that the ex-combatants would come back and implement all they had said into deeds, that never happened. And people felt cheated. People of the [rural] areas. Imagine, you are telling someone, next week we will be doing this, this and that. And you never come back, and nothing is ever done in relation to what was said. So what would you say? Even if we go down to our rural areas, people still ask, 'You used to tell us that you would do this, you would do this, and where is it?' And you have no answer to give.

FN: At the time of liberation, there was this 'hero' thing, like, an ex-combatant is a hero. And we felt fine, when people were saying that. It's like we were important everywhere we went. I would visit rural chiefs and they were all very happy, they all showed their appreciation for what I had done. And people who were not my relatives, they were all very happy. But I think that quickly faded out; by 1981 that had all faded out. Our popularity, in the sense that we were liberators, people who had actually gone to fight, to change the system, just faded out. Because there was very little attention given to the ex-combatants. Maybe that's one of the reasons why the people saw us like useless things.
   Maybe 'useless' is rather too harsh. I know that the majority of the people really feel bad about the way things have turned out. Especially those mothers and fathers who had their children out during the war, who also had these expectations that maybe something really good was going to happen to their son, that he was going to be doing a job, he wouldn't have to look for work, he was going to get help from every corner.
   I think a good number of ex-combatants were embarrassed when nothing was done for them. I remember when I was a commissariat in the bush, I would talk to people, saying, 'We would like to do this when we are liberated. We would like to give land to the people, we would make sure that everyone is treated equally, we would make sure that no White man would steal the land. We would also try and probably get as many industries as possible and try and upgrade most of the things so that we will prosper together.' And to think that we have come off worse than the people we were telling that we were going to do this and that. It makes one feel embarrassed. This is one of the reasons why many ex-combatants would rather not be called ex-combatants today.

I also have that feeling. When I am among people like, at a bus stop, there are a lot of people and someone [whom he hasn't seen in a long time] says, 'Comrade Nyika!' — I feel very tense, like, 'Who said Comrade Nyika?' You know?

WHAT DID YOU DECIDE TO DO AFTER INDEPENDENCE?

X: At the time of demobilization[15] in 1982, we formed a co-operative with some of my colleagues who were staying together at the assembly point. They were my colleagues, we had been fighting together. We started a farming co-op in Bulawayo. We decided to get [the demobilization money] in a lump sum so that we could buy this small farm. It's just about 20 kilometres out of Bulawayo. The co-op is still working there.

I stayed there up to 1984. My stay there was not really nice; I eventually decided to leave. On several occasions I was arrested, suspected of being a dissident; I was arrested, detained for some months, sometimes for weeks, sometimes for days, beaten up and things like that. Just because I was a former combatant, and I belonged to the other party. So most of the combatants were actually suspect. Somehow, somewhere if it was known that you were a former ZIPRA combatant, you ended up in jail [because of] a funny story that had been created against you.

I was picked up, detained and tortured. There was no case to prove against me, but just because I was detained several times, they were not satisfied with my explanations. They suspected me about the arms cache thing in 1982. 'What do you know about this arms cache, tell us, especially since you were at Gwaai [assembly point].' I was at Gwaai and was one of the commanders there. 'You were a commander there, you couldn't fail to know what was happening, you are telling us lies.' It was really a problem; my life was very difficult.

The other members of the co-op were also subjected to this kind of harassment. But with me it was even worse because I was the chairperson of the co-operative. So most cases when they came, they said, 'We want the leader of this group.' At some stage they thought we had an arms cache in the farm, so they came and started digging around! In some cases I know that at night they used to come to a farm and then dig in and put in some arms, and then the following morning they came and said 'We want to search the farm. We think you've got weapons here.' Then, there! There they are! It is very difficult for you to prove yourself innocent in this situation. But they could do it. They did it in some other places. In our farm they did not do that. But we were always alert and conscious that this is what they can do. Any time. So we used to have night patrols and we raised dogs. At some stage there were about eight dogs on the farm. The farm was just a small plot, ten acres. So we used the dogs, any movement within this plot and they would start barking. They were really vicious at night. We also used to have these patrols, because we were aware that, these people can come at night and put some weapons. Then they come tomorrow morning and say, 'We want to search your farm.' I know of one co-op [where this happened] . . . those guys were arrested, I don't know until today what happened to those guys, whether they are alive or dead, I don't know.

The last time they detained me, it was so serious, I was detained for three months, in 1984. So I just decided to say no. They knew where I was staying, so they could come up there and pick me up. In some cases, after a week they would come again, pick me up for questioning, then I stay for three days, then they come again, pick me up; and I said, 'No, I don't think this is the life for me.' So I left the co-op and got a job in government, in the Ministry of Co-ops [laughter].

TM: My demob [money] was used differently. I used it for the fees of my young brothers, and I also bought four cattle for myself. And I bought some clothes, since I was starting a new life. I didn't have anything! Except what I was wearing; I had to buy all sorts of clothes for myself.

My family had been in the keeps,[16] and that was the time when they were moving back to their original places. I had to build my own house there, as well as financing them for their houses: father, mother and grandmother. They had nothing at that time, they were impoverished from the war. That's how I used my demob payments.

I started my education again in 1981, at Chisumbanje. Then I did Form 1 at Rimbi Secondary School. Then there was the problem of school fees. The government did not pay for me there. There were some difficulties. And I had to move right here to Harare. That's when I went to Ruwa.[17] I started at Danhiko Secondary School in Harare in 1982, doing Form 2.

CM: How did I use the demob money? Well, I was coming from the bush. My parents had been shifted from their original place of residence. And I had brothers and sisters, well, I had to send them to school. I also had to buy myself something to put on, OK? I think I did all that, but not to my satisfaction. The way [the demob payments] were coming . . . per month, you couldn't really put down money to plan . . . $180 . . . I was staying in town, I had to pay my rent, buy my food, my parents wanted this and that. They also had to buy food in the rural areas, they were coming from protected villages. They also had no clothes. The difficulties with us people, what do you call it, the linkages of, the relationship, what do you call it? With us Africans, we are always attached from child to father . . . Up to now I'm still paying school fees for some of the people. My young brothers; there are still four — before I even have paid for my own child.

FN: [In 1981] we were staying at Harare Hospital repatriation camp. Most of the people who were staying there were disabled ex-combatants who had to be there because of the nature of their disability. They had to be near the hospital so that they could get treatment. So we met this lady, Sharon Ladin.[18] I think she just heard about the ex-combatants and she came to the camp. The first time she came there, she talked to a few people and asked whether they were interested in coming to school. She met with some resistance. People were all very worried that nothing was working for them. Just imagine, people just sitting there, waiting for lunch, waiting for supper, waiting for breakfast; just seated, doing nothing. They were very disheartened. [So with Sharon's questions] they were not interested. Then she came again for the second time. I'm sure this is the time when she met me and CM and friends. So she asked were we interested and we said we were interested. I think at first it was about 10 people we managed to recruit. We said, 'Well gentlemen, we are doing nothing, why can't we go back to school?' And it started off just like that. She told us where to go. I remember the first time she even gave us the bus fare to go to school.

To us it was not like, 'Now we are going to school.' It was like, 'Why can't we be doing something whilst we are waiting? The government is probably going to arrange something for us.'

WHAT WERE YOUR GENERAL EXPERIENCES WITH THE RULING PARTY AND GOVERNMENT STRUCTURES AFTER THE WAR?

X: Some people decided to be dissidents [and try to bring down the government]. They just did it as individuals, which I think was madness. But some of the people just decided to be dissidents because of this harassment, torture, things like that.[19] And especially when the Fifth Brigade came to Matabeleland, so many people were killed. And if the Fifth Brigade knew that you were a former combatant, you were not going to survive. Most of them were killed, those who did not run away. Some ran away and went to hide in town where it was safer. Some ran to Botswana or South Africa.

It's very difficult for me to say why [the army] had that attitude. It was not only the former combatants — it was also some ordinary peasants, some of them were killed. Even young children, some of them were killed! I don't know why these people had that sort of attitude. I have always asked myself that question . . . If you want to destroy an organization you have to get rid of its power base — the people.

After my demobilization I wouldn't say I was an active ZAPU member. And even now I am not a member of any political party.

Once I got a place in Hungary to study mechanical engineering. I was offered a place and I came here [Harare] to the Department of National Scholarships for a scholarship, and they refused! They refused to give me a scholarship. And I said, 'No, I'm an ex-combatant, I've got a place, so what I want is a scholarship.' They refused. Then I went back to [the Hungarians] and said, 'No, I can't get any sponsorship.' So that was the end of it.

I joined the Ministry of Co-ops in 1984. I was in Gwanda, my home area. It was not difficult for me to get a job [as a civil servant]. I mean, with my educational background it didn't take me three months to get a job. I did not have any problem, there was no discrimination [based on his ZAPU history]. In fact when I joined the Ministry of Co-ops, that's when I was sent to Domboshawa and did my certificate in co-operative management for a year. That was a full-time course, sponsored by the government. After I finished the course I found that there were better opportunities outside government, so that's why I got this job [with a local non-governmental organization].

TM: When the situation is ripe, cowards become heroes. What I mean is [in the 1970s] there were people who were very much aware of what was going to happen. And they were preparing for it, that Zimbabwe was going to be independent. They knew that. And instead of going to war, they went to school in America, Britain, especially to Western countries. Because the technology here is mostly from the West. So just after Independence they flooded in and took up some posts; some high, even the highest posts. They were educated enough; when the war was going on, they were getting educated.

As a result they had not much experience in the struggle, in the armed struggle. And it is hard for such type of people to think about the war. For them it's history; they read it from books. And they never think that it really happened. Therefore, they were not bound to cater for us, or to plan for us, for our lives. The people who are now planning for the country's economy, administration and the like, it is only less than a third with armed struggle experience. Most of them are chancers. Therefore we cannot expect such a person to bear fruitful results. It's very hard.

This is why most ex-combatants lost trust with the [ruling] party; because it's now being led by people who never participated. And [now] those people do not even want the participation of the ex-combatants. Although they seem as if they want, but they don't really want this person. Because these people know the truth, that they are not the right people to be leading the party.

We cannot mention by names [who should have been leading the party], but generally according to the experience of the armed struggle, the party should have been composed of the people with experience in the struggle. Including the faithful masses, who can actually recall what happened during the armed struggle. And those people could have been of great help to the country, to the government and to the party.

Those without experience cannot manoeuvre the party in the right direction. Because they don't have experience. They don't know what an ex-combatant is. They don't even want to chat with an ex-combatant. They don't have anything to say. Therefore, what do you expect from that? Adverse results. Which is detrimental to the ever-suffering of the ex-combatants.

CM: [There was once an incident of 'kidnapping' a government official at the National Rehabilitation Centre]. We [the ex-combatants at the centre] used to call some of these top people to ask them questions, because we wanted to know our future. We were very curious, I should say. The administration in the centre did not have an answer to our questions. We knew we were there, but for what purpose? So we had to have someone to answer that question. Then comes in the Deputy Director of Social Welfare. They ask him, 'Why are we here? You keep on spending government money, buying us sadza, meat, you know, all these foods you send down here. But are we malnourished children? There are better people to feed than us. All we want to know is why we are here. Do you intend to send us to school, or do you intend to give us jobs?' That was the question. And he could not answer that one. He said, 'Well, all I know is I should give you your compensation money. That's it.' And we said 'Who do you think should answer?' And he said, 'You call the Minister.' So the Minister was phoned and he said, 'There's no time to come down there.' So we asked the Deputy Director to phone his Director — who seemed not to be in his office. And we said, 'Why is it that whenever you come down here, your Director is never in his office? You are not going back until your director comes down here. When he comes then you can leave. You will stay.' And he said, 'I will stay, it's my pleasure, because I'm a man of the people!' He was given a room . . . [and eventually let go]. He retired. And he had worked for the Ministry of Labour for some thirty years.

The government had no straightforward plan about us being there. They did not plan to train us in any vocational field. Those of us who went to school, it was our own initiative. Some did not try and look for things to do, they were not far-sighted. And they spent all those years until the centre was closed in 1986, from 1980 when it was opened, they spent all those years seated there. Doing nothing. And the centre was closed after they had achieved nothing. Now by this time they are seated in Bulawayo, doing nothing.

Some of us [the ex-combatants at the National Rehabilitation Centre] got jobs through our own efforts. It didn't come from the government, we organized ourselves. We had a committee, the inmate committee. It was responsible for liaising with government ministries, boards and the like. We would say, 'Look, we have got some ex-combatants down there [in Ruwa]. Some have ['O' level] passes and the like. All we are asking is for you to secure them some jobs.' We went to see the Minister of Labour because we were dumped down there, and there was completely nothing taking place. We fought to see him, and he came down to Ruwa and we asked him, 'Don't you see that we should have something to do at this centre? This is a multi-million dollar complex which is lying idle, completely. Honestly, do you think — government money is being spent for f— all. Why can't you find us something to do?' That was when he issued a directive that each and every government ministry should at least if possible employ an ex-combatant, a disabled ex-combatant from Ruwa! One or two.

Then sometimes we were told that there was a vacancy somewhere [in a government ministry]. My boss now used to say that I talked too much [i.e. was articulate] while I was down there. So [one day] I was called by the superintendent of the National Rehabilitation Centre and he said, 'I want you to go to Sanders House [where the Ministry of Labour is housed]. And I went. When I got there I was asked for my certificate. I produced it and I was told, 'Well, you don't qualify for a job because you have no five ['O' level] passes.'[20] That was the staffing officer saying that. Just then the head of the office passed by and he said, 'Right how are you?' and I said, 'I'm OK'. And the staffing officer said, 'I wanted to hire two people but he can't qualify because he has no five 'Os'. And the head of the office said, 'I want you to do something! I want this guy here! I know he's intelligent. And by employing him I know we will have an asset in this office.'

So the staffing officer phoned the Public Service Commission and said, 'I have got this gentleman here, I think there is an instruction from the minister, saying we should give priority to ex-combatants from the National Rehabilitation Centre; he has got an A, a B, and a lot of Ds. What do I do with him?' And the Commission started going up and down, up and down, trying to make a decision. I spent the whole day there. And then it was two weeks after I had the interview — I was phoned to come to work the following day! That's how I got the job.

FN: I never had much to do with the party structures. At the start I used to go to these meetings, and I found out that I didn't really gain anything from that. It was saying the same thing over and over again. It was just a repetition of what I already knew. So I just didn't join in the structures. I just stayed home.

[The people who were staying at Ruwa] got thrown out in 1986. It really made me angry. Because I never thought the government could have made such a move, of removing people in such a manner. Especially as, I remember very well, there was a blind guy there. They didn't find them alternative accommodation. They were just told to move out, move out to their respective areas, whether in town or in the rural areas. 'Just go.' Gave them a twenty dollar note, dumped [them] at the Harare market bus terminus and told [them] to go! There was no warning. They came with guns to get them out. They did. And the people were removed.

WHAT IMPACT HAVE YOUR WAR EXPERIENCES HAD ON YOU IN THE LAST TEN YEARS?

X: I think that by joining the liberation struggle I was actually exposed to so many things which opened up my mind about what life is. I compare myself before and after I joined the struggle: there is a very big difference as to my approach to life. The biggest impact of course, was my assimilation of the Marxist-Leninist principles, which changed my perspective and outlook on life.

Not everybody who joined the liberation struggle actually believed that socialism will work. Of course, all of us were taught, but when we came back into the country, people started revealing their true colours as towards their attitudes towards socialism and capitalism.

I was born in a capitalist society, I knew what was involved. And I had a chance to stay in the socialist countries, especially the Soviet Union, where I stayed for a long time. At the end I decided that, 'Well, I think I know what capitalism is, and I have seen what socialism is. And I think this is what can work.' I still believe that socialism can work, though I know socialism worldwide is currently facing so many problems. But I still believe that if implemented in the right way, it can work, even for Zimbabwe. The most important thing I like about socialism is the distribution of wealth — wealth is distributed equally.

TM: Many of those who thought they were going to get something nice after Independence are crying. And those whom we thought were going to suffer are enjoying the fruits of Independence.

We used some guns like bazookas [during the struggle]. A bazooka is capable of blowing up one's ears, when you don't use it properly. If you don't follow the instructions your ears can be blown up. So sometimes you forget and you have some effects. And as well, these landmines, sometimes they blow up when you will be near them, near the minefield and the like, and you are likely to be affected. And as well in war, you do [things]. I was involved in a lot of killings when I was still young. For example I witnessed the bombardment of Tembwe, I was a field engineer at that time. And we were wanted to bury the corpses. But there were boobytraps, they even planted some mines after having bombed. So that when you try to bury the corpses you will be blown up as well. So the engineers were wanted to go and do that job because you could see that, 'That body has a boobytrap.' Then you just put on some branches of trees or you just tie a rope, pull the rope and it explodes — then you touch the body. You see? Therefore, you are likely to be affected mentally because you are involved in killings when you are too young. And witnessing some other horrible events. Then you tend to be more brave than you should be at that age. So I'm trying to tell you that I was more intelligent before the armed struggle, which could have helped me in going far, as far as the university!

CM: I think it has taught me to be self-reliant.

FN: I felt bad [about the situation] for the first few years, but now I have got this very strong feeling that, well, if you cannot succeed in one angle, why, you can always succeed in the other. It's like when I joined the struggle, I said, 'Well, I'll go and fight.' No one pushed me into fighting.

WHAT IS THE SITUATION OF MOST EX-COMBATANTS NOW?

X: Well, a lot has happened to ex-combatants. Some went back to school, some got good jobs, some joined the army. As I said, in Matabeleland most of them were killed, they died. Some ran away, left the country; most of them are working in South Africa. I was in South Africa in August. I met so many of them in Johannesburg. Yes! A lot of them, they would tell me, 'There are thousands of us, we are working here.' I was shocked. Some of the people who I thought died long back, but I met them in Johannesburg.

Most of those people who could not find jobs, mostly we find that it is those people who had very low education. Those who had a good educational background managed to get jobs here and there. But it is mostly those with a very poor educational background — Grade 1, 2 or 3 — they have really suffered. They can't get jobs anywhere. Some have retired to the Communal Lands and they just scratch a living out of the small plots of land there. Some of them are here on the streets, they are trying to look for jobs and some of them are living with friends or some relatives. Some of them are these street vendors; you see so many of them, trying to scratch a living out of that. So many of them are not working. It's really a pathetic situation.

TM: For the past ten years I've seen most of the ex-combatants living very poor lives. The reason is that there was not a stipulated law or an arrangement which was made for them to be employed somehow, somewhere. Many of them are not educated. There should have been a government policy for them to be employed, to have better lives. The policy should have stated clearly that so many ex-combatants should be employed in this field, depending on their qualifications; from 0 to Grade 7, from Grade 7 to Form 2, from Form 2 to Form 4. Let's say, for instance, 'From 0 to Grade 7, Ministry of Labour please try and employ ex-combatants as office orderlies, sweepers and the like.' It's better to have a low-paying job than to have nothing.

Those ex-combatants who are in the rural areas have no proper homes, they have no fields to plough. They went back to the farms, or to the small pieces of land in mountainous areas of their fathers, which they left before the armed struggle. They thought that it was going to be better for them after Independence. Only to find that they came back and it was worse! Because the father now is telling him, 'You are married, you have kids, find your own place!' And there is nowhere the ex-combatant can go now, because the resettlement programmes did not specify that ex-combatants should be given priority. There is nothing of that sort.

It was the government and the party's duty to say, 'We have got some people who are five years behind. What should be done to get them up? Should we leave them like that or should we upgrade them by the introduction of some policies?' Like what was done for the introduction of the two posts for deputy presidents, you see.[21] That could also have been done for the ex-combatants, because the president's directives cannot be resisted by anyone. Even in the parliament now, they don't speak about ex-combatants. We see an indication that this particular area was completely forgotten. It's one of my experiences.

CM: I know ex-combatants are suffering in the rural areas, especially. Those who are staying in towns are in economic crisis. Their living conditions are very unsatisfactory. I take as an example, this young man, BC. He leads an unbearable life. He is not working after he completed his 'O' levels. I don't think he has done anything. You know, he's a disabled person who is no longer in a position to handle anything like a plough, you know? I don't see him fending for himself. Had he not been receiving this little compensation for his injured leg [22] . . . I don't know. Some of them are leading very miserable lives.

FN: I would say that the majority of ex-combatants have married. Those who could not manage to get jobs in towns are in their home areas, doing some subsistence farming. Some have tried to join the co-operatives because there was this very big drive that the demob fund would work very well if the ex-combatants worked together and formed co-operatives. But I tell you, especially the ex-combatants' co-operatives, 99 per cent of them just fell off.

We have a few ex-combatants, of course, who have managed to get something going for their lives. I say a few — they are very few.

HAVE THE EXPECTATIONS THAT YOU HAD FOR
ZIMBABWE IN 1980 BEEN FULFILLED?

X: No, my expectations have not been fulfilled. There are so many things that
        I expected to see after liberating Zimbabwe. But they have not been fulfilled.
        Basically Zimbabwe is still a capitalist society, and despite the fact that we
        are having a so-called peoples' government, the situation is becoming
        worse and worse for the ordinary person than it was, even before
        Independence. Unemployment is increasing and the prices are going up.
        Capitalism is gaining ground every minute! And the people are feeling the
        pinch every minute.
        For all this, I would blame mostly the people who are pulling the strings of
        power. And the most important thing which I think some other liberation
        movements should learn from the Zimbabwean situation, and possibly
        from some other situations, is that nationalism is progressive at some
        stage. But as the years go by we find that it is very easy for nationalists to
        stand for capitalism. I mean, they are progressive during the period when
        people are struggling to liberate themselves. But with power in their hands,
        it is very easy for them to stand with capitalism. I've studied so many
        revolutions and that has always been the tendency for nationalism.
        One thing that is very important is that our leaders are not accountable to
        us. So if ever they are doing anything wrong, they don't stand to be
        corrected by anybody. The masses don't have that power to say, 'No, here
        you are not doing the right thing.' They do their own thing and impose it
        on the people! I think that's why our leaders have moved so much to the
        right. If they were accountable, I don't think we could be in this situation.

TM: What I have experienced is that the authorities were not capable of fulfilling
        their promises. Because we were inundated with promises when we were
        outside there. And we had to wait for ten years now after Independence
        without any of the promises being fulfilled. With the exception of a few I
        could mention, that education expanded, and the government encouraged
        everyone to go to school (although they knew very well that they had old
        people who could not go to school). But that is an achievement, and as
        well, roads were being constructed, and a lot of tall buildings being built.
        Some of them are white elephants and the like which we don't regard as
        very useful — economically anyway. But I regard those as achievements.
        Because if there is something where there was nothing, it's an achievement.
        My experience also covers the grumbling of the masses. They saw what
        they did not expect. They thought they were going to be given long fields
        where they could plough — and it didn't happen. They were left in their
        own places. Yet we used to sing songs like, 'Tinogaramumakomo' — 'We
        stay in the Mountains', and the like. This was an indication that the Smith
        regime was pushing us into the mountains and after Independence people
        were expecting to be shifted from the mountains to better land. The land
        question — it's intact, for the past ten years. The land is still in the hands
        of the minority.

CM: I used to think that after the war, I would have my own house, get married, and have a wife and kids who do not cry for sadza. Of course, taking care of my parents is stipulated by culture. I thought that we would lead a happy life — something like that. But we are still crying for money, and better living conditions, you know.

For the country as a whole, I think a lot has to be done. Because people are crying — it's sad to tell. A lot of development has got to take place for people to uplift their standards of living. I don't know what to recommend to the government, but this is how I see it.

FN: I would answer in two forms — no, and partly yes. Earlier on I said that when I joined the liberation struggle, one of the really piercing things which forced me to join was land; and my family actually got into a resettlement area and we've got some better land.

But I would say no in the sense that I would have expected our leaders definitely to have done much better than what they have done to ex-combatants. I find that its only those ex-combatants who were confined in the urban areas who managed to get some bit of education.

IS THERE ANYTHING ELSE YOU WOULD LIKE TO ADD?

FN: Yes. I think that if the present government would like to really do something for ex-combatants, I don't think it is too late. Not at all. We still have a lot of land in Zimbabwe, and some people are acquiring these big portions of land for no use at all . . . But government could buy tractors — like they did in Bulawayo when we had the ex-dissidents. They were given a farm. That's the idea, I would think. There are some people who are really experienced, they could little by little train those ex-combatants in agriculture. Someone who actually spent his time trying to fight for the country, I think land is the question! Of course, some people don't even know how to use land, but there is still a chance that people can be trained! I can be trained to drive a tractor; honestly, you just drive it, put furrows and plant the seeds!

CM: Now I have a [housing] plot in Budiriro.[23] I got it and I was given seven days to pay $4 580 for it, for that empty stand. Now it needs money to be constructed, about $45 000. Where am I going to get it? I've had quotations [to build a house of] seven rooms. And that was last year, when I got the last quotation. The prices are rising on a daily basis. I got the stand through thick and thin, a struggle; more than the struggle we had from 1975 to 1980. I had to crack my head with these ministers, all the way down to the Department of Community Welfare [of Harare]. It was worse. That was the worse struggle I have ever been in. And constructing the house now is going to be the worst struggle.

TM: For me, personally, being in the armed struggle was a waste of time. I did not achieve anything. I thought I was going to be recognized. My family was not so poor that it could not have sent me to school. But through excitement I ran away from school. And I thought that, when I came back, I would be far much better off than those whom I had left behind. Only to find out that the situation was a reverse! Those whom I left at the school had already obtained their degrees. And some of them are working outside [Zimbabwe] as ambassadors and the like, with their families, they are very happy, they can board aeroplanes at will, you see? And I was not dull at school; I could have gone as far as the University. But it did not happen, because of the war.

What I just appreciate is that Zimbabwe is independent. It's no longer in the hands of the foreigners. But personally it was a heavy setback on my part. If I could start again at [age] 13, I wouldn't join. Never ever.

X: I have met many people who say they are glad that they never joined the struggle. One thing that I've always told them is that they are ignorant. And not patriotic as Zimbabweans. The first and most important thing is that you must appreciate and love yourself for being a Zimbabwean. If you can not be so proud to say that you didn't waste your time to liberate your country, you are not fit to be a Zimbabwean! You are ignorant of yourself and you are very unfair with yourself.

I was reading the other day, something from Albie Sachs.[24] He was talking about languages in South Africa, saying that some people now have a problem with their identity, actually regretting that they are Afrikaners and things like that, wishing they could change. In Zimbabwe you find there are people who don't even speak to their kids in Ndebele or Shona. No! That's what you are! You must accept what you are! Even if I change my outlook on the world, I don't have to wish that I could change my skin. My ideas have nothing to do with my skin or where I come from. Ideas are ideas. So that is the kind of thinking which leads people to make careless remarks. I always consider such people to be fools.

I don't regret that I joined the liberation struggle. Not at all. I don't. I think that was part of my contribution to the liberation of this country. If I say I regret having joined the liberation struggle, then I would be saying that I regret having liberated my country. Which I don't think is right. Things are not OK now, but the fact is that we liberated ourselves (although some people actually hijacked the revolution!). I think I made an important contribution, and I'm proud of it.

8

The Politics of Creating National Heroes: The Search for Political Legitimacy and National Identity

NORMA J. KRIGER

In common with other newly-created nations, Zimbabwe has had to confront the international challenges of establishing a national identity and political legitimacy.[1] It is difficult to imagine a nation and state that could enjoy legitimacy and a shared national identity without access to national symbols. In this chapter I examine how Zimbabwe's ruling élite sought to enhance their political legitimacy and to foster a national identity through the discarding of colonial symbols and through attempts to establish their own heroes as national symbols. In its quest for heroes, the governing élite turned to the recent guerrilla war that had led to Zimbabwe's political Independence in April 1980.

The governing élite might reasonably have expected that drawing on the recent war of independence for symbols of legitimacy and national identity might capture the popular imagination. The war had claimed an estimated 30 000 to 80 000 lives and had contributed to liberation from colonial rule, thus making it an important emotional symbol and source of legitimacy for the governing élite. Whether ZANU(PF) élites governed the country alone (March 1982 – December 1987), or with ZAPU élites as junior coalition partners (April 1980 – March 1982 and December 1987 – December 1989), or in a united ZANU(PF) that had merged with ZAPU (December 1989 to the present), they could seek legitimacy from a war in which both parties had participated, albeit often as rivals. The fact that the two major ethnic groups, the Shona and the Ndebele, had participated in the liberation victory also made the war a symbol of potential national unity. The difference between the Zimbabwean and the Kenyan governing élite (who avoided and suppressed mention of the 'Mau Mau' war experience against colonial rule because they thought this experience would threaten their legitimacy and national unity) is striking. 'Mau Mau' guerrillas, drawn from the Kikuyu tribe, lost the war and, although the war contributed indirectly to Independence, those associated with the 'Mau Mau' did not inherit control of the state at Independence. Rather, state power went to those Kikuyu who had risen to political pre-eminence during the state of emergency which the colonial government had declared to crush the 'Mau Mau'. Consequently, the new governing élite had no positive emotional associations or common experiences with the 'Mau Mau' and appeals to the anti-colonial war were likely to threaten the new leadership's legitimacy. Élite appeals to 'Mau Mau' would also be potential threats to national unity because 'Mau Mau' recruits were from one ethnic group only, the Kikuyu. Rewards, compensation or war memorials to celebrate 'Mau Mau' would probably have raised fears from other ethnic groups which were already disadvantaged compared to the Kikuyu, and would have seemed like ethnic patronage, coming, as it would have done, from a Kikuyu governing élite.[2] In contrast, the Zimbabwean governing élite had no reason to expect the task of creating heroes to be contentious and they had no reason to anticipate any dissension from the indigenous population over eliminating colonial symbols.

Contrary to the ruling élites' expectations, their project of removing colonial symbols and replacing them with Zimbabwean ones has generated acute political controversy. For example, who should be the heroes — the dead or the living, the actual fighters or the politicians who orchestrated the war, the military leaders or the rank and file? Who should choose the heroes — the ruling party or the government? Should the living ex-combatants participate in the decision-making process and the commemoration of heroes? Should some heroes be more important than others or should all heroes enjoy the same status? The politics of choosing heroes has exposed the gap between the political rhetoric of equity, participation, and unity on the one hand, and the realities of an enormous disparity between party and government leaders and the masses, the leaders' desire for control and their imposition of decisions on the population, and overtly partisan decision-making by ZANU(PF) — at least until the signing of the Unity Accord in December 1987 when it merged with its rival party ZAPU to form a united ZANU(PF) — on the other. Ironically, a project designed to bolster political legitimacy and foster national identity, has generated highly emotional controversy, thereby producing another arena in which the governing élite has had to fight to establish its legitimacy and in which national unity has been threatened. In this sense, the self-conscious efforts of the governing élites to create national heroes has had the opposite effect to that intended.

In this chapter I rely on the Zimbabwean media for information on the public debates about heroes in Zimbabwe. Both *The Herald* and *The Sunday Mail* which are published in the capital, Harare, have been, together with the Bulawayo-based newspapers, *The Chronicle* and the *Sunday News*, governed by the Zimbabwe Mass Media Trust since shortly after Independence. Although the Trust proclaimed 'democratization' and 'decolonization' of the local press as its goals, these newspapers have been subject to strong political pressures. A former journalist at *The Herald* referred to 'several cases where news copy was tampered with because of political pressure . . . There was a 'ZANU(PF)ization' rather than a 'democratization' of the national public press.'[3] *The Chronicle* has also been subjected to political pressure, most publicly in the case of the journalist Geoffrey Nyarota who was dismissed for exposing the involvement of government leaders in illegally obtaining vehicles in the so-called 'Willowgate' scandal. I also draw on *Parade,* a popular, independent magazine published by Thomson Publications since 1984. *The Review of the Press*, published by the Zimbabwe-British Society, contains useful summaries of *The Herald* and *The Chronicle, Parade, Moto* (an independent newspaper), and other local papers. Parliamentary debates have also been a helpful source for the public debate about heroes.

The chapter begins with a discussion of how the governing élite's identification of controversial colonial monuments and statues not only incurred the anger of the settler population, which might have been expected, but also caused dissent between the central government and African local government officials. The second section discusses the politics surrounding the governing élite's creation of war heroes which in turn provoked debate about the nation's living and forgotten heroes, the ex-combatants. This debate on the 'forgotten heroes' is the subject of the final section. All these political debates have drawn attention to Zimbabwe's leaders' inability to create shared national values and thereby revealed the fragility of the legitimacy of their governance.

DESTROYING COLONIAL HEROES

Shortly after Independence in April 1980 the government began the politically delicate task of dismantling colonial symbols. In Harare, Cecil Rhodes's statue was removed on 31 July 1980, reportedly amidst jeers, chants, black power salutes, calls from a jubilant crowd to erect a statue of ZANLA's recently deceased General Tongogara, and attempts to deface the statue. On the same day, Jameson Avenue — named after an administrator of the British South Africa Company and leader of the infamous raid into the Transvaal — was renamed Samora Machel Avenue in honour of Mozambique's President and ZANU(PF)'s staunch war-time ally.[4] At the same time the government announced its policy on national monuments and statues. The Minister of Information, Nathan Shamuyarira, declared that the government would order the removal of only those colonial statues and monuments which by their presence raised political controversy. Statues and monuments of missionaries, explorers and doctors such as David Livingstone would remain where they were. A National Monuments Committee composed of cabinet members and chaired by Nathan Shamuyarira was set up to advise the government on the sensitive issue of which memorials belonging to the colonial past should be removed as well as other related issues such as the renaming of streets and towns. Anticipating an outcry from White settlers, Shamuyarira invoked the policy of reconciliation which was central to the relationship between the new government and the White community. However, the wording of his statement suggests that his concern was with reconciling Africans to their past, their present and their future rather than with inter-racial reconciliation. It stated

> The occasion of removing statues and monuments and erecting new ones is not one of recrimination, but rather a time of reconciliation — reconciling us to the reality of our independence, the death of colonialism and the national aspirations of the people. It is an occasion for the proper marriage of our past history and our dedication to the new social order.[5]

Ex-Premier Ian Smith's Rhodesia Front party interpreted the removals of statues and monuments that were sacred to the colonial past as a violation of the official policy of reconciliation. In September 1980 the Rhodesia Front party congress in Salisbury coincided with a government order to the city council to remove another four statues and memorials.[6] Delegates adopted the resolution that 'while fully supporting the principle of reconciliation in the development of the country, this congress does not accept that the White Zimbabwean must meekly accept the denigration of his achievements and past. On the contrary, reconciliation implies acceptance of the white man and his past.' A Rhodesia Front spokesman said: 'After all, you cannot remove history by taking away these memorials. It remains fact, and the Government's actions can only be described as stupid and nonsensical.'[7] Nathan Shamuyarira responded by saying that 'criticism that the Government was destroying the country's history was entirely inaccurate. The statues that have been, and are being, removed, represent no more than 2 per cent of all the statues and monuments in the country.' Moreover, these statues deserved to be removed because they were 'deeply and strongly' tied to an oppressive past and offended Africans.[8] The statues and monuments were not destroyed but merely moved to national galleries, archives and museums where they were less visible to Africans.[9] At least one Cabinet Minister, Herbert Ushewokunze, felt this was too dignified a fate for Rhodes's statue. Visiting the National Botanic Garden in Harare, Ushewokunze remarked that 'the greenery here is quite good, making the gardens an ideal place for colonial relics such as Rhodes's statue. We could find a spot here where we can dump them and allow creepers to grow over them until they disappear from the human eye.' Ushewokunze continued: 'I am worried it is taking too long for the moss to gather around the relics where they are now' — a reference to the visibility that the statues and monuments still enjoyed in the backyards of the National Archives and various museums in the country.[10]

The process of obliterating offensive historical edifices spread beyond Harare and touched not only the distant colonial past but also the raw wounds of the war of independence. White Rhodesians found that they were not free to erect memorials to those who had died in the war. In Shamva, the inscription on a war memorial that said 'In fond memory of Rhodesians murdered by communist terrorists' provoked a storm in the district. Minister of Local Government and Housing, Eddison Zvobgo, called it 'an insult to comrades who died during the war' and ordered its removal.[11] A war memorial carrying a list of servicemen from Marandellas district who had died in the two World Wars and the recent war became controversial because it bore the words 'Roll of honour in defence of Rhodesia'.[12] André Holland, leader of the Democratic Party, formed at Independence by Whites who wished to distance themselves from the Rhodesia Front party, deplored 'arbitrary acts of tearing down plaques' and called such actions 'contrary to reconciliation and repugnant in the extreme to whites in this country. Where the wording is offensive it can be altered to something acceptable to all people.' Rather than separate war monuments for those who fought for independence, he advocated that the flame of freedom be dedicated to the memory of 'all the young men from both sides who fell during our civil war'.[13] A private White citizen who was opposed to Umtali town council's plan for a statue to honour ZANLA and ZIPRA soldiers killed in the war proposed a similar implementation of the policy of reconciliation and advocated that war memorials be established to all who died in the war, regardless of political party or race.[14]

Deciding what was a politically controversial monument not only sparked conflicts between an edgy White community and an assertive new Black government but also, interestingly, between Harare's Black-dominated City Council and central government, for example, over whether or not World War II monuments were offensive to Blacks. The City Council signalled its feelings in July 1983 when it voted to remove from its property, *inter alia*, a World War II memorial and a book of names of those who died in that war which was displayed in the Town House. In the council debate, a White councillor asked that the memorial be kept as the war was against Hitler. A Black councillor objected: Whites who fought in World War II had got farms whereas his uncle who also fought, got 'f__ all'. Another Black councillor felt that the events of the two World Wars were not nearly as significant to the majority of people as the recent liberation war was. The council requested that it replace the book of names of those who perished in World War II with a list of freedom fighters who died in the liberation war.[15] When Harare City Council wanted to remove the Cenotaph commemorating Rhodesian soldiers who had died in both world wars from the Harare Gardens, it needed government permission because it did not own the property. The government showed little patience with the arguments that Black Councillors used to justify removing a World War II memorial from council property. In October 1984 a Black councillor described the memorial as offensive to Harare residents because it kept reminding them of colonial soldiers who had died for the British Empire. A government spokesman dismissed the councillor's concerns, asserting that the memorial had to stay because it commemorated those who died to resist fascism and the government was against fascism. 'Zimbabwe would rather ally itself to imperialist powers than allow fascism to thrive.'[16] *The Herald* supported the government's view. 'Harare City Council has fallen into the trap of missing the wood for the trees. There is a world of difference between the world wars statues and those set up to commemorate the occupation of our country by Cecil John Rhodes.'[17]

Several observations follow from the preceding description of the conflicts over representations of the colonial past. Firstly, when Nathan Shamuyarira, Minister of Information and Chairman of the National Monuments Committee, announced that the government would order the removal of only those colonial monuments and statues which raised political controversies, he seems to have expected more unanimity among Black Zimbabweans than actually existed. World War II memorials, for example, were much more politically explosive than he, or the government, had anticipated. The central government chose to remember World War II as first and foremost a war against fascism. Harare's Black city councillors' memories were less positive, and councillors invoked emotionally charged aspects of World War II such as the colony's support for the British Empire and the lack of reward for Black war veterans while generous land grants were made to White ex-soldiers. Significantly, where the government had the authority, as in the case of the Cenotaph in Harare Gardens, it would not permit the Harare City Council to remove the monument. The national government attempted at least to control the decisions as to which colonial monuments were politically controversial and should be removed.

Secondly, if the diversity of Black interpretation of the colonial past came as a surprise to the government, the conflicts between Whites and Blacks triggered by the removal of colonial monuments and statues was perhaps to have been expected. The participants in the disputes about the colonial past all invoked the concept of reconciliation, but what they meant by it was different. For the Minister of Information in 1980, reconciliation referred to reconciling Africans to their past (the death of colonialism), their present (the reality of Independence), and their future (their national aspirations). For Ian Smith's Rhodesia Front party in September 1980, reconciliation meant that the government should legitimize the colonial past and let its monuments and statues stand. Other Whites sought to promote reconciliation through war memorials which would represent all those who died in the liberation struggle regardless of race or political party. The national government could not accept such notions of reconciliation as regarded national monuments and statues. To leave all colonial monuments alone or to promote monuments that did not differentiate between those who died fighting for the survival of colonialism and those who fought for liberation would strike at the heart of the new African nation's quest for political legitimacy and a national, African identity.

Ironically, from at least 1983 onwards, rural people complained that the bodies of guerrillas and Rhodesian soldiers were often intermingled in shallow graves and were indistinguishable from each other. As I discuss later in the chapter, rural people sometimes ignored government requests to rebury guerrillas for this reason. In November 1986, Prime Minister Mugabe acknowledged in parliament that some people were concerned that the bodies of guerrillas and Rhodesian soldiers had sometimes been thrown into common graves. Seemingly aware of the difficulties this posed, but at the same time conscious of the need to rebury bodies that had surfaced from shallow graves dug during the war, Mugabe captured the dilemma of rural people: 'How do you distinguish the good bones from the bad bones? The heroic ones from the fascist ones and so on?'[18] Finally, debates about the colonial past were especially emotionally charged because they revived memories of those who had died in the wars, and such memories are intimately associated with questions of legitimacy and national identity.

Creating new national symbols by drawing on the recent liberation struggle was to be even more emotionally charged than the destruction of colonial symbols. At the heart of the contention were conflicts over who should control the process of establishing a national mythology, what that mythology should be, and the lack of popular consensus about the élite's projects for creating national symbols.

CREATING NATIONAL HEROES FROM THE DEAD

Two important national symbols were created soon after Independence. The first was the proclamation of public holidays on 11 and 12 August, which would be called Heroes' Days to commemorate those who gave their lives in the struggle. (Later, Heroes' Days were reduced to only one day, 11 August, and 12 August became Defence Forces Day.) The government also declared that a Heroes' Acre (57 hectares on a site seven kilometers west of Harare) would be built as a national monument to Zimbabwe's heroes. The main features of the Heroes Acre monument are: 1) a statue consisting of three heroic figures, one woman and two men, portraying the guerrillas; 2) a flag pole flying the Zimbabwe national flag; 3) a tomb for the unknown soldier; 4) a 40 metre-high tower carrying the Eternal Flame which was lit at the 1980 Independence Celebrations which depicts the spirit of independence; 5) on either side of the tomb of the unknown soldier are two high walls on which are engraved or painted scenes of the armed struggle; and 6) a revolutionary museum displaying war materials. Ironically, Zimbabwean artists, renowned internationally for their sculptures, were not commissioned to design the statue which was part of a monument to national identity. Instead, the government incurred the resentment of local artists by employing North Koreans who were co-sponsors of the monument.[19]

According to an official brochure, published in 1986, two categories of people qualified for burial at Heroes' Acre. One group includes 'national leaders, freedom fighters and the dedicated supporters of the national liberation who participated in or undertook revolutionary activities that contributed directly to the final victory of declaring independence on April 18 1980.' The other includes 'contemporary and future sons and daughters of Zimbabwe of the same calibre as those fallen heroes whose dedication and commitment to the new nation of Zimbabwe will justify their burial at this sacred spot.' The brochure continues, saying that the fallen heroes

> laid down their lives for Zimbabwe to be born and for the masses to be liberated. They subordinated their individual interests to the collective interests of Zimbabwe as a whole, cherishing qualities such as loyalty, dedication and patriotism. Their actions were guided by the ideals of comradeship and love. Theirs was an unwavering support for the cause of freedom and justice for which they accepted and endured pain, suffering and brutality with fortitude. These heroes had a firm conviction in the justness of their cause and they refused to surrender on matters of principle.

The brochure depicts Heroes' Acre as 'an expression as well as a symbol of the indefatigable collective will of Zimbabweans to be the makers of their own history, and to be their own liberators by participating in the protracted, arduous and bitter struggle for self-determination'. The brochure asserts that Heroes' Acre 'arouses national consciousness, forges national unity and identity'. The monument, it says, is 'a symbol of the masses' struggle for freedom that transcend [sic] tribalism, ethnicism, regionalism and racism'.[20]

In 1982 the government announced that the fallen heroes — the guerrillas — whose bodies lay scattered throughout the country should be reburied at local heroes' acres because they were known to the people in the localities where they had died. The government envisaged district and provincial heroes' acres corresponding to administrative jurisdictions. Only the Heroes' Acre in Harare was declared a national monument and it was decided that it would cater for national-level heroes only. However, the government made it clear that *all* those who died fighting for Zimbabwe's liberation were national heroes.[21]

Creating national heroes has been a politically turbulent process, one which has made mass–élite inequities highly visible. The entire project has revealed the governing élite's commitment to hierarchy, bureaucratic control, and top-down decision-making. These features of the project have alienated many ordinary people and so they no longer participate in the official commemorations of the heroes of the liberation struggle. The intense inter-party feuding — at least until December 1987 when the two parties signed a Unity Accord — also manifested itself in the context of the politics of creating war heroes. ZAPU party leaders persistently sought to undermine the ruling party's legitimacy by pointing out how partisan its process of choosing national heroes was and by refusing to participate in the entire project. The non-participation of a political party that was regionally based in Matabeleland and ethnically based among the Ndebele also exposed the vulnerability of national unity. Since the two rival parties, ZANU(PF) and ZAPU, merged in December 1989 to form a united ZANU(PF), discontent over who chooses national heroes, what criteria are used to select such heroes, and who funds which project has been fuelled by former ex-combatants from both parties.

HIERARCHY, BUREAUCRATIC CONTROL AND
TOP-DOWN DECISION-MAKING

The governing élite conceived of a hierarchy of heroes' acres and, along with the North Korean government, took responsibility for financing the National Heroes' Acre. The official estimate of construction costs is Z$12 million. Those buried at Heroes' Acre receive elaborate state-financed funerals and lie in expensive coffins. John Nkomo, ZAPU member of Parliament (and now a Cabinet Minister) conveyed the sense of extravagance of Heroes' Acre when he enquired about the $20 000 budgeted for the maintenance of the Eternal Flame and the War Museum at Heroes' Acre; he said 'I want to ensure that by the time I retire there, if I am going to retire there, it is going to be a five-star retirement place.'[22] With some prodding from parliamentarians, the government introduced provision for the dependants of national heroes in the National Heroes Act (No. 13 of 1984). The legislation provides for the President to appoint a board which is responsible for keeping a register of all national heroes and their families and for deciding who should be registered as a dependant in terms of the Act and the amount of State assistance, if any, that such dependants should receive.[23] National heroes' dependants have been the beneficiaries of extraordinary state largesse. This is apparent from the response of the Minister of Labour and Social Welfare to a question from ZAPU MP, Stephen Nkomo, in a debate on the Ministry's annual budget estimates. Nkomo said: 'I would like to know from the Minister why assistance to the National Heroes' dependants have gone down by $250 000 000 or is it that those dependants have become less or what has happened. . . ?'.[24] The Minister replied: 'The question of the families, now it is not so much a question of them receiving less but some of them have had their housing loans cleared. Therefore, what used to be given to them as housing loans has now been cut off because that has been cleared and what they are entitled to remains the same.'[25] It is noteworthy that these critical questions were asked by ZAPU leaders and were designed to undermine the legitimacy of the governing élite's project of creating national heroes. Why they were critical of the project is discussed below in the section describing the inter-party feuding.

How effectively the bureaucracy delivers these benefits to the dependants of national heroes is unclear. The widow of national hero Chief Rekai Tangwena confirmed that the government built her a beautiful house, electrified it and installed an engine-operated water tank. But she complained that she had not received her Z$100 monthly maintenance allowance from the government for four months and was unable to buy food.[26] Bureaucratic control affected the widows of national heroes in other ways too. Widows, in the same way as the general public, required government permission to visit Heroes' Acre to see their husbands' graves which were guarded by the army.[27] Ruth Chinamano, a ZAPU member of parliament and widow of a national hero, complained in 1985 that the government took foreign delegations to Heroes' Acre but widows were not invited to accompany such delegations.[28] Such restrictions symbolized the governing élite's idea that very important people, in death as in life, should be inaccessible to the public. These examples of government ill-treatment of widows of national heroes shows how even the beneficiaries of state largesse had grievances against the government.

Many government and high-ranking ZANU(PF) and army officials receive state funerals but are buried at home or at provincial heroes' acres. Former ZAPU members have begun to receive state funerals since the party merger at the end of 1989.[29] There is some evidence that the state also provides some assistance to the families of those who are buried at provincial heroes' acres. In January 1990 when Vhemba Mutandadzi, a former ZANLA commander and member of the general staff during the war who became a farmer after independence, was buried with full military honours at Mashonaland Central Provincial heroes' acre (the first person to be buried there), President Mugabe said that the government would see how it could help his 12 wives and 35 children.[30] In August 1991 the privilege of a state-assisted funeral was extended to any civil servant who died after serving the government for at least two years. The state agreed to provide Z$2 000 towards each civil servant's funeral expenses.[31]

Reburials at local heroes' acres get no direct state financial assistance. The costs of constructing heroes' acres are substantial and include paying spirit mediums and chiefs for selecting a site, preparing the site, digging the graves, and moving the bodies from the shallow graves where they were hastily buried during the war to the new graves. The standards that government sought to impose for reburials added to their cost. Government exhorted people to give their fallen heroes 'proper' and 'decent' burials, by which it usually meant providing each body that was still more-or-less intact with a coffin. For example, a provincial governor told a meeting that the government 'feels it imperative to provide coffins for the dead combatants in order to put together their bones as part of the state's respect for them'.[32] And at a reburial ceremony, a cabinet minister invoked the standards followed at Heroes' Acre: 'The way we respect heroes in Harare is the way it should be done throughout the country. Our heroes must be accorded the same respect no matter where they are buried.'[33] Frequently, however, the fallen heroes were buried in blankets to reduce the burden on local communities who often had to bury hundreds of bodies. One may speculate that rural people resented the financial burden of reburying those guerrillas whom they had supported materially during the war but with whom their relations had often been difficult.

Relatives of fallen heroes buried at local heroes' acres do not have access to the same kind of benefits as the families of heroes buried at Heroes' Acre. The War Victims Compensation Act (No. 22 of 1980) provides, in principle, for a monthly pension for dependants of those who died fighting or supporting the liberation struggle as well as for disabled war victims. However, in practice it is often impossible for dependants to meet the Act's stringent eligibility requirements, for example, applicants must submit a death certificate and a medical certificate stating the cause of death. Most guerrillas did not die in their home districts and many died outside the country in Mozambique or Zambia and their families live in hope that their relatives are merely missing. Dependants of missing persons (who may be dead) inundate the offices of the Department of Social Welfare seeking public assistance.[34]

Even the widow of national hero George Silundika was unable to receive compensation under the Act for injuries she sustained when tortured in detention between 1976 and 1977. Her story underlines how the bureaucracy applies eligibility criteria to war victims in order to restrict compensation payment. In 1987 Mrs Silundika approached the Department of Social Welfare for compensation for her war-related injuries. She received a medical certificate, as the department had requested, and as a result she received a payment number from the Department which entitled her to receive compensation. But then she was asked for her imprisonment number before she could receive compensation. 'I was naturally surprised that they were asking for my imprisonment number when I was never given one since I was being moved from one place to another by the Special Branch', she said. Her lawyer has not succeeded in intervening on her behalf. The Department then advised her to go to a doctor in Harare who was allegedly better than the one she had seen in Bulawayo on the grounds that this would facilitate her receiving compensation. Mrs Silundika complied with the request and also submitted her medical records from treatments she received in the Soviet Union, Britain and the German Democratic Republic. These records have never been returned to her, and she still has not received compensation.[35] Although Mrs Silundika thought she was being unfairly singled out by the bureaucracy, an editorial comment in The Chronicle stated that 'if it can happen to a high profile figure like the widow of a national hero then what about the ordinary peasant from the rural areas?'[36]

The élites' project of creating national heroes degenerated into an undisguised display of granting privileges to certain élites while advocating self-help for the rural people. It became a vivid example of how the leaders were willing to use even the sacred liberation struggle to promote divisions between themselves and the masses, or in the language of the masses, between the 'chefs' (leaders) and the 'povo' (people) and it fuelled popular resentment of these leaders. Bureaucratic requirements that made otherwise legitimate war victims ineligible for compensation also contributed to a lack of interest outside the capital in the national heroes project. Grassroots disinterest in the official commemoration of heroes' acres has manifested itself in low party interest in organizing reburials, in reluctance to contribute to reburial projects, and in low turnouts at official functions.[37]

Other factors may have also contributed to lack of interest in the local heroes' acres. In Shona society, the dead are buried according to their particular totem. Usually the guerrillas were from other districts and burying groups of them regardless of totem in alien territory may have raised concern about offending the ancestral spirits. This anxiety may be inferred from appeals made by government officials that people should not concern themselves with issues of tribe, region, or totem as these were not considerations during the war when people were united.[38] Also, some communities knew that some of the bodies they were being asked to rebury were not those of guerrillas but of Rhodesian soldiers or Bishop Muzorewa and Sithole's auxiliaries. For example, a young man wrote to *The Herald* claiming that he knew all the 'fallen comrades' in an extensive area including Charter district. People there were being asked to rebury 66 'comrades' yet he counted 20 at most. He complained: 'We cannot raise money to rebury *Sikuza Apos* (auxiliaries) when our brothers and sisters are in mass graves in Mozambique.'[39] Promises by politicians that the government would send trucks with coffins to bring back the bodies of those who died in Zambia and Mozambique never materialized.[40]

Between 1980 and 1987 a further reason for low turnouts in Matabeleland and the Midlands was a protest by ZAPU against the campaign that the government was waging against them. During the war, ZANU(PF) and ZAPU had formed an uneasy political alliance but, except for a brief period, had separate guerrilla armies. In the first independence elections, voting for the two parties was along ethnic and regional lines: the Shona (75 per cent of the African population) mostly voted for ZANU(PF); the Ndebele (25 per cent of the African population mostly resident in Matabeleland) for ZAPU. In the spirit of reconciliation, Prime Minister Mugabe included ZAPU leader Joshua Nkomo and several of his colleagues in his cabinet. Ethnic tensions were high from the beginning of Independence, as many in Matabeleland perceived that the new government did not represent them. Gangs of armed insurgents were reported to be roving around in the rural areas in Matabeleland. A major exercise involved integrating the two guerrilla forces and the Rhodesian forces into a single army, and then reducing the size of the army by demobilizing thousands of ex-guerrillas with a Z$185 per month stipend for two years. In late 1981 and again in early 1982, fighting broke out between ZIPRA (the military wing of ZAPU) and ZANLA (ZANU's military wing) ex-guerrillas in a camp in Bulawayo where they were awaiting reintegration into the Zimbabwe National Army. This incident provoked the first major defection of ex-ZIPRA officers from the army and strengthened the fledgling 'dissident' movement. In early 1982 Mugabe sacked Nkomo from the cabinet ostensibly because arms caches had been discovered on ZAPU properties. The most senior ex-ZIPRA officers in the army were detained and charged with treason. These events precipitated large-scale defections of ex-ZIPRA soldiers from the army and the 'dissident' movement grew.

The 'dissidents', numbering between 300 and 3 000, depending on the timing and source of the estimate, attacked government property, buses, civilians (especially White commercial farmers), and generally resumed the tactics that they had used in the war of independence. Their central grievances rested on a perception that the Ndebele people, and especially ZIPRA ex-combatants, were being discriminated against and excluded from power. Government figures estimate that 'dissidents' killed some 600 civilians, including more than 100 ZANU(PF) officials, between 1982 and 1986. The government responded to 'dissident' activity by sending in the army. From late 1982 to March 1983 the army, more specifically the exclusively Shona Fifth Brigade, killed at least 1500 civilians in Matabeleland for their alleged support of the 'dissidents'. Ndebele civilians in Matabeleland suffered terribly until December 1987 when the two warring parties signed a Unity Accord. In this period, the army beat up thousands of civilians, detained hundreds without charge, tortured many, and raped women and children. Unidentified gunmen abducted ZAPU supporters and ZIPRA ex-combatants in 1985. Ndebele families have been victims of civilian violence perpetrated by ZANU(PF) supporters. The government has denied any such abuses and, despite Nkomo's denials, insisted that Nkomo was linked to the 'dissident' campaign. This virtual civil war in Matabeleland provides the context for the inter-party feuding about the governing élite's national heroes' project.[41]

ZAPU challenged government efforts to control the process of identifying national heroes, thereby exposing the vulnerability of national unity and the ZANU(PF) government's national authority. One strategy of protest was for ZAPU to boycott Heroes' Days celebrations and the burials of national heroes. The first Heroes' Day in August 1980 was an occasion that both parties could celebrate. The bodies of ZIPRA's Jason Moyo and ZANLA's General Tongogara, both of whom had fought for political unity, were exhumed in Zambia and Mozambique, respectively, and returned to Zimbabwe. At Heroes' Acre, except for ZIPRA and ZANLA choirs trying to out-sing each other, there was no evidence of trouble brewing. Nkomo and Mugabe praised both men for their commitment to national unity, noted that neither were tribalistic, and urged people to emulate them. Nkomo said: 'We have not come here to bury heroes of ZAPU and ZANU — but heroes of Zimbabwe . . . It is the burial of the entire population of Zimbabwe — and not of a particular tribe . . . If you shout tribalism, then you are not with these two great young men.'[42] But in Bulawayo the celebrations were organized by ZANU(PF) and most ZAPU supporters stayed away. One ZANU(PF) official publicly blamed ZAPU for the low turnout and expressed the hope that 'there is no chicanery in their non-attendance'.[43] Another surveyed the empty seats and accused people of having an 'individualist mentality'. 'You go to Ndlodlo beer garden and you will find them.'[44] In July 1982, when ninety-two-year-old ZAPU central committee member Masotsha Ndlovu was buried at Heroes' Acre, Joshua Nkomo, now removed from the cabinet, did not even attend the burial.[45] When Robson Manyika, a ZANU(PF) Central Committee member and Deputy Minister of Labour, was buried at Heroes' Acre in June 1985, Joshua Nkomo was again absent.[46] Later that year, on Heroes' Day, ZAPU officials 'caused a stir' in Bulawayo when they failed to attend one of the Heroes' Day celebrations — apparently they had only received the invitations from the ZANU(PF) organizers on the day of the celebrations.[47] By Heroes' Day in 1987, unity talks were progressing and the celebrations were organized for the first time by both parties rather than ZANU(PF) only.[48] However, the turnout on Heroes' Day has remained very poor.

ZAPU also rejected the government's call to rebury its 'fallen heroes' at hierarchically graded heroes' acres for at least three (stated) reasons. ZAPU member of parliament John Nkomo told a crowd of about 200 at the Gwabalanda football grounds that it was against Ndebele custom to remove bodies from their original burial place: they should be left where they were and shrines could be constructed instead. This cultural argument against reburying ZIPRA dead at local and provincial heroes' acres persisted even after the Unity Accord was signed in 1987. Both Joshua Nkomo and John Nkomo opposed the idea of 'graded' heroes' acres — a national one at Harare, and provincial and local ones — when government, with ZAPU support, had legislated for only one heroes' acre in Harare where all the country's heroes were represented by the Tomb of the Unknown Soldier.

Furthermore, as John Nkomo said in August 1986, 'one could not ask people to go to the bush and exhume bones that might be confused with those of animals.'[49]

Provoked by John Nkomo's remarks about why ZAPU would not rebury its dead at local heroes' acres, an editorial in *The Chronicle* attacked ZAPU's rejection of local heroes' acres and its alleged failure to publish, as ZANU(PF) had on Heroes' Day in 1982 and on Heroes' Day 1983, a list of its guerrillas known to have died in the war. The editorial referred to the absence of published lists of ZIPRA heroes as a 'ticklish question' and held both ZAPU and the government responsible. The editor said that ZAPU had a duty 'to explain to those who had remained in this country the fate of their children or relatives who had joined the liberation forces, and for the Government to publish their names'. *The Chronicle* found John Nkomo's refusal to rebury the dead 'disrespectful' to ZIPRA ex-combatants who had died in the freedom struggle. The editorial found the cultural argument against reburials unconvincing and, provoked by John Nkomo's comment, asked, 'since when were animals in Zimbabwe buried in mass shallow graves?' It concluded provocatively: 'The unfortunate impression Cde Nkomo's remarks would give to a stranger to Zimbabwe is that there were no fighters killed and interred in shallow graves in Matabeleland by Rhodesian forces. We all know differently.'[50] Even if everyone knew differently, ZANU(PF) had insinuated, both during and after the war, that ZAPU was withholding guerrillas from the battlefield, and thus questioned ZAPU's contribution to the liberation struggle. ZAPU's failure to respond directly to the editorial's charges that it withheld a list of its war dead is puzzling. In August 1990 Dumiso Dabengwa, then Deputy Minister of Home Affairs, explained to *Parade* magazine that 'the ZIPRA records which were seized by the government in 1982 cannot now be located, and therefore we have had to carry out research from scratch to establish the names of those who died and the location of their graves.'[51] Why could ZAPU not say at the time that the ZANU(PF) government had confiscated its list of war dead?

What neither the newspapers nor the politicians spoke about as a reason for ZAPU to refuse to participate in reburying the dead from the liberation war dead was the fact that the same government that was appealing to villagers to rebury the guerrillas who had died in the liberation struggle was engaged in killing former ZIPRA combatants for their alleged 'dissidence' and civilians for their alleged support of the 'dissidents'. The government's war against the dissidents was at times more brutal than the war of independence, and produced its own mass graves — civilian victims of the Fifth Brigade.[52] It is difficult to imagine that the experience of this new war did not erode the ZANU(PF) government's legitimacy in rural Matabeleland and the Midlands.

ZAPU also engaged in initially veiled but increasingly open criticism of the sectarian process of selecting national heroes and the resulting omissions of worthy candidates. Coinciding with the reburial of Herbert Chitepo (ZANU(PF)'s leader when the party was in exile) at Heroes' Acre on Heroes' Day in 1981, Joshua Nkomo spoke at ZAPU member of parliament Boyson Mguni's funeral near Kezi in Matabeleland South province. 'If Zimbabwe had any heroes, it was difficult to imagine anyone who surpassed Mr Mguni.'[53] Joshua Nkomo also hinted that a ZAPU Central Committee member, Mrs Lois Sihwa, had a claim to being a national hero. At her funeral in Bulawayo in June 1982, he called on all Zimbabwean citizens to remember their fallen heroes such as Mrs Sihwa who, through their non-tribalism and non-racialism, had created a foundation for a stable Zimbabwe.[54] In August 1982 ZAPU member of parliament Ruth Chinamano asked the Minister of Information how national heroes were determined, and was told that a government committee forwarded names to the cabinet which made the decision.[55]

In November 1982 there was public debate over whether recently deceased Jairos Jiri, a man who had devoted 32 years to working with the disabled and had established the Jairos Jiri Association, should have been declared a national hero. Joshua Nkomo appealed to the government to consider giving him a heroes' funeral because 'heroes are not only the people who carried a gun or threw grenades to liberate Zimbabwe, but such people like Cde Jiri are heroes in their own fields.'[56] The *Sunday Mail* conceded that Jairos Jiri qualified as a certain type of hero: 'There was no iota of doubt that Cde Jairos Jiri was a great humanist, altruist and philanthropist — indeed, a great man.' It continued: 'It is true to say that greatness has the connotation of heroism. And a hero is variously defined as a man of distinguished bravery; an illustrious person; a person revered and idealised; an illustrious warrior; a person who has fought for his country, etc. Indeed as the definitions show, there are several types of heroes.' But ultimately, the *Sunday Mail* disagreed with Nkomo, alleging that Heroes' Acre had been established to honour a 'specific and exclusive type of hero. It is that hero whose courageous deeds were designed for and connected with one sole objective — the liberation of Zimbabwe.' Heroes' Acre was for those who risked their lives. 'The other fields of greatness, like philanthropy, did not have the element of risk.'[57]

Open party conflict broke out in September 1983 over whether ZAPU's Mrs Ruth Nyamurowa, who had been a commander of Victory Camp in Zambia, qualified to be buried at Heroes' Acre. In his funeral oration, Nkomo claimed she was a national hero: 'Ruth is a hero of the people of Zimbabwe and she has to be treated as such. We in ZAPU cannot claim her since her contribution goes far beyond these considerations.'[58] The government did give her a state-financed funeral, and at the funeral Joshua Nkomo stated that the government had been asked if she could be buried at Heroes' Acre, but since the Prime Minister was away, a decision could not be made. However, he was confident that she would qualify for reburial at Heroes' Acre.[59] Minister of Information Shamuyarira challenged Nkomo's optimism, publicly declared that the decision had been taken before her funeral not to honour her as a national hero.[60]

The issue of what criteria were used to decide who would be buried at Heroes' Acre was raised in December 1983 in Parliament by ZAPU Deputy Minister of Manpower Planning and Development, Daniel Ngwenya. The Prime Minister's response was not illuminating. 'Heroes are of different kinds: some are more heroes than others', he said. He stressed that anyone 'who really distinguished himself' would not be denied the right to be buried at Heroes' Acre.[61] In August 1984, shortly before her husband died and was declared a national hero, Ruth Chinamano asked the Minister of Information why ZAPU cadres, Nikita Mangena and Dr Parirenyatwa (both of whom had died years earlier), Mrs Nyamurowa and T. Makonese had not been declared national heroes. The Minister blamed ZAPU: 'At no time did ZAPU put to us a request that they wanted Cde Mangena to be buried at Heroes' Acre'. The only person's name the party had forwarded was that of Jason Moyo. Had ZAPU forwarded a request, 'we would have considered it, but that does not mean we would have accepted it'.[62] An article in the *The Herald* indicated that the Minister had used a political argument when there was an objective answer: Mangena was a 'lesser hero' than Moyo. The Minister's response had again raised questions about how heroes were chosen. His reply had suggested that parties were responsible for nominating national heroes. The same article in *The Herald* indicated that in some cases the government, undoubtedly guided by ZANU(PF)'s central committee, had decided on whether to confer national hero status; in other cases ZANU(PF)'s central committee had made the decision. The author of the article pleaded for the selection of national heroes to be divested of partisanship, not only because Zimbabwe still had a multi-party system but also because the concept of a national hero meant that there were objective criteria in the selection of a hero.[63]

A few months later, in October 1984, ZAPU's vice-president Josiah Chinamano was given a hero's burial at Heroes' Acre, but the partisan aspect to the celebration received adverse press. A commentator from *The Herald* observed that ZAPU, through enthusiastic partisanship, was more intent on making a political statement 'than according such a STATE and NATIONAL occasion the highest level of non-partisanship and solemnity'.[64] Denying the partisan ZANU(PF) government the legitimacy to make state and national decisions was precisely the point that ZAPU was intent on making. When ZANU(PF) Deputy Minister Robson Manyika was celebrated as a national hero in June 1985, the *Sunday Mail* asserted, as if to stifle controversy: 'We believe that the fact that one is a hero is objective: it is not subjective.'[65]

ZAPU's most unconstrained and indignant protest about the government's choice of national heroes occurred at the funeral of former ZIPRA commander, Lookout Masuku. Masuku died in April 1986 of a rare brain disease in hospital in Harare, having been transferred there from detention in February. He had been detained, along with Dumiso Dabengwa, since March 1982 despite having been acquitted in court. At the funeral in Bulawayo, which drew some 20 000 people, Joshua Nkomo deplored that 'this man, who contributed so much to the liberation of this country and after independence should today fail to find himself a place among our national heroes.' He asked: 'if Lookout Masuku is not a hero, who then is a hero in this country?' In a highly emotional speech, Nkomo charged that Masuku had died in prison: 'I am saying he died in prison because he died on the bed he was discharged onto from detention, and therefore he died in prison.' Nkomo then railed about corruption and those in high office stealing from the poor, the unemployed and the starving. He attacked the government's state of emergency and its disregard for the rule of law (Dabengwa — whom the High Court, Harare, had ruled could not be released from detention to attend the funeral — had been condemned to prison even though the highest court in the country had acquitted him of government charges). Nkomo continued: 'We accused and condemned the previous White minority government for creating a police state and yet we exceed them when we create a military state. We accused former colonisers who used detention without trial as well as torture and yet do exactly what they did, if not worse. We accused Whites of discrimination on grounds of colour yet we have discriminated on political and ethnic grounds.'[66] *The Herald* supported Nkomo's claim that Masuku deserved to be buried at Heroes' Acre but feared that Nkomo's funeral oration had 'revealed the inner feelings of the ZAPU leadership' and would threaten the progress that had been made in unity talks between ZAPU and ZANU(PF). 'It was a no-holds-barred oration which made it clear that ZAPU regards the unity talks as being between the good guys, them, and the bad ones, ZANU(PF), who have run the country to ground by being corrupt and being vindictive as not to bury Cde Masuku at Heroes' Acre.'[67] Past assertions by the *Sunday Mail* that identifying national heroes was an objective exercise and subsequent denials by the Minister of Information, Shamuyarira, that political affiliation was a factor in determining who was a national hero were unconvincing.[68] Two years later when Masuku's tombstone was unveiled, the political realities had been transformed by the Unity Accord.

Between 1980 and 1987 ZAPU persistently challenged the ZANU(PF) national government's project concerning national heroes and graded heroes' acres. ZAPU denied the right of the government to make state and national decisions about national heroes by attacking the partisan nature of its decision-making process and its actual selection of national heroes, and by being conspicuously absent from national heroes' burial ceremonies. ZAPU also rejected the concept of graded heroes' acres as a ZANU(PF) party decision in which ZAPU had not participated because the issue had never been placed before parliament. By not attending Heroes' Day celebrations that were organized by ZANU(PF), it protested against the partisan nature of what should have been national commemorations. ZAPU's actions threatened national unity and challenged the ZANU(PF) government's legitimacy.

DEBATES ABOUT FALLEN HEROES SINCE THE UNITY ACCORD

The Unity Accord and the subsequent party merger in December 1989 has not stifled debate about national heroes and graded heroes' acres. Nor has the Unity Accord led to improved attendance at Heroes' Day celebrations outside the capital. Many reasons for low turnouts at Heroes' Day functions are offered, as they were before the Unity Accord.[69] But Mr Chamakuhwa, writing in the *The Chronicle* after the Heroes' Day holiday in 1990, dismissed most of these reasons and accepted the view of 'the brutal ones' who 'put it (low turn-outs) down to a clear case of a protest stay-away from the politicians' now well-known harangues and tired slogans most of which have no relevance to the occasion being marked.'[70] One man, listening to President Mugabe deliver his Heroes' Day address at Heroes' Acre in August 1991 was unable to contain his frustration as the President listed the alleged successes of the ZANU(PF) government. The man shouted, in Shona: 'You are saying rubbish. Smith was better than you. Prices are going up all the time. Those fallen heroes you are talking about died for nothing.' He later appeared in court, and was charged with insulting the President.[71]

In March 1989 the ZIPRA War Shrines Committee was established on the instructions of the then ZAPU central committee. Its task is to locate the grave sites of ZIPRA freedom fighters, both inside and outside the country, and to identify the names of all ZAPU members who died in the war of liberation — something that ZANU(PF) has never tried to do. The War Shrines Committee, directed by the former ZIPRA intelligence chief, now Deputy Minister of Home Affairs, Dumiso Dabengwa, is following the ZAPU central committee's resolution of 1989 that confirms earlier ZAPU practice of not reburying its fallen heroes. The Shrines Committee has begun the process of locating grave sites inside Zimbabwe, marking them with gravestones and building shrines that contain the names of the fallen heroes. Since the party merger and the dissolution of ZAPU's central committee, the War Shrines Committee's work is being continued under the auspices of the Mafela Trust. Mafela means 'the fallen one', and was the chimurenga name of the former ZIPRA commander, the late Lt.-Gen. Lookout Masuku.[72] Dabengwa, a trustee of the Mafela Trust, and, as Deputy Minister of Home Affairs, responsible for national monuments, explained to *Parade* that the Mafela Trust was formed 'because we cannot leave all these tasks to the government alone. It is government policy that the people should involve themselves in activities to commemorate the liberation war and honour those who gave their lives to free Zimbabwe. The Trust will support and work closely with the government departments responsible for the war heroes.'[73] This sounds very conciliatory, yet it remains the case that the Mafela Trust is currently taking care of ZAPU's fallen heroes only. It seems as if the Mafela Trust exists partly (and unofficially) to keep alive ZAPU's legitimacy in its strongholds.

Increasingly frequently ex-combatants, and for the first time since Independence, ZANLA ex-combatants, are now questioning publicly the process of choosing national heroes. The formation of a War Veterans' Association in 1989 has also given ex-combatants a platform from which to criticize the commemoration of heroes. Ex-combatants are now asking for a role in organizing Heroes' Day celebrations, and have drawn attention to the absurdity of their non-participation in these festivities. They have also criticized the system of graded heroes' acres and have blamed this system for the many anomalies and contradictions in the definition of a national hero.[74]

In April 1991 Mrs Dongo, herself a ZANLA ex-combatant, member of parliament for Harare East and a member of the united ZANU(PF) central committee, sparked an emotional debate in the House of Assembly when she asked what criteria were used to determine national heroes, who made the decisions, and whether the party or the government funded the burials of national heroes. Dongo gave examples of people who were supposed to have been declared national heroes but were not, including Ashwet Masango who was a member of the ZANLA general staff. She also noted that no ex-ZIPRA commanders and ex-combatants have been declared heroes, 'even at district level'. Dongo questioned, as others had earlier, whether only high-ranking politicians and government officials were heroes. There were no answers to Dongo's questions. The Minister of Justice, Legal and Parliamentary Affairs, Emmerson Mnangagwa, and the Minister of State for the Public Service, Eddison Zvobgo, appealed to Dongo to withdraw her motion. Minister Zvobgo said 'Mr Speaker, there are matters too sacred for any nation to discuss in a forum of this kind.'[75] This evasive reply suggests the importance of the national heroes project for government legitimacy.

Another former ZANLA detachment commissar, Amos Sigauke, who is now a senior budget officer with a parastatal organization in Harare, told *Parade* in 1991 that the committee who made decisions about who should be a national hero 'should come out in the open. People want to know who they are.' He expressed bitterness that only government employees with close contact with the central committee were being buried at Heroes' Acre. Sigauke argued that the government should exhume Lookout Masuku's body and rebury him at Heroes' Acre if it wanted the unity between ZANU(PF) and ZAPU 'to look genuine'. He said: 'there are people who decided to be politically inactive after independence, yet they contributed so much. Should they not be declared heroes because they are no longer politically active?'[76]

That almost all the national heroes have been high-ranking government employees and politicians has raised questions about what kind of national values the government is trying to promote. *Parade* asked in its August 1990 edition: 'What then does a national hero represent in Zimbabwe? He (and we have no heroines yet)[77] must make it in politics, must cultivate patronage from the powerful and must aspire to be a chef. Is this the example that we wish our people to live up to? Surely these were not the motivations of our Tongogaras and J. Z. Moyos.' *Parade* asks if the nation wishes to encourage qualities that are 'élitist, self-serving, unquestioning and remote?'[78]

After the Unity Accord, the debate about how national heroes are chosen became intertwined with controversies about the status of ex-combatants. The controversy about the governing élite's national heroes project struck at the legitimacy of national symbols. The more recent public debate about the status of ex-combatants strikes at government legitimacy derived from effective performance, in that it raises questions about what the government has actually done for ex-combatants. Ex-combatants have also become a symbol of government and party leaders' betrayal of the socialist principles espoused by the leaders during the liberation struggle. The next section shows how the debate about ex-combatants is intimately associated with issues of government and party legitimacy.

FORGOTTEN HEROES

With preparations under way for ZANU(PF) and ZAPU to dissolve their separate constitutions and unite, parliamentarians turned to the plight of the nation's living heroes, the ex-combatants, in March 1988. The motion on ex-combatants, introduced in parliament by a White non-constituency member of parliament, Sean Hundermark,[79] ended the virtual silence on the grim situation of an estimated 25 000–35 000 unemployed ex-combatants. Parliamentarians who spoke in support of the motion portrayed the unemployed ex-combatants as poor, desperate, disgraced, jobless and roaming the streets, despite their contribution to the liberation of Zimbabwe. Alexio Mudzingwa, (ZANU(PF) MP for Chegutu) spoke of how those who had fought the war had been neglected while others benefited from their sacrifices. 'They are being treated like dogs because after a good catch while in the bush, hunters sit in their homes and eat the meat with their families, leaving the bones to the very same dogs that caught the animal. This is what we are doing to our liberators.'[80] Hundermark spoke for the ex-combatants, saying that they 'now consider themselves as rejects in society . . . used during the war as cannon fodder.'[81] Sabina Mugabe (ZANU(PF) MP for Makonde East and the sister of President Mugabe), highlighted how dependant the former freedom fighters were on their relatives for their basic needs and how they felt government had neglected them.[82] Kembo Mohadi (ZANU(PF) MP for Beitbridge) deplored the neglect of former freedom fighters that had resulted in the 'disgraceful situation' of many of them becoming push-cart operators to earn a living.[83] Some ex-combatants had even gone to South Africa, said Sean Hundermark, humbling themselves to cross the enemy border to seek jobs on the mines.[84]

In July 1988 parliament heard more about the plight of ex-combatants, although usually in the context of war victims generally. Sidney Malunga (ZAPU MP for Mpopoma), introducing a motion on the problems of the disabled, called for national legislation and a national policy on the disabled to eliminate discriminatory practices against them and allow them equal opportunities to participate fully in society. Malunga spoke about how most of those disabled during the war 'are today stranded, they are today starving'.[85] N. K. Ndlovu (ZAPU MP) also referred to the war disabled, both ex-combatants and civilians, whom he estimated to number 15 000.[86] 'Just now, as I speak here, it would be right for me to say: what a disappointment to the nation — not only the people who suffered through the acts of war — Government has done nothing or very little to improve the quality and life [sic] among the disabled.'[87] It was 'amazing', said MP Simela, that Zimbabwe, which 'emerged from a war of liberation with many disabled people' had not assimilated its war disabled 'into industries or into the public sector' and did not have a Ministry of Disabled Affairs, yet had established a Ministry of Women's Affairs.[88] Why had the previous Minister of Labour, Manpower Planning and Social Welfare dismissed disabled ex-combatants from Ruwa Rehabilitation Centre,[89] asked Mr Lazarus Nzarayebani, himself an ex-Methodist minister in the Honde Valley who had joined the guerrillas during the liberation struggle.[90] 'I have seen a number of these ex-combatants, they are living untold hazardous lives and it is not in the national interest that the fighters, the heroes of the struggle, should live in that manner. I have already pointed out that that is a national issue . . . We do not want to talk about NGOs, wealthy organisations et cetera. It is our problem. Those people have to be looked after by us. It is their inalienable right, not a privilege that the nation should look after them.'[91]

Since the motion on the plight of ex-combatants in March 1988, the image of 'forgotten heroes' is frequently invoked in the press. In its Independence Day Supplement in April 1988, *The Chronicle* ran a story on the 'forgotten army'.[92] On Heroes' Day in August 1988, *The Chronicle* reminded its readers that respect was due not only to the fallen heroes but also 'to the thousands of freedom fighters who survived the liberation war, many of whom came back maimed'. It cautioned that 'these ex-combatants, thousands of whom are today living in desperate poverty with nothing to show for what they fought for', should not be allowed to become 'forgotten heroes'.[93] When non-constituency MP Obert Mpofu, himself a ZIPRA ex-combatant, addressed the War Veterans' Association meeting in Bulawayo in January 1990, he criticized the Department of Social Welfare's attitude to the ex-combatants, stating 'They treat them like beggars instead of liberation war veterans.'[94]

BLAMING THE LEADERSHIP FOR THE PLIGHT OF EX-COMBATANTS

Those who promote the cause of the 'forgotten heroes' target the leadership, usually depicted as wealthy and uncaring, for their neglect. In August 1988 *The Chronicle* placed the plight of the 'forgotten heroes' in the context of 'some who are today enjoying the fruits of freedom, seemingly unmindful of the plight of their former comrades-in-arms. How frustrating and disillusioning it must be to the thousands of the ex-combatants in dire straits to observe those with whom they shared the perils of the war of liberation now virtually wallowing in the lap of luxury, while they live in poverty.'[95]

After the introduction of the scheme allowing ex-combatants employed in the public service to count their years in the guerrilla army towards their pensions, an unemployed ex-combatant wrote to The Chronicle in January 1990 pointing out the injustice of the government in not providing them with life pensions. He explained that many of them were demobilized 'on the pretext that Zimbabwe's economy could not sustain a large army. Surprisingly, a few months later, a new brigade was formed. Following this exercise some of the ex-fighters were gradually forced to resign from the armed forces because they had not attained at least a Grade Seven standard of education. The army was meant for the élite, most of whom never contributed anything to the liberation of our country.' The public service could not absorb all the ex-fighters — it was not by choice that unemployed ex-combatants were not in the public service. He then went on to talk about the leadership

> Depressingly and painfully, the pension scheme was drafted by no other than people with whom we suffered together in the long protracted war. Those are the same people who have in turn given the ex-fighters a raw deal . . . We bleed from the wounds of the unfair treatment we are receiving from the government we helped bring into being.

Their former colleagues having become callous leaders, the ex-combatant appealed to his dead comrades. 'I wish even the dead heroes of our struggle could rise from their graves and see what we are going through, even in a free Zimbabwe that we suffered for.' The letter concluded: 'We love our motherland. But some people in high places are in love with their ministerial posts and they view us as a thorn in their flesh and hate to hear about us.'[96]

Another letter to the The Chronicle's editor in March 1988 acknowledged that 'some of our leaders' were 'in the bush too as combatants. But the $64 million question is: can't they see the plight of their former comrades-in-arms?' The writer then proposed that the Ministers volunteer 'to have their enormously fat salaries cut'. He asked rhetorically: 'Do they each need $1 000 per month as housing allowances? Do our socialist 'comrades' need two drivers each? Do they need a Benz when they can do with more modern cars such as 504s? All this money 'seemingly spent without foresight' could go towards a fund to create jobs.[97] A month later, also in The Chronicle an unemployed demobilized ex-combatant blamed the leaders, exempting Maj.-Gen. Jevan Maseko and Sidney Malunga who spoke on behalf of ex-combatants in parliament, for his situation. 'I agreed to be demobilised thinking it would be easy to get a job. It seems our leaders are to blame as their promises were not fulfilled. They are living in luxury while we are suffering. It seems the exercise to demobilise us was not done properly.'[98]

Another writer to The Chronicle in April 1988 found it disturbing that a recently appointed non-constituency White member of parliament had taken up the issue of the plight of ex-combatants, 'we have been independent for eight years now and have had Black MPs all along, 80 of them to be precise. But that they were quiet all this time only to take up the issue after it had been brought up by someone who entered Parliament only six months ago does not give a good picture of our representatives.' He questioned whether the members of parliament were representing the people. 'Surely they must have known about the plight of our ex-combatants all along? After all, some of the MPs, and even Cabinet Ministers, are former combatants. Do they not really know what is happening to their colleagues? Or just like any other Zimbabweans of high standing they have become too busy with the running of the affairs of the State, or personal ones to notice that the very people who fought for this country are not well looked after?' Finally, the writer was concerned that the government might not have the capacity to do anything about the ex-combatants' situation, and that their rhetoric and promises would raise hopes they could not fulfill.[99] In the same newspaper and during the same time period, still another ex-combatant charged that the rewards that should have gone to the ex-combatants had gone to 'those who were in universities or who were somewhere in London or Washington during the most difficult times of the struggle in the bush.'[100]

In a poignant statement in parliament in February 1989, MP N. K. Ndlovu, a vocal participant in the motions on the plight of ex-combatants and on the disabled, evoked the grim plight of ex-combatants and blamed the leaders, associating himself with them.

Talking about the heroes — who are they? Are we referring to the dead heroes, if we are referring to our heroes, do we not have living heroes? I believe if we had declared those dead as heroes, surely there should be some living heroes declared. When it comes to performing on Heroes' Days, the living heroes should be seen to be taking the forefront in parading in front of the graves of the dead heroes. I think eight years back. I have lived to wonder why we have shunned to bring forward our living heroes. Are we waiting to know them when they are dead, and recognised now when they are living because the dead ones fought side by side with those who are living? This is one of the anomalies which I believe we should address ourselves to in order that we pay due respect to those of us we would like to honour. The very fact that they are not being mentioned, I think it is a cover up because most of the living heroes are walking the streets of Harare bare-footed, dressed in torn trousers without jobs. They are walking the streets of Mutare, Masvingo, Gweru, Bulawayo, Kwekwe, et cetera, or any other city in this country without actually mentioning those who have backed away from the city centres and are living in communal centres without anybody realising what their plight is about. I think this is a deliberate omission of our living heroes because we want to hide the truth. We do not want them to be known but they are the real people who brought about this independence which we are enjoying, and they are looking forward to the leadership to see what leadership is going to do for them, but they have waited for too long. Their hopes are dying and in fact their hopes are dead already because nothing has come forward.

Mr Ndlovu ended with a strong indictment of the celebration of Heroes' Day when the nation would not recognize its living heroes. His speech is an illuminating illustration of how the efforts to create national symbols by drawing on the fallen heroes became intertwined with the image of neglected ex-combatants — an image that complicated further the governing élite's project to create national heroes that would serve as symbols of political legitimacy. 'This is the unfortunate part of our struggle which perhaps will remain unwritten purposely because we shun to mention out who was a hero here and there. It is needless to talk about Heroes' Day or to recognize that as a day when we remember our struggle without really putting forward people with such courage who have suffered and without realising their problems.'[101]

In January 1990 *The Chronicle* reminded readers that nothing had been heard of the special committee that the government was supposed to set up to investigate the situation of ex-combatants and that would lay the basis for formulating a program of rehabilitation. 'Nothing has been heard of that committee since. And nobody seems to care.'[102]

The Chronicle, ex-combatants and some leaders themselves portrayed the government and party leadership as having enriched itself while ex-combatants were starving, homeless and jobless. Repeatedly, leaders are described as uncaring, as having used the ex-combatants to acquire positions of power, and as having failed to meet the promises they made to the ex-combatants during the war. The plight of the ex-combatants has thus become another arena in which the leadership's legitimacy is questioned. Criticism of the leadership's neglect of the ex-combatants is particularly sensitive because the leaders are perpetually referring to their war sacrifices to legitimate their positions and rule.

ARE EX-COMBATANTS A SPECIAL GROUP?

Proponents of the 'forgotten heroes' thesis believe that the living ex-combatants deserve a reward or compensation for their sacrifices on behalf of the nation. Following the motion on the plight of ex-combatants, members of parliament appealed to government to set up a special committee to study the current status, employment, education, accommodation and welfare of the ex-combatants, and to devise a program to rehabilitate and restore them to dignity.[103] Underlying the proposal was the perception that the ex-combatants faced special problems, in part because of their contribution to the liberation struggle. Many had interrupted their schooling to fight and were disadvantaged *vis-à-vis* those who had been able to complete their schooling during the war. This made them uncompetitive on the job market. They lacked the capital for self-improvement, and their lack of skills and access to funds contributed to the failure of the co-operatives in which many initially enthusiastically participated.[104] In his statement in response to this motion, Minister of Labour, Manpower Planning and Social Welfare, John Nkomo, acknowledged the special status of ex-combatants, at least in the short term. He assured the House of Assembly that his Government, 'born out of revolutionary struggle' had a 'special responsibility' towards the ex-combatants that it 'cannot possibly and should not ignore'. As a 'short term solution', government still hoped to renew its call for organizations to give priority to the employment of ex-combatants; in the long term, policies had to be formulated to cater for unemployed ex-combatants and unemployed youth.[105]

Other ministerial statements contradict the government's stated commitment to preferential treatment for the ex-combatants. Shortly after the motion on the plight of ex-combatants, John Nkomo told *The Chronicle* that he dissociated himself from those members of parliament who argued that the problem of unemployment affected ex-combatants more than anyone else. He objected to singling out a group for preferential treatment eight years after Independence. 'I think in the eight years we have gone through, too many things have been evened out between the ex-combatants and the non-ex-combatant. We should now be addressing unemployment as a national problem that faces both the veterans of the war and those who were young during the war, but who have now attained the age of majority.'[106] Joshua Nkomo, appointed as Senior Minister of Political Affairs after the Unity Accord in 1987, felt the same way. A few months after the parliamentary discussion on the plight of ex-combatants, he addressed a May Day rally in Bulawayo where he appealed to ex-combatants to appreciate the country's unemployment problems and not consider themselves as special cases because they fought the war for liberation. 'You went to fight for the liberation of the country, you were not mercenaries', he said.[107] Minister Joshua Nkomo returned to the theme that ex-combatants were not a special case when replying to a question by member of parliament Obert Mpofu about whether the government, which had reportedly organized a 'high-powered delegation' to discuss the plight of 'ex-dissidents', would arrange a similar meeting to consider the plight of ex-combatants. Joshua Nkomo argued that the question of the 'ex-dissidents', who had accepted the offer of amnesty made by the government on Independence Day in April 1988, was different from that of the ex-combatants. The 'ex-dissidents were not wanted by the people where they came from and they became a problem and it was therefore necessary to meet and discover what could be done, in order to avoid a security situation . . . When they get out and they cannot be accepted, the next thing is that they will be in the bush and we will have that problem.' The ex-combatants, he acknowledged, had 'a problem', but he presented their problems of unemployment as similar to those of youth generally. 'It is not just the ex-combatant — it is the young people who have no jobs . . . The problem is not for those who carried the gun during the war, it is the problem facing all the young people in this country and, therefore, we would like to have only an all-embracing answer to this problem . . .'[108]

Despite government's contradictory statements about its intentions to accord ex-combatants preferential treatment in the socio-economic sphere, it has given ex-combatants special rights in the political realm. During the discussion on the plight of ex-combatants, Obert Mpofu proposed that ex-combatants set up a national association with branches countrywide.[109] In early 1989, ZANLA and ZIPRA ex-combatants formed a War Veterans' Association. Despite opposition in some quarters, the constitution of the new united party provides for the War Veterans' Association to choose two representatives on the central committee.[110] The united ZANU(PF) has asked the War Veterans' Association to seek associate status in the party.[111] Moreover, the President of the united ZANU(PF), Mugabe, has promised the War Veterans' Association financial assistance if it comes up with ideas for employment projects.[112] By giving the ex-combatants special representation in the central committee, the ruling party seems to be pursuing a strategy of incorporating a potentially hostile group.

How effective will the war veterans be in furthering their very different interests? Those who are employed have different concerns from their unemployed former colleagues. Employed ex-combatants in the police and army complain of discrimination in promotions *vis-à-vis* those who never were in the guerrilla forces,[113] and former ZIPRA ex-combatants perceive that former ZANLA ex-combatants are favoured for promotions and pay in the police force.[114] Educated ex-combatants who obtained degrees in socialist countries complain that they suffer discrimination in favour of those who obtained degrees in western countries and that they have difficulty finding jobs.[115] However, from the perspective of unemployed ex-combatants, their former colleagues who have jobs in the police, armed forces and civil service are well-provided for. Regulations introduced in 1989 make it possible for ex-combatants in the armed forces, police, prison service, and the public service to receive pensions for their years in the liberation struggle. Also, ex-combatants who are civil servants, members of parliament, the armed forces and the police force can obtain mortgages from building societies without the ten per cent deposit usually required because the government gives them 100 per cent guaranteed loans.[116] Unemployed ex-combatants enjoy none of these benefits, rewards or compensation. The unemployed ex-combatants, it should be emphasized, are themselves a diverse group. They include an estimated 13 000 people who do not hold even a primary-school certificate and are unqualified for any type of job as well as those who, on their return from the war, resumed their interrupted studies and managed to attain high academic qualifications.[117] Despite these differences, the mere existence of an organization that believes that ex-combatants have special interests and are entitled to rewards and compensation from the government will ensure that they will be a persistent voice that will keep alive the public debate about whether or not they constitute a special group. Representing themselves as the conscience of the nation and an embodiment of the ideals of the liberation struggle, they pose a potential threat to the legitimacy of a government that itself relies on its war credentials for legitimacy.

CONCLUSION

The élites' implementation of its national heroes' project and their neglect of ex-combatants have exposed the tensions that exist between the élite and the masses as well as the ethnic-regional rivalries that dominate Zimbabwean politics. In a sense, then, public debates about war heroes have merely reflected the tensions in Zimbabwean society and politics, and have highlighted how fragile national authority and national unity are in a new nation. Because the war led to the founding of Zimbabwe, political controversies surrounding the governing and party élites' efforts to create national heroes out of the war experience have been intensely emotional. The élites sought to attain legitimacy and national unity through creating national war heroes but the project has backfired and revealed the fragility of the government and nation instead. However, it is conceivable that in time, the right to debate such sacred national issues will itself become a shared value that will foster national identity and legitimate governments that permit that debate.

9

Making Peace with the Past: War Victims and the Work of the Mafela Trust[1]

JEREMY BRICKHILL

INTRODUCTION

There is no more effective way of understanding the terrible cost of war than by remembering the individual who died fighting it . . . Those who lived through the war do not need to be told of its horrors, but younger generations have to make an imaginative leap to understand.[2]

The unmarked graves of the liberation war dead, the plight of their dependants and the unresolved traumas of war and violence are a neglected aspect of the legacy of the liberation war in Zimbabwe. This chapter explores some of these issues through a review of the work of the Mafela Trust.

The Trust originated in a programme of the Zimbabwe African People's Union (ZAPU) to identify and commemorate its war dead. This work, which took ex-combatant researchers into the rural areas, soon opened up wider questions of the legacy of trauma and dislocation in rural communities. In responding to these problems the Mafela Trust has turned its attention more and more to issues which rural communities from all parts of the country have themselves brought forward. Rural communities, who contributed so much to the liberation of Zimbabwe, remain scarred by the liberation war.

The conflict between ZANU and ZAPU in the 1980s has left its own bitter legacy. It was this conflict and the attempted suppression of ZAPU which prevented ZAPU from commemorating its own war dead immediately after Independence. When unity was achieved and it became possible for this work to be carried out, former ZAPU fighters returned to their operational zones to carry out research on their war dead. In seeking to propitiate the dead they had to attend to the problems of the living, those whose own memories of war and conflict are not yet healed.

Appropriately, the origins of the Mafela Trust itself can be traced to the last wishes of a liberation war hero who died after Independence had been achieved.

THE LAST COMMAND

On 5 April 1986 Lt-Gen. Lookout Masuku, the last war-time commander of the Zimbabwe People's Revolutionary Army (ZIPRA), died in Harare's Parirenyatwa Hospital. Arrested in March 1982 during the arms cache crisis, he was tried for treason with Dumiso Dabengwa, acquitted and then re-detained.[3] In detention Masuku's health deteriorated rapidly but the authorities failed to transfer him to hospital. Finally, in desperation, his closest friend and fellow detainee, Dumiso Dabengwa, threatened a hunger strike, as a result of which Masuku was transferred to Parirenyatwa Hospital. But Masuku's condition continued to deteriorate despite treatment and he died a few weeks later of a rare brain disease.

Masuku's role in the liberation struggle is legendary. He joined the National Democratic Party and soon became a prominent member of the Youth League. In the early 1960s he was a member of one of the secret 'Action Groups' of the Youth League and participated in the early sabotage campaign. After he left the country and had undergone his own military training, he became one of ZAPU's first military instructors and trained many of Zimbabwe's guerrillas, including the former Commander of the Zimbabwe National Army, Solomon Mujuru (Rex Nhongo). Later he became ZIPRA Commissar and after the death of Alfred 'Nikita' Mangena in 1978, was himself appointed Commander of ZIPRA. He played a vital role in securing the cease-fire before and after Independence and was a prominent architect of the integration exercise which led to the creation of the Zimbabwe National Army (ZNA), of which he was appointed Deputy Commander.

Less well known outside ZAPU circles was Masuku's concern for the demobilized ex-combatants. Together with ZAPU's former intelligence chief, Dumiso Dabengwa, and ZAPU leader, Isaac Nyathi, Masuku established the ZIPRA co-operative company, NITRAM, to provide employment, training, welfare benefits and project funding for ZIPRA ex-combatants.[4] He personally assisted several ex-combatant co-operatives, and involved himself in the earliest efforts of the ex-combatants to organize self-help schemes. It was Lookout Masuku who introduced Sir Garfield Todd to the disabled ex-combatants who today form the Vukuzenzele War Disabled Foundation and who farm a portion of the Todd ranch in Zvishavane donated to them by Sir Garfield.

Masuku's concern for the ex-combatants was also part of a wider concern about the legacies of the liberation war. In the last days of his life Lookout Masuku was anxious to establish a Trust to look after his own children, but he insisted that the L. K. V. Masuku Trust, as it was to be called, had two further objectives: these were: 'to promote publications concerning the liberation war in Zimbabwe, and generally to assist the ex-combatants of the liberation war in Zimbabwe'.[5]

From his hospital bed Masuku dictated several letters dealing with ZIPRA affairs and the plight of the ex-combatants. One of these letters was addressed to National Archives Director, Angeline Kamba, requesting that the ZIPRA war records be donated to the National Archives. 'I am most anxious', he wrote, 'that these records should not be lost to the nation. They will provide, I believe, a most useful source of historical record.'[6] Masuku also gave instructions that the list of ZIPRA War Dead should be collated and published and that the deeds of the liberation war fighters should be commemorated.

These concerns — history, the propitiation of the war dead and the welfare of the ex-combatants and their dependants — were an important part of Lookout Masuku's legacy. 'Mafela' (the Fallen One) was Masuku's chimurenga name, and his own contribution to Zimbabwe's liberation is today commemorated as part of this larger legacy in the Mafela Trust, whose work brings together many of the concerns of the last years of Masuku's own life.

RAISING THE FALLEN HEROES

Lookout Masuku was buried at the Lady Stanley Cemetery in Bulawayo at a highly emotional funeral attended by 30 000 people. The government's failure to declare him a national hero or send any representatives to his funeral provoked a fiery speech from Joshua Nkomo in which he accused ZANU(PF) of turning the national liberation war into party property. 'If Lookout Masuku is not a hero', he asked, 'who then is a hero in this country?'[7]

Masuku's funeral took place at the height of the inter-party conflict of the mid-1980s, and ZANU's ignoring of ZAPU's contribution to the war was part of their broader campaign against ZAPU at that time. The issue of war heroes and the plight of the ex-combatants was too sensitive an issue to be tackled at that time. But two years later, after the successful conclusion of the Unity Accord between ZAPU and ZANU, a parliamentary debate finally took place on liberation war heroes and the plight of ex-combatants and war victims.

A White non-constituency member of parliament, Sean Hundermark, was the first to raise the matter by introducing a private members' motion in March 1988. His voice was soon drowned out by contributions from ZANU(PF) and former ZAPU backbench radicals. It was clear from this debate that many MPs knew that the war legacy was not simply a question of heroic myths. Following this debate the state-owned media introduced, for the first time, the notion of 'forgotten heroes' into its annual Heroes' Day homage. The government too took note and set up a committee to investigate the problems of ex-combatants.[8]

Norma Kriger argues that the exclusion of ZAPU's national heroes was part of a wider appropriation of the symbol of The National Hero by the new ruling élite.[9] Contrasting Zimbabwe with independent Kenya where the government sought 'to stifle discussion about the war' she proposes a metaphor for class and power relations in Zimbabwe in which the hierarchy of heroes created by the government mirrors the post-war political dispensation. This hierarchy, Kriger says, symbolizes the politics of resource allocation in which the capital and the governing élite enjoy privileges that are denied to the masses. National heroes, she says, belong in the capital and their funerals are glorious and expensive occasions paid for by the state. The rank-and-file heroes are buried in rural communities and the local people foot the bill.[10]

A correspondent writing to *Parade* magazine makes the point explicit that, not only have the heroes been appropriated by the ruling élite, but the criteria for their selection now reflects the values of that élite. The correspondent writes that, in order to be a hero, '(you) must make it in politics, must cultivate patronage from the powerful and must aspire to be a chef. Surely these were not the motivations of our Tongogaras and J. Z. Moyos'.[11]

This appropriation of the war heroes compounded many ex-combatants' feeling that they had been abandoned after they had been disarmed and cleared from the Assembly Points.[12] ZAPU's ex-combatants, in particular, suffered greatly during the period of inter-party conflict. They were excluded from many job opportunities within the state sector and were singled out in the hunt for 'dissidents' during the deployment of the Fifth Brigade in Matabeleland. Many were killed, several hundred ZAPU ex-combatants were detained, and many more were harassed during this period.

After his release from detention in December 1986, Dumiso Dabengwa raised the problems of the ZAPU ex-combatants in the ZAPU Central Committee. Although there were some who counselled caution in the delicate atmosphere of resumed unity negotiations between the two parties, Dabengwa and others argued that the plight of the ZAPU ex-combatants was an urgent responsibility of the ZAPU leadership. As part of this process the ZAPU Central Committee resolved in 1987 to resume its programme of identifying the ZIPRA war dead.[13] A ZIPRA War Shrines Committee was appointed, headed by Dabengwa, to carry out this work.

As Kriger relates, ZAPU had originally opposed two aspects of the government 'heroes' reburial' programme. Firstly, ZAPU did not approve of the hierarchical system of heroes' acres at national, provincial and district level. Instead, ZAPU proposed that the tomb of the unknown soldier should be the key national shrine of homage to the liberation war dead and that war heroes should be buried in their home areas. Secondly, ZAPU was opposed to the exhumation and reburial of the war dead who died inside the country, proposing instead that gravestones for the war dead should be erected in the places where they lay.[14]

The ZIPRA War Shrines Committee endorsed both these decisions and referred them to the Central Committee for approval as part of a package of proposals to commemorate the ZAPU war dead. In one of its final decisions before its dissolution the ZAPU Central Committee approved the proposals which called for the publication of a list of ZAPU war dead and the erection of shrines and monuments, both within Zimbabwe and in neighbouring states. It was also agreed that bodies would not be exhumed, except in exceptional cases, but that graves would be marked with headstones.[15]

During 1988 the ZIPRA War Shrines Committee discussed and planned its work. At this time the complex process of uniting the two parties was starting and this led to a discussion over whether the committee should be absorbed into the new united ZANU(PF). It was eventually decided that the incorporation of the committee would hinder the work at that stage, and this led to the curious anomaly that a ZAPU Central Committee organ was still functioning after the party itself had been dissolved.[16]

A RESEARCH PROGRAMME TO LOCATE THE DEAD

In early 1989 a team was appointed to carry out the research work of the ZAPU War Shrines Committee. It was headed by the ZIPRA former Deputy Commissar, Col. Richard Dube, who was released from the National Army to carry out this work.[17] The three other members of the team were also former members of ZIPRA. Nicholas Nkomo was a former commander in ZIPRA's northern front and Mark

Ndlovu was a former commander in ZIPRA's regular forces based in Zambia. The fourth member of the team was myself, with overall responsibility for designing the research programme.

The principal aim of the research programme as defined by the War Shrines Committee was:

> To establish the exact locations of the graves of the fallen heroes, their names, areas of origin (homes) and next of kin. The ultimate aim being that the ZAPU President announce to the entire nation the fate of their sons and daughters who died during the liberation struggle.[18]

The research work was planned to take place in three phases. The first phase involved the physical location and mapping of actual burial sites of ZIPRA members. The second phase aimed at identifying the names and biographical details of the ZIPRA dead.[19] The third phase required the researchers to match the graves with names, thereby enabling each grave to be marked with a headstone identifying its occupant.

The research programme began in Harare and Bulawayo, where a series of interviews were conducted with former members of ZIPRA. The project was carefully explained to the veterans who were asked to provide details from their personal experience of the details of battles with Rhodesian forces and the numbers and names of ZIPRA casualties. On the basis of this information, which was recorded in notes and on maps, 21 out of the 55 districts of Zimbabwe were identified as requiring field work.[20]

Anticipating a wide range of problems in the field, the research team conducted some preliminary field work before a final research methodology and procedure were agreed and adopted. Two major problems were encountered in these field tests. The first concerned the sensitivity of the issue and involved dealing with the suspicions with which rural communities greeted the arrival of young men asking questions about former guerrillas. In those parts of Matabeleland which had only recently suffered the tragic consequences of Fifth Brigade operations, this suspicion was acute. The second, related, problem involved the suspicions and jealousies of government officials, some of whom still behaved as if any mention of ZAPU and ZIPRA was a security matter.

To deal with these and other related problems a multi-pronged strategy was adopted to gain access to rural communities. Contact was first made officially with Governors and Provincial and District Administrators in each area and requests were made for appointments to enable the team to explain the programme to them. The laborious task of explaining, persuading and assuaging their fears then began. Col. Dube's status in the National Army was crucial in this process. Many problems arose, not least of which was the continual suspicion of local state security officers. Dealing with these problems required patience and diplomacy.

The research team had decided that the co-operation of both traditional and local political leaders would be essential to the success of the field work. Chiefs and headmen and local councillors were, therefore, invited to briefings by the team in the next stage of the programme.[21] They were asked by the research team to convey their request for assistance in tracing the ZIPRA dead to their communities. To avoid jealousies, and to ease administration, the research team asked the chiefs and headmen to communicate with the team through the local District Administrator. The research team then followed up the offers of help by visiting those local communities who had volunteered information. At the same time the team, now more acceptable in the eyes of the local government structures, began making contact with the (often almost clandestine) local ZAPU structures.

This apparently cumbersome procedure certainly delayed the start of actual research. But because it involved all the local power structures and provided a role for each of them, it eventually enabled the researchers to gain almost unhindered access to local people. Given the nature of the project this access was essential.

After these circuitous preparation stages, the researchers began the follow-up visits and conducted interviews in local communities, investigating further leads and eventually piecing together much of the information they required. Finally the researchers moved through the rural areas identifying and mapping burial sites.

Questions of gender were discussed many times by the research team and were always seen as an important issue for the research methodology. Guerrilla relations with local girls were a complex and controversial aspect of the rural politics of the liberation war, but guerrillas undoubtedly had frequent contact with local girls and anyone wishing to trace detailed local guerrilla history would ignore this fact at their peril. The War Shrines Committee and the research team recognised this, but were also aware that local communities might consider improper the appearance of a female researcher enquiring about dead guerrillas. The researchers also expressed unease at travelling with a female researcher on a mission concerning the location of the dead — and being seen to be doing so. Nevertheless it was clear that accessing the local female population was essential and required a female interviewer. The solution adopted was to use local female researchers chosen by the local communities at the request of the team. This deprived the programme as a whole of a considered and continuous female perspective, but it worked well as a research method.

The mass of data obtained through the procedures outlined above was processed through journals in which detailed daily records were kept and entered onto a series of card indexes. The names of the dead, the gravesites and details of the circumstances of death, together with other information, were then matched together in a painstaking processing exercise.

HAMBA KHALE QHAWE LETHU LEZIMBABWE[22]

Having established the location of 400 gravesites and accounted for 533 dead ZIPRA fighters, the Mafela Trust purchased space in the popular Zimbabwean magazine, *Parade*, and published a list of ZIPRA war dead in August 1990. In an accompanying article the establishment of the Mafela Trust was announced to continue the work started by the ZIPRA War Shrines Committee and the research team appealed for more information from the public. A second list was published in December 1990.

These publications resulted in a massive public response, not only from former ZIPRA operational areas but from all parts of the country, concerning a range of issues associated with the legacies of the liberation war. Before reviewing these issues, however, I will briefly summarize the results of the research programme of the Mafela Trust and the plans of the Trust for commemorating the ZIPRA war dead. By the end of 1991 the research team had located 1 087 gravesites and established the circumstances of the death of 1 414 guerrilla fighters out of an estimated 2 500. (These included 35 ZANLA and 16 South African ANC members.) The real names of 657 dead ZIPRA fighters had been established and their next of kin informed.[23]

Preliminary analysis of this data reveals much new information on aspects of the guerrilla war. The chronological and geographical spread of ZIPRA operations can be ascertained from this data, as can many insights into guerrilla strategy and tactics and Rhodesian counter-insurgency methods. The causes of death provide new perspectives on the guerrilla war experience. For example, five per cent of ZIPRA fatalities were found to be accounted for in non-combat situations; including suicide, disease, drowning and training accidents. Forty per cent of fatalities took place during air and ground raids into the Frontline States, and eight per cent of fatalities are accounted for by those taken captives who were never seen again. This information helps shed light on the conditions which guerrillas endured and provides a deeper meaning to their war effort.

A more sinister revelation suggests that a larger percentage, possibly as high as 10 per cent, of fatalities were caused by a hitherto unexplored aspect of Rhodesian counter-insurgency — chemical and biological warfare. At least 150 ZIPRA guerrillas died of poisoning and the evidence suggests that the civilian death toll caused by poison warfare is far higher than this. The use of poisons by the Rhodesian forces can now be clearly linked to the destabilization of rural communities during the war. The breakdown in guerrilla-peasant relations and the rise in witchcraft accusations in Lupane in 1978–9 coincides with the extensive use of poison warfare in the area at this time, and this factor clearly now needs to be examined in relation to similar phenomena in ZANLA operational areas.[24]

These and other topics for further research on the history of the liberation war and its legacy have been brought to light through the efforts of the Mafela Trust. Before turning to the legacy of the war in rural communities, however, a few words are necessary concerning the Mafela Trust's own plans, programmes and objectives.

COMMEMORATING THE FALLEN ONES

Remembrance of the liberation war, as Kriger argues, also involves the present and the future. The contribution of the Mafela Trust to this contestation is to argue for a return of the historical legacy of the war to the rural people who fought and sacrificed the most for the liberation of Zimbabwe. The Trust proposes to place headstones on all the graves of ZIPRA fighters and to erect shrines in 'all the districts where ZIPRA forces operated because this will enable locals of the respective areas to visit shrine sites'. With the National Heroes' Acre in Harare, and most other Heroes' Acres in urban centres, the Trust has argued that shrines should be built in rural areas because 'mostly the war was fought in rural areas and the people who were physically involved in the war are peasants in the outlying areas, and most of the recruits came from the same areas'.[25]

The Trust also proposes to build simple museums at shrine sites in rural areas where exhibits from the liberation war can be displayed, together with a register of all the gravesites in the area. Meetings with rural communities and investigations into the major battles of the liberation war have elicited a number of proposals for shrine sites. These include Inyantue in Hwange, Mabhongani in Tsholotsho and a site in Guruve. The choice of sites for the shrines is also intended to take account of the early resistance to colonial occupation. As the researchers report: 'The last war was a continuation of that of our forefathers (1893–6) and therefore some places of historical significance like Pupu in Lupane and Enungwini in Matobo can be used as sites'.[26]

At present the research team is preparing detailed proposals, designs and costings for the gravesites, shrines and museums in consultation with the Department of National Museums and Monuments, and as the researchers point out '(This) exercise requires co-ordination with the locals of those areas so as to come out with decisions which will be acceptable to those whom this exercise is designed to benefit.'[27]

Under the circumstances, the work of the Mafela Trust so far is an exceptional achievement, though perhaps it is not surprising as the research was conducted by former guerrillas turned researchers who had a wealth of experience of the dynamics of rural society and who were able to work with rather than on rural communities. As Mark Ndlovu pointed out, 'We are not alone in this work. The information we need comes from the people.'[28]

The effect of the liberation war and its aftermath on the rural people is the focus of the remainder of this chapter.

THE OTHER 'FORGOTTEN HEROES'

The Mafela Trust, which began with the relatively simple objective of locating the ZIPRA war dead, has become involved in understanding and responding to the peasant experience of the liberation war. When collecting information from rural communities the research team heard of the many unresolved problems created by the war. Richard Dube's report to the Trustees in May 1990 concluded with these words:

> Initially the team lacked co-operation from the local authorities and the people, who viewed our presence with suspicion and distrust. This problem had to be overcome by careful and patient explanation to all concerned, until the people understood what the purpose of the exercise was and trusted members of the team to carry it out.

> There are very many unsolved problems and worries which the people explained to the team, and which arise from their experiences during and after the liberation war. These include lack of information on the whereabouts of their relatives who are still missing, absence of birth and death certificates caused by the circumstances of the liberation war.

> Above all, there are people whose sons and daughters gave their lives for the liberation of Zimbabwe, but who today face many problems and who have not received any information or gratitude from the nation for their sacrifices.

> Their silent suffering touched our hearts.[29]

The visit of one elderly couple to the Mafela Trust offices is poignantly recorded in an article published in *Parade*:

> The old lady was weeping quietly. The old man spoke with dignity. 'Our hearts will rest now that we know what became of our son. We thank you deeply for the great work you are doing.'
>
> When the couple had left, Comrade Nicholas Nkomo told me about their visit. 'These old people last saw their son in 1977 when he left the country with their blessing to join the liberation struggle. He never returned and they have waited and searched for him since independence . . . We think we know where his grave is, as he was buried by locals. But we must confirm it along with the graves of many others and then we will make arrangements for the parents to go there.'[30]

These contacts with rural communities have added a new dimension to the work of the Trust, as researcher Mark Ndlovu explains:

> We are having to be social workers. We have to break the news to parents who have never given up hope. Some believe that their children are still on scholarships overseas, or that they are in Angola trapped by the war there.[31]

Numerous compensation claims and requests for assistance in obtaining birth and death certificates are now handled by the Trust, which assists applicants in making approaches to the relevant authorities. Sometimes the authorities also request help from the Trust in authenticating claims, as in the case of a district social welfare officer who wrote

> His whereabouts were not known until his father read about his fate in the August *Parade*. The applicant has applied for compensation so that he can maintain the deceased's child as he is unemployed himself. Will you please confirm.[32]

It is clear from the letters received at the Trust office that there are still many missing persons from all parts of the country. From Mutare a father wrote about his son

> At the time everyone assumed that he had joined ZANLA, but when the ZANLA war dead were released his name never appeared. It was only when we heard of *Parade* that we raised hopes of getting the details of his death. On the list of fallen heroes there did appear a name which coincided with the name of my son. We are therefore kindly asking you for further information.[33]

In response to these requests the Trust has established a register of missing persons, and is seeking to involve churches, welfare organizations and government bodies in creating a programme to identify missing persons and investigate their fate.

The work with rural communities has also drawn attention to the other 'forgotten heroes' of the liberation war, the peasants themselves. Rural communities invariably provided the research team with names of civilians killed in the war, and included many of these people in their lists of local heroes. Others identified as 'sellouts' were specifically excluded from such lists. The Mafela Trust is shortly to publish a list of civilian war heroes, together with information about their deeds. It is proposed to include these liberation heroes in the shrine programme.

In some areas local communities have already created shrines, and at a guerrilla shrine and gravesite in Gokwe, civilian war heroes are buried with guerrillas. Such shrines are a powerful reminder of the peasant perspective of the war. Local legends of war-time heroic exploits and tragedies were often told to the researchers and are an important part of local oral history. The Trust is discussing ways in which these histories can be recorded and disseminated to a wider audience.

The Mafela Trust Research team has also been made aware of the sense of betrayal and outrage rural communities feel at the way in which their history has been appropriated. On many occasions the researchers received lectures from peasants who felt the team was also attempting to 'steal' their history. The neglect of the role of rural people in the war is also reflected in another new aspect of the work of the Trust concerning the obvious evidence the researchers have acquired on the traumatic legacy of the war.

OVERCOMING THE TRAUMA OF WAR

A male patient was brought to Gororo (a spirit medium) because he was disturbed and spoke nonsense. Gororo became possessed and instructed her acolyte to make an infusion of herbs and incense, over which the patient had to lean covered with a blanket. After some time he called out that he was ready to talk. He admitted to killing nine people in the war as a fighter against the Rhodesian Army. Some he killed in battle; some he killed as *varoyi* ('witches') because he believed they had eaten the corpses of comrades killed in battle; and others he killed for being sellouts. Gororo divined that two spirits of the last category had returned to trouble him as they had been wrongfully accused. Had they been guilty they would not have sought revenge. Gororo cleansed the patient. The purification ritual would not have been effective (she said) if the patient had not revealed the truth.[34]

The story of Gororo's purification of the guerrilla fighter illustrates how people may survive the trauma of war but bear its scars. Overcoming the trauma of war, Gororo suggests, requires that we identify the sources of trauma, reveal the truth of its origin and then cleanse ourselves and make amends.

When the chairperson of the Mafela Trust, Dumiso Dabengwa, visited the site of the proposed ZIPRA shrine at Pupu in Lupane, he held discussions with the custodian of an existing shrine to the High God. Dabengwa consulted the shrine keeper to obtain his support for the erection of the ZIPRA shrine at that site. He was told that *Mwali* (the High God) was angry because the soldiers of the liberation war had still not come to be cleansed of their sins committed during the war. According to the custodian the suffering which rural people had endured since

Independence was the result of this failure to deal with the legacy of the war.[35] These two illustrations of the legacy of the war from opposite ends of the country reflect a widespread phenomena of disturbance, conflict and trauma which the Mafela Trust researchers have frequently encountered in their work.

Witchcraft accusations and *ngozi* possession — cases in which the wrongfully killed seek redress through the innocent living — are only two of the many forms through which divisions in rural communities created by the violence of the past express themselves today. Rural families who are still unable to trace their missing relatives have been unable to perform the necessary death ceremonies. They remain deeply troubled by this failure to mark and mourn the loss of their kin. Conflicts between families and clans, and even within families, remain unresolved.

In parts of Matabeleland this destabilization of rural communities has been profoundly deepened by the government counter-insurgency campaign of the mid-1980s. Hostility to Shona-speaking people is very evident among children who witnessed the Fifth Brigade rampaging through their villages. Rural communities, unable to make sense of their suffering, are profoundly alienated from political authority and have been effectively disenfranchised as a result.

Distrust, division and demobilization in rural communities scarred by the violence of the past undermine present and future development. Understanding and addressing these issues is clearly an essential element of any development programme but few, if any, development plans take this into account. Moreover, the legacies of the conflicts of the past are the seeds of future conflict.

The Mafela Trust is presently discussing ways in which this legacy might be addressed. Social scientists and politicians need to be made more aware of these problems and the fact that they have a role to play in their solution. Programmes of identification of the dead and commemoration are only a starting point. Very little work has been done in Africa on localized conflict resolution, and yet the conflicts throughout the Southern African region have created a widespread and bitter harvest. Making peace with this violent past is essential for a peaceful future.

Notes

General Introduction

1. An excellent summary of much of the work already done on the war and on Zimbabwean society can be found in the opening pages of Jocelyn Alexander's chapter in *Volume Two*.

2. N. Kriger, *Zimbabwe's Guerrilla War: Peasant Voices* (Cambridge, Cambridge Univ. Press, 1992); K. Manungo, 'The Role Peasants Played in the Zimbabwe War of Liberation, with Special Emphasis on Chiweshe District' (Ohio, Ohio University, Ph.D. thesis, 1991); T. Ranger, *Peasant Consciousness and Guerrilla War in Zimbabwe* (London, James Currey; Harare, Zimbabwe Publishing House, 1985); R. Werbner, *Tears of The Dead: The Social Biography of an African Family* (Edinburgh, Edinburgh Univ. Press; Harare, Baobab, 1991).

3. I. Staunton (ed.), *Mothers of the Revolution* (Harare, Baobab, 1990).

4. D. Lan, *Guns and Rain: Guerrillas and Spirit Mediums in Zimbabwe* (London, James Currey; Harare, Zimbabwe Publishing House, 1985); A. Moyo and C. Hallencreutz (eds.), *Church and State in Zimbabwe* (Gweru, Mambo, 1988).

5. P. Reynolds, 'Children of Tribulation: the need to heal and the means to heal war trauma', *Africa* (1990), LX.

6. J. K. Cilliers, *Counter-Insurgency in Rhodesia* (London, Croom Helm, 1985); H. Ellert, *The Rhodesia Front War* (Gweru, Mambo, 1989); P. Moorcraft and P. McLaughlin, *Chimurenga: The War in Rhodesia 1965–1980* (Marshalltown, Sygma/Collins, 1985).

7. K. Flower, *Serving Secretly: An Intelligence Chief on Record* (London, Murray; Harare, Quest, 1987); P. Stiff, *See You in November: Rhodesia's No-holds Barrred Intelligence War* (Alberton, Galago, 1985).

8. R. Reid Daly and P. Stiff, *Selous Scouts: Top Secret War* (Alberton, Galago, 1982).

9. P. Stiff, *Selous Scouts: Rhodesian War — A Pictorial Account* (Alberton, Galago, 1984).

10. B. Moore-King, *White Man Black War* (Harare, Baobab, 1989).

11. The most illuminating study of White Rhodesia during the war is that by D. Caute, *Under the Skin: The Death of White Rhodesia* (London, Allen Lane, 1983); a recent history is P. Godewin and I. Hancock: *Rhodesians Never Die: The Impact of War and Political Change on White Rhodesia, C. 1970–1980* (Oxford, Oxford University Press, 1993).

12. Two of Ngwabi Bhebe's research students, Josiah Tungamirai and Janice McLaughlin, have had access to the ZANLA files and make use of them in their chapters in these volumes. Josephine Nhongo is currently working on an Oxford M. Litt. making use of material relating to women in the ZANLA files.

13. Jeremy Brickhill was able to work on the ZIPRA files before their seizure by the police and draws upon them for his chapter in *Volume One*.

14. A. Nyathi with J. Hoffman, *Tomorrow is Built Today: Experiences of War, Colonialism and the Struggle for Collective Co-operatives in Zimbabwe* (Harare, Anvil, 1990). There is one invaluable book by a *chimbwido*, P. Chater, *Caught in the Crossfire* (Harare, Zimbabwe Publishing House, 1985).

15. D. Martin and P. Johnson, *The Struggle for Zimbabwe: The Chimurenga War* (Harare, Zimbabwe Publishing House; London, Faber, 1981), is *often cited* as having established this 'official version'.

Introduction
Soldiers in Zimbabwe's Liberation War: Volume One

1. D. Martin and P. Johnson, *The Struggle for Zimbabwe: The Chimurenga War* (Harare, Zimbabwe Publishing House; London, Faber, 1981).

2. Kingsley Dube wrote to Stanlake Samkange from New York on 18 October 1967 to describe a recent visit to Lusaka:

> Just about one week after our arrival, ZAPU press-gangs, as they were called by the Zambian press, began raiding the homes of fellow Rhodesians (or Zimbabweans) on the Copperbelt, carrying the men away for military training. This excited hostility to ZAPU leadership among Rhodesians there. They told me they were not against military training in principle, but they wanted to be approached properly so as to make arrangements for the continued upkeep of their families while they were away. George Nyandoro is quoted in the press as saying that the operation was quite in keeping with normal conscription practice. The drama of it all consisted in the rounding up of a few Zambians . . . because they were married to Mandebele girls.
> File: 'Private Letters From Friends', Samkange Archives, Harare.

3. B. Cole, *The Elite, The Story of the Rhodesian Special Air Service* (Three Knights, 1984); K. Flower, *Serving Secretly* (London, Murray, 1987); R. Reid Daly and Peter Stiff, *Selous Scouts: Top Secret War* (Alberton, Galago, 1982).

4. In this summary we draw on documents made available to us by Makatini Guduza.

5. R. Werbner, *The Tears of the Dead* (Edinburgh, Edinburgh Univ. Press, 1991).

6. N. Kriger, 'Struggles for Independence: Rural Conflicts in Zimbabwe's War for Liberation' (Harvard, MIT, Ph.D. thesis, 1985); N. Kriger, *Zimbabwe's Guerrilla War: Peasant Voices* (Cambridge, Cambridge Univ. Press, 1991).

Chapter 2
Recruitment to ZANLA: Building up a War Machine

1. Zvobgo Series Article No. 13, Patterns of Conflict: 1965–1972, 2; Interview with Richard Hove, Minister of Trade and Commerce, Harare, July 1984; Interview with Bernard Mutuma, Deputy Secretary in the Ministry of Mines, Harare, 18 July 1984.
2. Interview with Major-General Vitalis Zvinavashe, Chief of General Staff Army Headquarters and Colonel Tshinga Dube, Deputy Secretary Research and Development, Ministry of Defence, Harare, 20 Nov. 1990.
3. Report of the Constitutional Conference Lancaster House, London, Sept.–Dec. 1979, 19.
4. R. Ridell, *The Land Question* (Gwelo, Mambo Press and Catholic Commission for Justice and Peace in Rhodesia; London, Catholic Institute for International Relations, Rhodesia to Zimbabwe, 1978), 5.
5. Ibid.
6. International Defence and Aid Fund, *Zimbabwe: The Facts About Rhodesia* (London, International Defence and Aid Fund, 1977), 10.
7. Ridell, *The Land Question*, 6.
8. International Defence and Aid Fund, *Zimbabwe: The Facts About Rhodesia*, 22.
9. Ibid., 14.
10. Catholic Commission for Justice and Peace in Rhodesia, *Civil War in Rhodesia: Abduction, Torture and Death in the Counter-Insurgency Campaign* (Salisbury, The Commission, 1976), 1.
11. International Labour Office, *Labour Conditions and Discrimination in Southern Rhodesia (Zimbabwe)* (Geneva, International Labour Office, 1978), 111.
12. [Rhodesia], *Annual Report of the Secretary for Education for the Year Ended 31st December 1977* (Salisbury, Govt. Printer, 1978).
13. *Annual Report of the Secretary for Education for the Year Ended 31st December 1978* (Salisbury, Govt. Printer, 1979).
14. Interview with Justin Chauke, Superintendent at Beatrice Rehabilitation Centre, Beatrice, 30 Nov. 1990.
15. D. Martin and P. Johnson, *The Struggle for Zimbabwe: The Chimurenga War* (Harare, Zimbabwe Publishing House; London, Faber and Faber, 1981), 23.
16. Ibid.
17. Ibid.
18. Interview with Major-General Vitalis Zvinavashe and Colonel Tshinga Dube.
19. Ibid.
20. N. Bhebe, *ZAPU and ZANU Guerrilla Warfare and the Evangelical Lutheran Church in Zimbabwe* (forthcoming).
21. '"Umtali attack: The beginning of the end of our war" says Comrade Tongogara', *Zimbabwe News* (1979), X, v, 28; personal recollections.
22. Interview with Sarudzai Chinamaropa, Ruwa Rehabilitation Centre, Ruwa, 20 Nov. 1989.
23. Interview with Spirit Medium Chipfeni, Chifombo Base, July 1973.
24. D. Lan, *Guns and Rain: Guerrillas and Spirit Mediums in Zimbabwe* (Harare, Zimbabwe Publishing House, 1985), 5. ·
25. Interview with Spirit Medium Chipfeni.

26. ZANU's Department of Personnel Records, Chimoio, Dec. 1979.
27. Ibid.
28. Ibid.
29. Ibid.
30. Joint High Command, ZIPRA Assembly Points Records, January 1980.
31. P. Pandya, *Mao Tse Tung and Chimurenga: An Investigation into ZANU's Strategies* (Cape Town, Skotaville, 1988), 81.

Chapter 3
Daring to Storm the Heavens: The Military Strategy of ZAPU 1976 to 1979

1. A. Neuberg, *Armed Insurrection* (London, 1970 [originally published in German in 1928]), 264. A. Neuberg was the pseudonym for a group of Comintern revolutionaries including Ho Chi Minh.
2. The acronyms ZIPRA and ZPRA are used interchangeably although the army referred to itself as ZIPRA and this is the term I prefer to use.
3. ZAPU, *Our Path to Liberation* (Lusaka, The Party, 1976), 3.
4. Ibid., 4.
5. Ibid., 8.
6. Interview with Dumiso Dabengwa, Bulawayo, 6 July 1981.
7. Ibid.
8. Interview with Jerry Mtethwa, ZIPRA Regional Commissar, Mashumbi Pools Assembly Point, 10 July 1981.
9. Ibid.
10. Interview with Todd Mpisi, ZIPRA Deputy Regional Commander, Salisbury, 12 June 1981.
11. Interview with Richard Mataure, ZIPRA Regional Commander, Mashumbi Pools Assembly Point, 10 July 1981.
12. Interview with Dumiso Dabengwa, Oxford, 21 October 1988.
13. Vo Nguyen Giap, *People's War: People's Army* (Hanoi, Foreign Languages Press, 1961), 107.
14. Interview with Dumiso Dabengwa, Oxford, 21 October 1988.
15. Interview with Fibion Mutero, ZIPRA Platoon Commander, 5 Aug. 1981. The incident cited by Mutero occurred shortly before one of the few active revolts inside the country by ZIPRA forces. Led by a local ZIPRA commander named Maphuta, the survivors of the units which had been 'combed' by the Rhodesian forces, refused to comply with High Command orders, and remained outside the control of the High Command for the rest of the war.
16. Interview with Jerry Mtethwa, ZIPRA Regional Commissar, Mashumbi Pools Assembly Point, 10 July 1981.
17. J. K. Cilliers, *Counter-Insurgency in Rhodesia* (London, Croom Helm, 1985), 238–40.
18. This account represents the views of the post-crisis ZAPU and ZIPRA leadership. The ZAPU-FROLIZI faction, which split from ZAPU, emphasize other points of difference.

19. There were two military fronts, the Northern and Southern, and five operational regions within them, designated as NF1, 2 and 3 and SF1 and 2.
20. This summarized account of ZIPRA structures is drawn from a variety of documentary and interview sources.
21. Interview with Dumiso Dabengwa, Bulawayo, 6 July 1981.
22. Ibid.
23. Giap, *People's War: People's Army*, 104.
24. Ibid., 105.
25. ZAPU, *The Turning Point* (Lusaka, The Party, 1979)
26. Summarized from interview sources.
27. Interview with Richard Mataure, ZIPRA Regional Commander, Salisbury, 10 July 1981.
28. Interview with Todd Mpisi, ZIPRA Deputy Regional Commander, Salisbury, 12 June 1981.
29. Interview with Dumiso Dabengwa, Bulawayo, 6 July 1981.
30. J. Nkomo, *Nkomo: The Story of My Life* (London, Methuen, 1984), 196.
31. Ken Flower offers an ingeniously misleading account of this strategy, in which he depicts the architects of the plan as pro-South African 'Total War' Rhodesian military commanders, and deflects attention away from the CIO's key role in orchestrating the strategy. K. Flower, *Serving Secretly* (Harare, Quest; London, Murray, 1987), 245. Dabengwa and T. S. Ndlovu, a senior NSO officer, provided me with details of the role of the CIO.
32. Cilliers, *Counter-Insurgency in Rhodesia*, 190–1.
33. Interview with Joshua Nkomo, Bulawayo, April 1990.
34. Interviews with Joshua Nkomo, Bulawayo, April 1990 and Lookout Masuku (1981).
35. Interview with Dumiso Dabengwa, Oxford, 21 Oct. 1988.
36. Interviews with Dumiso Dabengwa, Oxford, 21 Oct. 1988 and Joshua Nkomo, Bulawayo, April 1990.
37. Interview with Richard Chimba, ZIPRA Regional Security Chief, 1 Aug. 1981.
38. Interview with Jerry Mtethwa, ZIPRA Regional Commissar, Mashumbi Pools Assembly Point, 10 July 1981.
39. Interviews with Dabengwa, Bulawayo, 6 July 1981 and Masuku (1981).
40. Interview with Peter Ndebele, ZIPRA Deputy Regional Commander, 12 June 1981.
41. B. Cole, *The Elite: The Story of the Rhodesian SAS* (Amanzimtoti, Three Knights Press, 1984), 388.
42. Ibid., 388.
43. Ibid., 393.
44. Interview with Mark Ndlovu, ZIPRA Camp Commander, Bulawayo, 29 Nov. 1991.
45. Wreckage from two aircraft was recovered by ZIPRA inside Zambia. The third aircraft fell on the Rhodesian side of the escarpment.
46. Interview with Mark Ndlovu, ZIPRA Camp Commander, Bulawayo, 29 Nov. 1991.
47. Interview with Dumiso Dabengwa, Oxford, 21 Oct. 1988.
48. Interview with Dumiso Dabengwa, Bulawayo, 6 July 1981.
49. Interview with Joshua Nkomo, Bulawayo, April 1990.

50. Ibid.
51. The statistics and other data employed in this section of the essay are derived from a questionnaire survey carried out in ZIPRA Assembly Points in early 1981. There were 250 respondents from several military units, drawn in equal proportions from officers, NCOs and rank-and-file soldiers.
52. Unfortunately my survey did not include female combatants so the analysis which follows excludes the women in ZIPRA.
53. From ZIPRA survey questionnaires.
54. Interview with Dennis Mpofu, ZIPRA Regional Commissar, Gwaai Assembly Point, 25 July 1981.
55. Interview with Curtain Sibanda, ZIPRA Zone Commissar, Gwaai Assembly Point, 2 Aug. 1981.
56. Interview with Fibion Mtero, ZIPRA Regional Commander, Gwaai Assembly Point, 5 Aug. 1981.
57. Ibid.
58. Richard Chimba, ZIPRA Intelligence Officer for the Southern Front, Gwaai Assembly Point, 1 Aug. 1981.
59. These and other factors gave rise to many observations on the war suggesting that ZIPRA was less 'political' and more 'militaristic' than ZANLA in its conduct of the war. These observations do not take account of the role and functions of the party structures, and hence provide a misleading impression of how the war was actually fought.
60. Interview with Fibion Mtero, ZIPRA Regional Commander, Gwaai Assembly Point, 5 Aug. 1981.
61. Interview with Richard Mataure, ZIPRA Regional Commander, Salisbury, 10 July 1981.

Chapter 4
The Zimbabwe People's Army: Strategic Innovation or More of the Same?

1. J. K. Cilliers, *Counter-Insurgency in Rhodesia* (London, Croom Helm, 1985).
2. See David Moore, 'The Contradictory Construction of Hegemony in Zimbabwe: Politics, Ideology and Class in the Formation of a New African State', Ph.D. Thesis, York University, North York, Canada, 1990, for more ruminations on this theme. Antonio Gramsci's classic is, of course, *Selections from the Prison Notebooks* (London, 1971). On similar themes see Moore, 'The ideological formation of the Zimbabwean ruling class', *Journal of Southern African Studies* (September 1991), 17, 3 and Christine Sylvester, 'Simultaneous revolutions: The Zimbabwean case', *Journal of Southern African Studies* (September 1990), 16, 3.
3. For example, André Astrow, *Zimbabwe: A Revolution That Lost Its Way?* (London, Zed, 1983), who sees ZIPA as little more had a slightly more militant form of nationalism in the Zimbabwean liberation movement.
4. Eg. Robert Mugabe, 'Comrade Mugabe lays down the line at historic Chimoio Central Committee Meetings', *Zimbabwe News* (July–December 1988), 9, 5–6, 9–14, and *idem.*, 'Zimbabwe African National Union Central Committee Report', *Zimbabwe News*, ed. 'ZANU (PF) Second Congress, 8th–13th August 1984', (January 1985) 16, 1, 4–32, and David Martin and Phyllis Johnson,

The Struggle for Zimbabwe: The Chimurenga War (Boston and London, Faber; Harare, ZPH, 1981).

5. Emmerson D. Mnangagwa, 'The formation of the Zimbabwe People's Army: Zipa', Canaan S. Banana, (ed.), *Turmoil and Tenacity: Zimbabwe 1890–1990* (Harare, College Press, 1989), 143–146. Stephen John Stedman, *Peacemaking in Civil War: International Mediation in Zimbabwe 1974–1980* (Boulder, Rienner, 1991), conflates ZIPA with ZANLA at one point (p. 93) and then states that it was the single army of the Patriotic Front (p. 107). Neither was the case. Such misinterpretation allows Stedman to consider that Robert Mugabe was the 'radical' Kissinger was so concerned to keep out of a settlement, whereas if he had good intelligence it is more likely that ZIPA was his concern.

6. 'Mwenje 2' is the common name for the *Political Programme, Zimbabwe African National Union (ZANU)*, 27 November 1973.

7. To elaborate: such a distinction is based on the premise that guerrilla warfare is not necessarily a radical make. Those committed to armed struggle against the settler regime had various degrees of commitment to democratic and socialist transformation, although in the mid-1970s all within this group were opposed to détente. With the availability of various meanings attributable to the notion of guerrilla war and armed struggle, those who preferred a non-transformational 'militarist' option — i.e. one that would use military pressure to force the demise of the Rhodesian settler state, but would stop short of social transformation and would even consider serious discussion of socialist change as diversionary and, as such, 'reactionary' — could dress their discourse in somewhat populist terms. Thus, to the extent that 'populism' could now include strains of anti-Marxism as well as anti-élitism, there was an elision of the old nationalist 'populist/élitist' partition with the 'Marxist versus bourgeois' ideological bifurcation emerging within ZANU's hegemonic struggles. If the tendency towards 'authoritarian populism' had to be identified with one individual, the name of Josiah Tongogara — the general commander of ZANLA, who was imprisoned in Zambia after the Chitepo assassination and was primarily responsible for the elimination of ZIPA soon after he was released — fits the bill. I have labelled ZIPA the 'transformation militants' — as those who carried the 'populist' meanings of the nationalist struggle to their furthest socialist expression. One should also note that J. Z. Moyo stated that fascists, as well as guerrilla soldiers, are 'militant militarists.' ('Our Path to Liberation, Being Comments at a ZAPU Consultation and Information Meeting, Now Issued as a Party Document', 20 November 1976, p. 9). The phrase 'authoritarian militarism' is based on what Stuart Hall has called 'authoritarian populism', in his 'Popular-democratic versus authoritarian populism: Two ways of taking democracy seriously', *The Hard Road to Renewal: Thatcherism and the Crisis of the Left* (London, Verso, 1988), 125–149.

8. Fay Chung, 'Education and the Liberation Struggle', paper presented to the *International Conference on the History of the Zimbabwean Liberation War*, Harare, University of Zimbabwe, July 12–18 1991, 3–4 on some of the conflicts leading up to and surrounding the Nhari Rebellion of early 1975.

9. Many of the interviewees remarked that on arriving in Botswana from Rhodesia and waiting in refugee camps, what party they joined depended on what planes arrived from Zambia first. Similarly, for those who crossed the Zambezi into Zambia, much depended on what party got to them first.

10. Interview, David Todlana, Harare, July 1991. Todlana became director of Wampoa College, ZIPA's ideological institution. He also merits mention in Martin and Johnson, op. cit., p. 260, as one of the ZIPA commanders who in October 1976 told Tongogara that ZIPA was now in charge of the liberation war. ZIPA members do not give much credence to Martin and Johnson's version of the liberation war.

11. Todlana recalled being evicted from the Soviet training camps he had been sent to as a result of a joke made during a drinking session with some of his instructors. When one of the instructors intended to elicit the answer 'study, study, and study again' from Todlana in response to a question about one of Lenin's maxims to aspiring cadres, Todlana replied 'drink, drink, and drink some more.' He was sent back to Zambia for that indiscretion.

12. It should be noted that the time of this indiscretion was probably in late 1968, significantly before the eruption of the 'Chikerema-Moyo' dispute in 1970 and 1971.

13. I use quotations around the term 'Shona' to emphasize the fact that such identities are 'constructed', not necessarily pre-given. See John S. Saul, 'The dialectic of class and tribe', John S. Saul, *The State and Revolution in Eastern Africa* (New York, Heinemann, 1979), and Leroy Vail, (ed.), *The Creation of Tribalism in Southern Africa* (London, James Currey, 1989).

14. Of course, the interviewee's 'slip' here is another indication of how deeply the ethnicization of the struggle reaches — stills.

15. Interview, David Todlana, Harare, July 1991. During and after the ZAPU crisis, about 130 soldiers left ZIPRA to join ZANLA. See Moore, 'The Contradictory Construction . . . ', Chapter 5 for an interpretation of ZAPU's 1970s crisis which gives the 'March 11 Movement' due credence in this crisis. See also Owen Tshabangu, *Revolution within the Revolution*: does not rely solely on the 'ethnicist' perspective of Zimbabwean political history.

16. M. Mamarkin, *The Making of Zimbabwe: Decolonization in Regional and International Politics* (London, 1990).

17. Vo Nguyen Giap, *People's War, People's Army* (Hanoi, Foreign Languages Press, 1961), 105, quoted in Jeremy Brickhill, 'A Step Further: ZAPU Military Strategy (1976–1979)', paper presented to the *International Conference on the History of the Zimbabwean Liberation War*, Harare, University of Zimbabwe, July 12–18 1991, p. 7, wherein the ZIPRA plans for mobile warfare are described as unique. The data indicated here suggests that ZIPA preceded ZIPRA with these plans.

18. Interview, Parker Chipoera, Harare, July 1991.

19. Tamarkin, op. cit., p. 112, states that in early April 1976, high-ranking Zambians and a Soviet met with ZIPA in Mozambique. Interviews with ZIPA actors confirm that Soviet support was imminent, and surmise the information was leaked to the Americans. There is little doubt that regardless of the quality of information fed to them, the Americans were worried about Soviet involvement, given the Angolan and Mozambican situations.

20. Interview, Dzinashe Machingura, Harare, July 1991.

21. Interview, Parker Chipoera, Harare, July 1991.

22. Interview, Dzinashe Machingura, Harare, July 1991.

23. Ibid.

24. Dzinashe Machingura, 'A Treatise on the Theoretical Problems in the National Democratic Revolution in Zimbabwe', unpublished manuscript, May 1978.

25. Interview, Dzinashe Machingura and Parker Chipoera, Harare, July 1991.

26. Ibid.

27. As Martin and Johnson's information put it, op. cit., 262.

28. Interview, David Todlana, Harare, July 1991.

29. Ibid. It may have been after debates like this that Todlana was nicknamed 'J. V.'

30. Ibid.

31. Ibid.

32. Chapter 11, 'Ideology: Fear of Communism', of Sister Janice McLaughlin's doctoral thesis on the relations between ZANU and the Roman Catholic church in the liberation war, University of Zimbabwe, quotes Tongogara's remarks on his attendance at Chitepo College on 25 July 1977, after ZIPA was eliminated, but during which time ZANU Central Committee members such as Rugare Gumbo and Henry Hamadziripi attempted to keep up some of the ZIPA tradition.

>   I spent the whole day. The lesson was about 'Space and Time.' In the afternoon, we had discussions about the lesson which was taught in the morning. Comrades raised so many questions . . . I told them to concentrate on the situation we have now, *teaching party line*, not philosophy . . . I said we should not be talking about space and time (emphasis mine).

>   Aside from the fact that this appears to be the discourse of an 'authoritarian militant', Chitepo College was not run by ZIPA.

>   Mugabe also ridiculed the notion of 'the negation of the negation' at the rally accounted for in 'Robert Mugabe lays down the line', *Zimbabwe News*, op. cit., stating that if the concept had any meaning, the comrades who had been killed in combat should arise from the dead.

33. Interview, David Todlana, Harare, July 1991.

34. Ibid.

35. Machingura, 'A Treatise . . . ', 25. The paper goes on to remark on the contraction inherent in the fact that such a non-revolutionary leadership could not avoid.

36. Machingura, 'A Treatise . . . ', 25.

37. *Loc. cit.*

38. Ibid., 25–26.

39. Interview, David Todlana, Harare, July 1991.

40. Ibid.

Chapter 5
The Rhodesian Security and Intelligence Community 1960–1980

1. This chapter was written without access to any files and my memory may be faulty on points of detail.
2. I. Hancock, *White Liberals, Moderates and Radicals in Rhodesia, 1953–1980* (New York, St Martin's Press, 1984).
3. D. Lessing, *Going Home* (London, Michael Joseph, 1957).
4. H. Ellert, *Rhodesian Front War* (Gweru, Mambo, 1989).

Chapter 6
The Metamorphosis of the 'Unorthodox': The Integration and Early Development of the Zimbabwean National Army

1. Some issues the nationalists found objectionable were the reserved White seats in parliament, land distribution and the provision that civil service pensions, commutations of pensions and private insurance were to be made remittable to non-residents without exchange control restriction.
2. Many of those in government realized the enormity of the exercise. The first President of Zimbabwe, Rev. Canaan Banana, described the exercise as 'one of the three wonders of Independent Zimbabwe' (the other two are the winning of Independence itself and the 1987 Unity Accord). See *The Herald* , 18 Apr. 1990.
3. After the American civil war, those who had fought on either side were brought together in the reconstituted army. A similar thing happened at the end of the British Civil War. Similarly, after the defeat of the Biafran attempt at secession in 1970, some of those soldiers who had left the Nigerian army to join the rebellion were reintegrated into the Nigerian Army.
4. See IDAF, *Smith's Settlement: Events in Zimbabwe During The Internal Settlement* (London, IDAF Publication, 1978), 9. During the years preceding, and in the early years of, independence the phrase 'lowering of standards' was used to describe Black involvement.
5. For example, membership of the War Council — the supreme security authority in the country — was altered. Since the Internal Settlement would produce a Black prime minister, the prime minister's membership of the council was abolished. The seats previously reserved for cabinet ministers were also removed. This was probably to prevent Muzorewa, Sithole, Chirau and/or any of their colleagues from assuming automatic membership of the council should they become cabinet ministers.
6. IDAF, *Smith's Settlement*, 9.
7. W. Burchett, *Southern Africa Stands Up: The Revolutions in Angola, Mozambique, Zimbabwe, Namibia and South Africa* (New York, Urizen Books, 1978), 238.
8. Ibid.
9. This position was often repeated after Independence. Whenever the White parliamentarians were too critical of anything they perceived as injustice in the new army, Mugabe was quick to remind them that it was only because of

the Lancaster House Agreement that White soldiers were able to remain in the army at all.

10. Discussion with ex-ZIPRA officer.

11. The exercise was under the command of Col. Peter Davis of Shaw Barracks, but the training was done by Major Richard Hatton of the Royal Artillery assisted by six Rhodesian Army Regiment instructors.

12. Both ZANLA and ZIPRA guerrillas brought in a diversity of weapons but were all issued with AK assault rifles. This marked the beginning of uniformity in weapons in the ZNA.

13. The JHC had power to co-opt any expert into its membership. Thus representatives of the Treasury Department and the British Military Training Team were present at most of its meetings.

14. Zimbabwe, *Parliamentary Debates, House of Assembly. First Session, First Parliament, comprising periods from 14th May to 26th June 1980, 23rd July 1980 to 15th August 1980*; I, 30 May 1980, 403.

15. A Rhodesia Front member of parliament argued with the Prime Minister that both ZANLA and ZIPRA were also forces established for a specific purpose, that is to overthrow the government of the day, and since the task had been completed they should also be disbanded.

16. Interview with General Vitalis Zvinavashe.

17. Many people in Zimbabwe did not like this codename, as it presupposed mass production with little regard for quality. When the government requested an increase in the production of officers, the codename was changed to 'Super Sausage Machine'.

18. The Chinese Ambassador to Zimbabwe, Chu Qiyuan had, on 18 July 1980, made an offer on behalf of his country to establish 'garrison farms' in Zimbabwe for former guerrillas. These farms would be for agricultural production during peace time, but could be turned into military garrisons during a war. See *The Herald*, 19 July 1980.

19. This position could be seen in the early defence speeches of the Prime Minister to Parliament.

20. ZANLA troops were sent to the middle Save area while ZIPRA troops went to the Silabuhara scheme, about 30 kms from Filabusi. Both groups worked on irrigation projects.

21. This should not be considered abnormal or unusual, especially in an African context. Every uprising or struggle has its own leaders, and it is usual for the leaders of such a struggle to be rewarded with an elevation of their rank after the successful completion of the struggle.

22. The guerrillas resented these training sessions and many complained that the sessions were conducted maliciously.

23. Many of the guerrillas did not expect that members of the former Rhodesian Security Forces would like to be treated as they were after Independence. Even the most sympathetic had thought that the Rhodesian forces would be disbanded.

24. An ex-ZIPRA guerrilla still in the army told me that, after the second riot at Entumbane, he became convinced that total confusion in the army was imminent. According to him, many of them who stayed on in the army only did so because of pressure from Nkomo, Masuku and Dabengwa. He said that

after the conflict, former ZANLA guerrillas were in the habit of floating another ruthless suppression if they dare embark on another revolt. It is only fair to add that this was denied by a former ZANLA combatant with whom I had an informal discussion.

25. Discussion with a former ZIPRA leader.
26. General Walls told a BBC reporter in an interview that he had written a letter to Mrs Thatcher after the 1980 general election, asking her not to recognize the election that had brought Mugabe into power. He also said that civil war was a distinct possibility in Zimbabwe.
27. There can be no doubt that the handling of the Zimbabwean integration and retraining exercises impressed many Southern African countries which were facing similar problems. One of the earliest defence policy statements of President Nujoma of Namibia was to invite the British to assist in the building up of his army.
28. An army source.
29. I owe this information to Dumiso Dabengwa. He said that the Patriotic Front had agreed that the new army should comprise 15 000 men — 5 000 from each military unit — but this was impossible to implement because of the activities of the British Monitoring Team.
30. Britain had used its veto against a United Nations Security Council Resolution ordering the division of the military equipment of the Federation of Rhodesia and Nyasaland to be divided between the three nations that had formed the Federation.
31. *The Herald*, 28 Dec. 1981.
32. *African Concord*, 9 Apr. 1987.
33. During my field trip to Zimbabwe in 1990, I came across a story in an old magazine which was full of praise for the toughness and physical strength of members of the Fifth Brigade. The article cited the performance of the members of the Brigade during a celebration, when some of its members used their hands to break cement blocks. I later asked a member of the ZNA who was a former ZIPRA member to validate this claim. He dismissed the performance as a public relations gimmick. He said the blocks were already broken and neatly packed together to trick the audience. All the brigade members did was to separate broken blocks. However, I later confirmed from an independent reliable source that the blocks were in fact intact, and that members of the Fifth Brigade can lay claim to some strength.
34. S. Sarkesian, 'African military regimes: Institutionalized instability or cohesive development?', in S. Simmon (ed.), *The Military Regime and Security in the Third World: Domestic and International Impact* (Boulder, Westview, 1978), 19.
35. *Zimbabwe National Army Magazine* (1982), I, 3 (my emphasis).
36. *Zimbabwe National Army Magazine* V, ii, 12.
37. Interview with Josiah Tungamirai.
38. Informal discussions with former members of the Rhodesian Security Forces.
39. Informal discussions with former ZANLA members.
40. Many of the former ZIPRA guerrillas with whom I discussed this issue believed that the elimination of the office of the Deputy Army Commander was to prevent it from being occupied by a member of ZIPRA.

41. A former ZANLA officer of the ZNA told me that promotion up to the rank of a Lt.–Col. is straightforward. Candidates write exams, and successful candidates are promoted accordingly. However, from the rank of Lt.-Col. upwards, he confirmed that extra-military factors come into play. This he said 'is only natural', as officers of this rank and above could be given political duties and their loyalty should not be in doubt. He hastened to add that political considerations in this context does not mean along ZANLA-ZIPRA-Rhodesian Security Forces lines but rather loyalty to the governing authority.

42. While in Zimbabwe I discovered that this rivalry has in fact already started in the ZNA. I noticed subtle rivalries between combatants and support units. It is almost certain that in the years ahead such rivalries will not only continue but will increase.

Chapter 7
The Heroes' Struggle: Life after the Liberation War
for Four Ex-combatants in Zimbabwe

1. Nyasha and Rose, 'Four years of armed struggle in Zimbabwe', in M. Davies (ed.), *Third World Second Sex* (London, Zed, 1983), 106.

2. Ex-combatant TM. See Introduction.

3. People were mobilized and politicized internally. Opinions differ on the legitimacy of this mobilization; see N. Kriger, 'The Zimbabwean war of liberation: Struggles within the struggle', *Journal of Southern African Studies* (1988), XIV, ii, 309–322. For an opposing view, asserting the voluntary co-operation of rural people with the liberation movements, see K. Manungo, 'The Role of Peasants in the Struggle for Zimbabwe' (Harare, unpubl., 1988). Moral and material support for the struggle also came from a variety of outside sources.

4. The popular response in the United States to the Gulf War is an example of the manufacture of an aggressive culture which greatly depends on the production of jingoist histories and the near-canonization of national leaders. An example of a quasi-official history in Zimbabwe which depends solely on official sources and the recollections of leaders is P. Martin and D. Johnson's *The Struggle for Zimbabwe* (Harare, Zimbabwe Publishing House; London, Faber, 1981). A point strongly made in B. Moore-King's *White Man, Black War* (Harare, Baobab, 1989) is the way in which histories of the Rhodesian side of the war ignored the experiences of the common soldier and as a result mythologized and glorified the war. An exception to the observation on popular memory is the None but Ourselves Oral History Project, undertaken by the Oral Traditions Association of Zimbabwe. This is a project to encourage the recording and preservation of experiences of ordinary people related to the struggle for Independence. Hopefully it will help to restore some balance in the national historiography of the war.

5. It has been estimated that of the 100 000 combatants of the three armed forces (the Rhodesian Security Forces, ZANLA and ZIPRA) at the time of Independence in 1980, 36 000 were demobilized by 1984. Of these 16 000 had

obtained training in some field by 1985, see S. Moyo, 'The Socio-economic Status and Needs of Ex-Combatants: The Case of Masvingo Province' (Harare, Zimbabwe Institute of Development Studies, 1985), 2.

6. Mr Peter Njerere, late oral historian of the National Archives of Zimbabwe carried out several interviews with ex-combatants which I was unable to use for this chapter. I hope other researchers will take advantage of his work.

7. 'Chimurenga' is the name given to the first anti-colonial struggle of 1896–7 and the second of 1966–80. For security reasons, a combatant in the liberation armies was either given a new name or selected one for himself or herself for the duration of the struggle. Chimurenga names were a constant reminder of one's new identity as a fighter whose life was dedicated to the liberation of the country.

8. Bishop Abel Muzorewa was the leader of the United African National Congress, which by that time had become a reactionary organization. It joined the Rhodesian government in the 'internal settlement' of 1979.

9. ZAPU was the premier nationalist organization in the country from the time of its creation in 1961 until ZANU was created in 1963 as a result of an internal split. ZAPU remained the main liberation organization operating in the southern and western areas of the country.

10. The Zimbabwe Peoples' Revolutionary Army, the armed wing of ZAPU. The armed wing of ZANU was ZANLA, the Zimbabwe African National Liberation Army.

11. Josiah Magama Tongogara, commander of ZANLA until his death in 1979.

12. White City Stadium is in Bulawayo. Enos Nkala, member of ZANU(PF), became Minister of Home Affairs in Independent Zimbabwe. He was disgraced and resigned his government post after the scandals revealed by the Sandura Commission in 1989.

13. *Mujibas* were village boys who assisted guerrillas in the field. Girls who helped were called *chimbwidos*.

14. The Patriotic Front between ZANU and ZAPU was formed in 1979.

15. The 'demobilization exercise' was the government's programme for removing guerrillas from the army and compensating them for their time spent in the bush. It consisted of a cash payment to each person of $185 a month for two years, or a lump sum payment of $4 300. Most, but not all, ex-combatants received this money.

16. The colloquial name for 'protected villages'. In rural areas where there was a lot of fighting, the Rhodesian Security Forces moved people into new villages, surrounded by fences and guards. This was to try to ensure that rural people had no contact with the guerrillas.

17. Ruwa is a small town about 22 kilometres south-east of Harare where the National Rehabilitation Centre was situated. After the war it was used for the physical rehabilitation of disabled ex-combatants. It was a residential treatment centre open to ex-combatants until 1985.

18. Dr Sharon Ladin, from the USA, was one of the founders and the director of Danhiko Secondary School from 1981–6. Danhiko is now an academic and vocational school for disabled adults situated on the eastern outskirts of Harare.

19. See page 128.

20. It was and is Zimbabwean government policy that the minimum qualification for employment as a civil servant is five 'O' level passes, at the standard of C or better.

21. As part of an exercise to restructure the government in 1989, Robert Mugabe became executive president of Zimbabwe. The post of deputy president was split in two, and shared between Joshua Nkomo and Simon Muzenda.

22. Under the War Victims Compensation Act (No. 22 of 1980), some permanently disabled soldiers and injured civilians receive monthly compensation payments. For FN this now amounts to $150 a month.

23. A new high-density suburb south-east of Harare. The policy of the Harare City Council is that once a stand is finally allocated (some people have been on the waiting list for housing for more than 15 years), it must be paid for in cash in no less than five working days. Residents are only allowed to build houses of seven rooms or more. At the time this chapter was being written the Council had placed a moratorium on all construction in Budiriro.

24. A South African writer and activist and member of the African National Congress of South Africa.

Chapter 8
The Politics of Creating National Heroes: the Search for
Political Legitimacy and National Identity

1. S. M. Lipset, *The First New Nation: The United States in Historical and Comparative Perspective* (London, Heinemann, 1964).

2. R. Buijtenhuijs, *Mau Mau: Twenty Years After* (Leiden, Afrika-Studiecentrum, 1973). Buijtenhuijs argues that Kenyatta feared that rewards or compensation to 'Mau Mau' fighters would have scared off White capital. Mugabe's government, having come to power through guerrilla warfare, was unconcerned about the effect on White capital of rewards, compensation or memorials for the ex-fighters.

3 Britain Zimbabwe Society, *Review of the Press* (mid-Feb. – mid-Apr.1991), No. 58, 17.

4. *The Herald*, 1 Aug. 1980, 'Rhodes statue moved'.

5. Ibid.

6. Two of the four statues that the government initially ordered to be removed ultimately remained where they were. The two that were removed were the Physical Energy statue and the Pioneer Flagpole. The former had been commissioned by Northern Rhodesia to honour Cecil Rhodes, but when Zambia became independent it saw the statue as a racist symbol and gave it to Salisbury City Council. The statue seemed destined to continue on its southward journey when Rhodes University offered to take it in exchange for a computer. But the government turned down the offer and the statue remains at the back of the National Archives where it was resited. The Pioneer Flagpole had been used to fly the Union Jack annually in commemoration of the first raising of the flag by the Pioneer Column on 12 September 1890. After some equivocation, the government decided not to remove either Alfred Beit's

statue — because of his humanitarian and philanthropic work — nor the memorial to those who had died in the 1896-7 African rebellion against the British South African Company. See *The Herald*, 27 Sept. 1980, 'Axe for statues'; *Sunday Mail*, 21 Dec. 1980, 'Reprieve for two statues'; *The Herald*, 21 July 1982, 'Rhodes statue to move to the archives'; *The Herald*, 23 July 1983, 'Colonial relics will give way to heroes'; *The Herald*, 24 Oct. 1983, 'Offer is rejected'; *The Herald*, 11 Sept. 1984, 'Cabinet "no" to request for statue'.

7. *The Herald*, 28 Sept. 1980, 'RF slams removal of old monuments'.
8. *Sunday Mail*, 21 Dec. 1980, 'Reprieve for two statues'.
9. Ibid.
10. *The Herald*, 15 Feb. 1983, 'Old relics to be dumped in gardens?'. A Professor of Botany, alarmed at this idea, wrote to *The Herald*, pleading that colonial relics not be 'dumped' in the botanic gardens because they would spoil the tranquillity and beauty of the gardens. He asserted, moreover, that botany was a progressive subject which should not be associated with symbols of conservatism. *The Herald*, 10 Mar. 1983, 'No dumping in the garden'.
11. *The Herald*, 14 Nov. 1981, 'Remove this colonial memorial — Shamva folk'; *The Herald*, 18 Nov. 1981, 'War memorial to be smashed'.
12. *The Herald*, 2 Dec. 1981, ' "Offensive" memorial is taken down'; *The Herald*, 10 Dec. 1981, 'Memorial was not offensive'.
13. *The Herald*, 3 Dec. 1981, 'Honour the dead of both sides, urges Holland'.
14. *The Herald*, 26 Nov. 1981, 'Build a monument to all the fighters'.
15. *The Herald*, 23 July 1983, 'Colonial relics will give way to heroes'.
16. *The Herald*, 22 Oct. 1984, 'Cenotaph must stay — official'.
17. *The Herald*, 22 Oct. 1984, 'Spare the Cenotaph'.
18. Zimbabwe, *Parliamentary Debates, House of Assembly. Second Session, Second Parliament, comprising periods from 24 June 1986 to 22 August 1986; 9 September 1986 to 19 November 1986; 17 February 1987 to 15 April 1987*, XIII, 5 Nov. 1986, 1279–80.
19. *Sunday Mail*, 28 Mar. 1982, 'Local artists take a swing at plan for heroes' statue'; *The Chronicle*, 22 May 1982, 'Heroes scheme forges on'. Sculptors from Zimbabwe Co-operative Craft Workshop in Harare expressed similar sentiments: 'Everything about the statue looks foreign. We feel local artists and craftsmen would have come up with something better.' One of Zimbabwe's leading sculptors, John Takawira, was also critical, 'Our young liberators didn't stand on bricks, they stood on rocks.' He too felt that the design should have been the work of Zimbabweans. *The Herald* was guardedly critical: 'From the artist's impression of the bronze group statue of freedom fighters published yesterday, some might not recognize the typical freedom fighter who swam with the people during the bitter years of the struggle. Perhaps at close range the centre-piece of the new Heroes' Acre does in its grandeur bear authentic Zimbabwean characteristics. Otherwise the centre-piece might deserve another look. The design could be improved, by local sculptors, if necessary.' *The Herald*, 20 Mar. 1982, 'Designing a hero'.
20. Zimbabwe, *A Guide to Heroes Acre . . . Some Basic Facts about Zimbabwe's Heroes and Heroes' Acre* (Harare, Ministry of Information, 1986), 3–4.
21. *The Chronicle*, 8 Jan. 1982, 'Call for more heroes' acres'; *The Herald*, 8 Jan. 1982, 'Acres for other heroes?'; *The Herald*, 2 Dec. 1984, 'Bulawayo to decide on

heroes' acre plan'; *The Herald*, 14 Jan. 1984, 'Local heroes' acres urged'.

22. Zimbabwe, *Parliamentary Debates, House of Assembly. Second Session, Second Parliament, comprising periods from 24 June 1986 to 22 August 1986; 9 September 1986 to 19 November 1986; 17 February 1987 to 15 April 1987*, XIII, 21 Aug. 1986, 1021, 1031–2.

23. *Sunday Mail*, 27 Oct. 1985, 'Heroes board named'. In July 1981 the Minister of Labour and Social Security submitted a memorandum to the parliamentary committee on pensions, grants and gratuities requesting that the widows of those buried at Heroes' Acre be provided with state pensions stating that because of their outstanding contribution to liberating Zimbabwe, 'it is fitting that the people of Zimbabwe, through their representatives in Parliament, recognise the heroes' deeds and ensure that their widows and children are not exposed to economic hardships' (*The Herald*, 23 July 1981, 'House rises for heroes' reburial'). In early 1985 Ruth Chinamano, a ZAPU parliamentary representative whose husband had been buried at Heroes' Acre, called on government to define a policy regarding heroes' widows (*The Herald*, 16 Jan. 1985, 'What about widows? — Ruth Chinamano').

24. Zimbabwe, *Parliamentary Debates, House of Assembly. Fourth Session, Second Parliament, comprising periods 28 June 1988 to 17 August 1988; 18 August 1988 to 29 November 1988; 30 November 1988 to 7 December 1988; 24 January 1989 to 8 February 1989; 7 May 1989 to 31 May 1989*, XV, 30 Aug. 1988, 1285.

25. Ibid., 1307.

26. *The Chronicle*, 12 Aug. 1991, 'Hero's widow speaks of hardship', 2.

27. *The Herald*, 27 Sept. 1982, 'A rough reception at Heroes' Acre'; *The Herald*, 4 Oct. 1983, 'Minister tells of plan for Heroes' Acre'; *The Herald*, 19 Oct. 1983, letter to editor. Several letters to *The Herald* complained that foreign tourists who went to Heroes' Acre encountered hostile Zimbabwe National Army soldiers and were prevented from visiting the national monument. The Ministry of Information justified the presence of the army guarding the graves as being 'normal practice' for protecting one's heroes and also invoked security concerns, alluding to the recent bombing of Independence Arch on the airport road in Harare.

28. *The Herald*, 16 Jan. 1985, 'What about widows? — Ruth Chinamano'.

29. *The Herald*, 31 Oct. 1984; *The Herald*, 7 Feb. 1986; *The Herald*, 1 Mar. 1988; *The Herald*, 17 Mar. 1988; *The Chronicle*, 17 Mar. 1988; *The Herald*, 15 July 1988; *The Chronicle*, 11 Apr. 1990; *The Chronicle*, 12 Apr. 1990; *The Chronicle*, 6 Aug. 1991; *The Chronicle*, 7 Aug. 1991. State funerals were given to, *inter alia*, James Bassoppo-Moyo, Ndongwe, Ngara, Benson Ndemera, Tarisai Ziyambi, Sheila Hove, Elmond Ndhlovu, and even Chief Chirau, a co-signatory with Prime Minister Ian Smith in the internal agreement of 1978. Ndiweni was given a state-assisted funeral when he was buried at Lady Stanley cemetery in April 1990: he was a former ZIPRA commander who became an officer in the Zimbabwe National Army.

30. *The Chronicle*, 3 Jan. 1990, 'Veteran fighter buried'; *The Herald*, 3 Jan. 1990, 'Farewell to Mutandadzi'.

31. *The Chronicle*, 16 Aug. 1991, 'Funeral aid for civil servants'.

32. *The Herald*, 16 Sept. 1986, 'Heroes reburial to be state task'. The governor erroneously informed the people that the government had been moved by

their efforts to cover the dead comrades with blankets and henceforth would pay for coffins for the fallen heroes.

33. *The Herald*, 10 June 1985, 'Villagers in Mudzi give 27 ZANLA fighters heroes' burials'.

34. Zimbabwe, *Parliamentary Debates, House of Assembly. Fourth Session, Second Parliament, comprising periods 28 June 1988 to 17 August 1988; 18 August 1988 to 29 November 1988; 30 November 1988 to 7 December 1988; 24 January 1989 to 8 February 1989; 7 May 1989 to 31 May 1989*, XV, 31 Aug. 1988, 1368–70: Zimbabwe, *Parliamentary Debates, House of Assembly. Fifth Session, First Parliament, comprising periods 26 June 1984 to 7 September 1984; 11 September 1984 to 30 November 1984; 15 January 1985 to 7 May 1985*, XI, 17 Jan. 1985.

35. *Sunday News*, 22 Apr. 1990, 'National hero's widow seeks compensation'.

36. *The Chronicle*, 29 Apr. 1990, 'Comment — War victim'.

37. Several newspaper reports lend support to this interpretation, although the interpretations offered in the articles for low turnout at reburials or lack of party interest in local heroes' acres sometimes differ. For instance, the *Sunday Mail*, 21 Dec. 1986, 'Mass graves: Party silent on burial bid', reported that the reburial of guerrillas was delayed in Beatrice district because 'unresponsive provincial party authorities' had disturbed the spirit mediums while the *Sunday Mail*, 16 Aug. 1987, 'Mystery surrounds mass grave', described how, in Wedza, three ZANU(PF) officials had to work through the night to erect a fence around the sagging graves of 65 ZANLA combatants in preparation for Heroes' Day. A ZANU(PF) representative complained of the 'outright lack of interest' by party officials in organizing reburial programmes. The *Sunday Mail* visited the graves and found the fence hanging loosely on poles. 'Poor turnout at the occasion also added to the tension', said the *Sunday Mail*. The ZANU(PF) representative, seemingly forgetful of his earlier comment, said people failed to turn up because of lack of transport. *The Herald*, 23 July 1987, 'Appeal for reburial funds', reported that in Guruve, ex-combatants had formed a reburial committee and raised $475. Each of 14 party districts was supposed to contribute $30 but only 3 did, bringing party contributions to $90. The rest of the money had been raised by donations from government departments and schools. *The Herald*, 12 Aug. 1988, 'Masvingo heroes' reburial delayed until September', wrote of the reburial ceremony for 135 'comrades' at Masvingo having to be postponed because only 30 graves had been dug and that the scheduled ceremony was poorly attended. Local people had contributed money to buy 100 coffins. The Minister of State for Political Affairs, Eddison Zvobgo, suggested the poor attendance may have been caused by the cold weather. *The Herald*, 15 Aug. 1988, 'Zvishavane reburies 52 combatants', reported that at a reburial ceremony at Zvishavane heroes' acre on Heroes' Day, the turnout was so poor that Cabinet Minister Mnangagwa rebuked people who stayed away, and made a general statement about the poor attendance nationwide. Local people had raised $25 000 for this heroes' acre, which the district administrator claimed ranked only behind the National Heroes' Acre. Finally, the Minister of Information complimented the Zimbabwe Broadcasting Corporation for its coverage of Heroes' Holidays, but said: 'alas, these people deliberately decided not to be covered by their non-attendance at most of these functions in many areas' (Zimbabwe, *Parliamentary Debates*,

House of Assembly. Fourth Session, Second Parliament, comprising periods 28 June 1988 to 17 August 1988; 18 August 1988 to 29 November 1988; 30 November 1988 to 7 December 1988; 24 January 1989 to 8 February 1989; 7 May 1989 to 31 May 1989, XV, 16 Aug. 1988).

38. In fact totems *had* been significant during the war. In some wards, people belonging to subject clans grouped together to try to wrest power from chiefly clans. The fact that guerrillas were from other districts made their acceptance by rural people more difficult.

39. *The Herald,* 17 Nov. 1987, 'Charter bodies are of Sithole's men'. See also *The Herald,* 24 May 1983, 'Mass grave in Chivhu: Police to investigate'; *The Chronicle,* 4 Aug. 1983, 'Burial of liberation war victims'; and Zimbabwe, *Parliamentary Debates, House of Assembly. Second Session, Second Parliament, comprising periods 24 June 1986 to 22 August 1986; 9 September 1986 to 19 November 1986; 17 February 1987 to 15 April 1987,* XIII, 5 Nov. 1986, 1279–80, in which Mugabe refers (seemingly dismissively) to people's concerns about how they could differentiate the bones of Rhodesian soldiers and guerrillas who were sometimes in common graves, or, as he put it, 'how do you distinguish the good bones from the bad bones? The heroic ones from the fascist ones and so on?'

40. *The Chronicle,* 23 May 1981, 'War dead will be brought home'.

41. Lawyers Committee for Human Rights, *Zimbabwe: Wages of War* (New York, The Committee, 1986).

42. *The Herald,* 12 Aug. 1980, 'Nkomo calls for national unity'; Ibid., 'Personal tribute by Prime Minister'.

43. *The Herald,* 13 Aug. 1980, 'Zimbabwe's heroes laid to rest'.

44. *The Herald,* 12 Aug. 1980.

45. *The Chronicle,* 11 July 1982, 'Leaders must learn from Masotsha, says Mugabe'.

46. *The Chronicle,* 29 June 1985, 'For the sake of unity' (comment).

47. *The Chronicle,* 24 Jan. 1987, 'Nkomo no to local heroe's acre'.

48. *The Herald,* 17 Aug. 1987, 'Call to honour heroes'.

49. *The Herald,* 16 Aug. 1986, 'ZAPU rejects call to rebury heroes'; *The Chronicle,* 18 Aug. 1986, 'ZAPU no to local heroes' acre idea'; for Joshua Nkomo's rejection, see *The Chronicle,* 24 January 1987, 'Nkomo no to local heroes' acre'; *The Chronicle,* 6 Nov. 1989, '287 graves located', *The Chronicle,* 11 Apr. 1988, 'Memorials for combatants planned', *The Chronicle,* 19 Apr. 1988, *The Herald,* 30 Nov. 1988, 'Reburial of heroes meets opposition'.

50. *The Chronicle,* 19 Aug. 1986, 'Rebury war dead' (editorial).

51. *Parade,* Aug. 1990, 'War shrines team brings out first list of ZIPRA war dead'.

52. British Zimbabwe Society, *Review of the Press* (Jan.-Feb.1989), No. 43, 14 cites an article in *Parade* on how villagers were willing to reveal where new graves were after the unity accord.

53. *The Chronicle,* 12 Aug. 1981, 'Mguni 'a man among men' says Nkomo'.

54. *The Chronicle,* 20 June 1982, 'Nkomo calls for probe'.

55. *The Chronicle,* 28 Aug. 1982, 'Second phase to start at acre'.

56. *The Chronicle,* 27 Nov. 1982.

57. *Sunday Mail,* 28 Nov. 1982, 'Heroes' Acre'.

58. *The Chronicle,* 18 Sept. 1983, 'Nkomo calls on all to live in unity and peace'.

59. *Sunday Mail,* 18 Sept. 1983, 'Heroine to be buried at acre?'.

60. *The Herald*, 20 Sept. 1983, 'No second burial for Nyamurowa'.
61. *The Chronicle*, 8 Dec. 1983, 'Why not all go to Heroes' Acre'.
62. *The Herald*, 16 Aug. 1984.
63. *The Herald*, 20 Oct. 1984, 'Seeking the definition of a national hero'.
64. Ibid.
65. *Sunday Mail*, 30 June 1985, 'A true hero' (editorial).
66. Britain Zimbabwe Society, *Review of the Press* (1 Mar. – 18 Apr. 1986), 9; *The Chronicle*, 13 Apr. 1986, 'Why not at Heroes' Acre? asks Nkomo'.
67. Britain Zimbabwe Society, *Review of the Press* (1 Mar.– 19 Apr. 1986), 9.
68. *The Herald*, 7 Aug. 1986, 'Weekend burial for heroes'; *Sunday Mail*, 30 June 1985, 'A true hero' (editorial).
69. *The Chronicle*, 17 Aug. 1991, 'Friction blamed for Gwanda Heroes' Day flop'; *The Chronicle*, 12 Aug. 1991, 'Fallen heroes honoured'; *Sunday News*, 12 Aug. 1990, 'Poor attendance at festivities'; *The Chronicle*, 13 Aug. 1990, 'Why there were low turn-outs'.
70. *The Chronicle*, 18 Aug. 1990, 'Yawning empty stadiums'.
71. *The Chronicle*, 15 Aug. 1991, 'Insulted President'.
72. *Parade*, Aug. 1990, 'War shrines team brings out list of ZIPRA war dead', 56–7.
73. *Parade*, Aug. 1990, 'Mafela Trust honours fallen fighters', 59.
74. *Moto*, Nov. 1990, 'War veterans wary of political 'hijackers'; *The Chronicle*, 13 Aug. 1990, 'Why there were low turn-outs'.
75. *Parade*, July 1991, 'Who is a hero?'; *The Chronicle*, 10 Aug. 1991, 'Miserable heroes' (comment).
76. *Parade*, July 1991, 'Who is a hero', 12–13.
77. The President's wife, Sally Mugabe, died in February 1992 and became the first heroine to be buried at Heroes' Acre.
78. *Parade*, Aug. 1990, 'Who is a hero', 28–9.
79. In 1987 constitutional changes eliminated the 20 reserved White seats in the House of Assembly and provided instead for the appointment of a number of non-constituency members.
80. *The Chronicle*, 17 Mar. 1988, 'Govt. urged to help ex-combatants'.
81. *The Chronicle*, 25 Mar. 1988, 'Redress ex-fighters' plight, urges MP'.
82. *The Chronicle*, 18 Mar. 1988, 'Appeal to help ex-combatants'.
83. *The Chronicle*, 24 Mar. 1988, 'Call to reward ex-fighters'.
84. British Zimbabwe Society, *Review of the Press* (13 Feb.–8 Apr. 1988), 11, citing *The Herald*, 21 Mar. 1988; see also *Sunday News*, 3 December 1989, 'Solve this problem' (letter to the Editor). This letter is one of several on the subject of the growing numbers of young people illegally crossing the border to look for work in South Africa or Botswana. It is a response to another letter expressing the view that border jumpers should be subjected to harsher court punishments. 'I think Nkosenstha must be a well-educated somebody enjoying to the fullest extent the fruits of a genuinely independent Zimbabwe. And yet the same border jumpers that he is so willing to see locked behind bars comprise mainly of the gallant fighters who sacrificed their lives, education and their chances for a brighter future to bring about this independence whose fruits and freedom we cherish.'

85. Zimbabwe, *Parliamentary Debates, House of Assembly. Fourth Session, Second Parliament, comprising periods 28 June 1988 to 17 August 1988; 18 August 1988 to 29 November 1988; 30 November 1988 to 7 December 1988; 24 January 1989 to 8 February 1989; 7 May 1989 to 31 May 1989*, XV, 13 July 1988, 148.

86. In 1982 the Minister of Labour and Social Services estimated that there were more than 5 000 disabled ex-combatants. According to him, almost all of them had been placed in employment or skill acquisition programmes, and only just over 200 still needed rehabilitation. Zimbabwe, *Report on the National Disability Survey of Zimbabwe* (Harare, Ministry of Labour and Social Services and Unicef 1983), 26.

87. Zimbabwe, *Parliamentary Debates, House of Assembly. Fourth Session, Second Parliament, comprising periods 28 June 1988 to 17 August 1988; 18 August 1988 to 29 November 1988; 30 November 1988 to 7 December 1988; 24 January 1989 to 8 February 1989; 7 May 1989 to 31 May 1989*, XV, 13 July 1988, 156.

88. Ibid., 165. The Ministry of Women's Affairs (and the Ministry of Youth) which were created because of the role of women and youth in the war have since been absorbed in the Ministry of Political Affairs.

89. There are several allusions to problems at Ruwa Rehabilitation Centre. The government had allegedly spent $60 million on the centre, set up specifically to cater for disabled ex-combatants. Although well-equipped and employing about 70 instructors, there were reported to be only 15 inmates. Zimbabwe, *Parliamentary Debates, House of Assembly. Fourth Session, Second Parliament, comprising periods 28 June 1988 to 17 August 1988; 18 August 1988 to 29 November 1988; 30 November 1988 to 7 December 1988; 24 January 1989 to 8 February 1989; 7 May 1989 to 31 May 1989*, XV, 29 Nov. 1988, 1933.

90. British Zimbabwe Society, *Review of the Press* (17 Feb. – 6 Apr. 1990), No. 51, 7.

91. Zimbabwe, *Parliamentary Debates, House of Assembly. Fourth Session, Second Parliament, comprising periods 28 June 1988 to 17 August 1988; 18 August 1988 to 29 November 1988; 30 November 1988 to 7 December 1988; 24 January 1989 to 8 February 1989; 7 May 1989 to 31 May 1989*, XV, 13 July 1988, 584–5.

92. *The Chronicle*, 18 Apr. 1988, Independence anniversary supplement.

93. *The Chronicle*, 11 Aug. 1988, 'Ex-combatants are heroes too!' (comment).

94. *The Chronicle*, 15 Jan. 1990, 'War veterans gear for provincial pools'.

95. *The Chronicle*, 11 Aug. 1988, 'Ex-combatants are heroes too?'.

96. *The Chronicle*, 5 Jan. 1990, 'Pension for ex-fighters' (letter to the Editor).

97. *The Chronicle*, 30 Mar. 1988, 'Yes, fighters are forgotten' (letter to the Editor).

98. *The Chronicle*, 13 Apr. 1988, 'MPs spoke well' (letter to the Editor).

99. *The Chronicle*, 4 Apr. 1988, 'Why speak out only now?' (letter to the Editor).

100. *The Chronicle*, 31 Mar. 1988, 'No material returns' (letter to the Editor).

101. Zimbabwe, *Parliamentary Debates, House of Assembly. Fourth Session, Second Parliament, comprising periods 28 June 1988 to 17 August 1988; 18 August 1988 to 29 November 1988; 30 November 1988 to 7 December 1988; 24 January 1989 to 8 February 1989; 7 May 1989 to 31 May 1989*, XV, 7 Feb 1980, 2389–90.

102. *The Chronicle*, 16 Jan. 1990, 'The forgotten heroes'.

103. *The Chronicle*, 25 Mar. 1988, 'The plight of ex-combatants'.

104. Britain Zimbabwe Society, *Review of the Press* (13 Feb. – 8 Apr. 1988), 11, citing *The Herald*, 21 Mar. 1988.

105. Zimbabwe, *Parliamentary Debates, House of Assembly. Fourth Session, Second Parliament, comprising periods 28 June 1988 to 17 August 1988; 18 August 1988 to 29 November 1988, 30 November 1988 to 7 December 1988; 24 January 1989 to 8 February 1989; 7 May 1989 to 31 May 1989*, XV, 4 August 1988, 781–6.

106. *The Chronicle*, 24 March 1988, 'Jobless ranks continue to grow'. An estimated 25 per cent of the workforce are unemployed. What makes the problem especially acute is that many of the unemployed have had secondary and even higher education. While the number of secondary school-leavers increased from less than 30 000 in 1984 to 185 000 in 1989, only 167 000 new non-agricultural jobs were created between 1980 and 1988 (*Facts and Reports*, 1989, XIX, No. D, 'Zimbank Economic Review' 24 Feb.; *Financial Times* [London], 8 Jan. 1989, 'Zimbabwe faces a survival test in economic jungle'; *Financial Gazette*, 15 Dec. 1989, 'Zimbank Economic Review'.

107. *The Chronicle*, 21 May 1988.

108. Zimbabwe, *Parliamentary Debates, House of Assembly. Fourth Session, Second Parliament, comprising periods 28 June 1988 to 17 August 1988; 18 August 1988 to 29 November 1988; 30 November 1988 to 7 December 1988; 24 January 1989 to 8 February 1989; 7 May 1989 to 31 May 1989*, XV, 13 July 1988, 131–2.

109. *The Chronicle*, 17 Mar. 1988, 'Govt. urged to help ex-combatants'.

110. *Sunday News*, 3 Dec. 1980, 'New party's top leaders hold talks'. *The Herald* objected to special provision for the direct representation of war veterans on the Central Committee when peasants and workers did not have such rights, and noted that some people felt that the party's power base, peasants and workers, was not acknowledged in the constitution. *The Herald* was of the opinion that 'if ZANU-PF is to establish itself as a mass party it cannot afford to encourage power blocs within its ranks. The mass organisations are a different proposition altogether. There must be no encouragement of distinctions between the workers and the separate electorates but only a recognition and sensitivity to the unique interests and problems of the peasants and workers which must be addressed by the party as a whole' (*The Herald*, 5 Dec. 1989, 'No power blocs in new party'). But Didymus Mutasa, a member of ZANU(PF)'s politburo and Speaker of the House of Assembly, justified the provision for war veterans to be directly represented on the central committee under the proposed constitution of the new united party that would be born when ZANU(PF) and ZAPU dissolved themselves at a party congress in December 1989. Some ex-combatants would be on the Central Committee through their positions in the party at the provincial level and their positions in the mass organizations such as the Women's League and the Youth League and so come into the Central Committee, but he saw no harm in having ex-combatants representing ex-combatants even though the War Veterans' Association was not a mass organisation (*The Herald*, 7 Dec. 1989, 'Ex-fighters deserve special deal — Mutasa').

111. *The Chronicle*, 21 Dec. 1989, 'Speculation on party posts'.

112. *The Chronicle*, 15 Jan. 1990, 'War veterans gear for provincial polls'.

113. Zimbabwe, *Parliamentary Debates, House of Assembly*.

114. Zimbabwe, *Parliamentary Debates, House of Assembly. Fourth Session, Second Parliament, comprising periods 28 June 1988 to 17 August 1988; 18 August 1988*

to 29 November 1988; 30 November 1988 to 7 December 1988; 24 January 1989 to 8 February 1989; 7 May 1989 to 31 May 1989, XV, 16 Aug. 1988, 886.

115. Zimbabwe, *Parliamentary Debates, House of Assembly. Fourth Session, Second Parliament, comprising periods 28 June 1988 to 17 August 1988; 18 August 1988 to 29 November 1988; 30 November 1988 to 7 December 1988; 24 January 1989 to 8 February 1989; 7 May 1989 to 31 May 1989,* XV, 6 July 1988, 71–2.

116. Zimbabwe, *Parliamentary Debates, House of Assembly. Fifth Session, Second Parliament, comprising periods 27 June 1989 to* 9 Aug. 1989, XVI, 888.

117. *The Chronicle,* 11 Aug. 1988, 'Ex-combatants are heroes too!' (Comment).

Chapter 9
Making Peace with the Past: War Victims and the Work of the Mafela Trust

1. First presented at a seminar on 'Religion and War and Swedish Relationships', Uppsala, Sweden, 23–8 March 1992.

2. Mafela Trust, *Report of the Mafela Trust Research Team* (Bulawayo, The Trust, 1990), 2.

3. Masuku and other ZAPU and ZIPRA leaders were charged with treason and several other offences related to arms caches found in several locations near ZIPRA Assembly Points. Recent disclosures have suggested that South African intelligence agents engineered the arms cache crisis as part of a bid to destabilize newly independent Zimbabwe. See *Southscan,* 16 Nov. 1990, and *Parade,* June 1990 on the South African connection; see *Africa Now,* June 1982, for an account of the arrests and *Moto,* March 1983, for an account of the charges and subsequent trial and acquittal.

4. NITRAM was a pioneering attempt to address the problems of the ex-combatants in a practical way, involving the ex-combatants themselves in a variety of commercial projects as well as providing welfare benefits. Trustees included Joshua Nkomo but NITRAM was effectively controlled by a board of directors comprising ZIPRA commanders and representatives of its ZIPRA shareholders elected in the Assembly Points.

5. Draft Deed of Donation Upon Trust (The L. K. V. Masuku Trust) original copy, p. 2.

6. Letter to Mrs Kamba (no date) but dictated to me on 1 April 1986. I spent most of the last three weeks of Lookout Masuku's life at his bedside, taking notes and carrying out his instructions. The letter to Mrs Kamba was prepared but not sent as the records had not been located. Unfortunately these records, which were confiscated by the government, are still missing.

7. *The Chronicle,* 13 Apr. 1986.

8. Four years later a bill is before parliament proposing a variety of measures to assist ex-combatants, but it has been widely criticized by ex-combatants and the War Veterans' Association as being inadequate.

9. N. Kriger, 'The politics of creating national heroes: The search for political legitimacy and national identity' (this volume).

10. Ibid.

11. *Parade,* Aug. 1990, 29.

12. See *Vanguard*, the newspaper of the ex-combatant-led co-operative movement, OCCZIM, from 1983 to 1985.

13. The detention of the ZIPRA leadership in 1982 and the confiscation of ZAPU's war records had prevented the publication of the list of ZIPRA war dead and the planned erection of shrines. The failure by ZAPU to carry this programme through in 1982 was not a protest, as Kriger suggests ('The politics of creating national heroes'), but was the result of its leaders being detained and the confiscation of its records.

14. See Kriger, 'The politics of creating national heroes', 17. The political aspect of the opposition to reburials arose from fears, later borne out in ZANU(PF)'s reburial programme, that it would lead to a competition for the biggest heroes' acre and that former Rhodesian forces — mainly auxiliaries — would accidentally be exhumed and reburied as heroes. ZAPU also argued that local communities should accept the dead guerrillas in their midst just as they had received the living guerrillas during the liberation war.

15. Personal Notebook 1987. Notes of a briefing from D. Dabengwa.

16. This uncomfortable position was only resolved in September 1990 when the Mafela Trust was formed.

17. The National Army continued to pay Col. Dube and also provided a vehicle and fuel in a generous gesture of support for the project and a sign of the new attitudes after the Unity Accord.

18. ZAPU, 'General Report on ZIPRA Fallen Heroes: Phase One', 1989, 1.

19. Having failed to locate the ZIPRA war records, which had been confiscated in 1982 and were reported missing, the research team had to devise methods of reconstructing identities of ZIPRA soldiers which had been deliberately concealed through the use of pseudonyms.

20. Sites of graves in neighbouring countries were also identified in this procedure. This will be followed up in a later stage of the programme.

21. Traditional leaders, it was felt, could be brought to support the programme because, as the custodians of tradition, they could rise above party conflict and encourage their communities to participate in a programme of homage to the unpropitiated dead. Moreover, having recently been stripped of some of their roles by ZANU(PF), it was hoped they would be enthusiastic in endorsing and supporting a project which would remind everyone of the central role played by traditional leaders in rural society in the past.

22. 'Go well [peacefully] hero of Zimbabwe'.

23. Mafela Trust, *Projects Report* (Bulawayo, The Trust, 1991).

24. The official list of ZANLA war dead names 69 fighters killed by poisons, although this is certainly an under-estimate. See Zimbabwe, *The Fallen Heroes of Zimbabwe* (Harare, Prime Minister's Office, 1983). A detailed presentation of the evidence of the use of chemical and biological warfare is published in *Horizon*, March 1992.

25. Mafela Trust, *Museums and Shrines: Site Proposals* (Bulawayo, The Trust, 1991), 1.

26. Ibid.

27. Ibid.

28. *Parade*, Dec. 1990, 75. One of the missed opportunities in Zimbabwe has been the failure of the government to use guerrilla expertise in these areas in

    government rural development programmes.
29. Mafela Trust, *Report to the Trustees*, May 1990.
30. *Parade*, Dec. 1990, 74.
31. Ibid., 75.
32. Letter to the Mafela Trust 1990.
33. Letter to the Mafela Trust 1990.
34. P. Reynolds, 'Children of tribulation: The need to heal and the means to heal war trauma', *Africa* (1990), LX, 14.
35. Notes from a discussion with Dumiso Dabengwa, Dec. 1991.

Bibliography

Astrow, A. *Zimbabwe: A Revolution That Lost Its Way?* (London, Zed, 1983).

Banana, C. S. (ed.) *Turmoil and Tenacity: Zimbabwe 1890-1990* (Harare, College Press, 1989).

Baumhögger, G. *The Struggle for Independence: Documents on the Recent Development of Zimbabwe (1975-1980)*, Vol. II (Hamburg, Institute for African Studies, 7 vols., 1984).

Bhebe, N. *ZAPU and ZANU Guerrilla Warfare and the Evangelical Lutheran Church in Zimbabwe* (Braamfontein, Skotaville, forthcoming).

Buijtenhuijs, R. *Mau Mau: Twenty Years After* (Leiden, Afrika-Studiecentrum, 1973).

Burchett, W. *Southern Africa Stands Up: The Revolutions in Angola, Mozambique, Zimbabwe, Namibia and South Africa* (New York, Urizen Books, 1978).

Catholic Commission for Justice and Peace in Rhodesia, *Civil War in Rhodesia: Abduction, Torture and Death in the Counter-Insurgency Campaign* (Salisbury, The Commission, 1976).

Caute, D. *Under the Skin: The Death of White Rhodesia* (Harmondsworth, Penguin, 1983).

Charlton, M. *The Last Colony in Africa: Diplomacy and the Independence of Rhodesia* (Oxford, Blackwell, 1990).

Chater, P. *Caught in the Crossfire* (Harare, Zimbabwe Publishing House, 1985).

Cilliers, J. K. *Counter-Insurgency in Rhodesia* (London, Croom Helm, 1985).

Cole, B. *The Elite, The Story of the Rhodesian Special Air Service* (Amanzimtoti, Three Knights Press, 1984).

Ellert, H. *Rhodesian Front War: Counter-Insurgency and Guerrilla War in Rhodesia, 1962–1980* (Gweru, Mambo Press, 1989).

Flower, K. *Serving Secretly: An Intelligence Chief on Record* (Harare, Quest; London, Murray, 1987).

Frederikse, J. *None But Ourselves: Masses vs. the Media in the Making of Zimbabwe* (Harare, Zimbabwe Publishing House, 1982).

Hall, S. 'Popular-democratic versus authoritarian populism: Two ways of taking democracy seriously', in his *The Hard Road to Renewal: Thatcherism and the Crisis of the Left* (London, Verso, 1988) 9.

Hancock, I. *White Liberals, Moderates and Radicals in Rhodesia, 1953–1980* (New York, St. Martin's Press; London, Croom Helm, 1984).

International Defence and Aid Fund, *Zimbabwe: The Facts About Rhodesia* (London, International Defence and Aid Fund, 1977).

International Labour Office, *Labour Conditions and Discrimination in Southern Rhodesia (Zimbabwe)* (Geneva, International Labour Office, 1978).

Kriger, N. 'Struggles for Independence: Rural Conflicts in Zimbabwe's War for Liberation' (Harvard, MIT, Ph.D. thesis, 1985).

_____. 'The Zimbabwean war of liberation: Struggles within the struggle', *Journal of Southern African Studies* (1988), XIV, ii.

_____. *Zimbabwe's Guerrilla War: Peasant Voices* (Cambridge, Cambridge Univ. Press, 1992).

Lan, D. *Guns and Rain: Guerrillas and Spirit Mediums in Zimbabwe* (Harare, Zimbabwe Publishing House; London, James Currey, 1985).

Lawyers Committee for Human Rights, *Zimbabwe: Wages of War* (New York, The Committee, 1986).

Lessing, D. *Going Home* (London, Michael Joseph, 1957).

Lipset, S. M. *The First New Nation* (London, Heinemann, 1964).

Machingura, D. 'A Treatise on Some Theoretical Problems on the National Democratic Revolution in Zimbabwe' (unpubl., 1978) [written in a Mozambican prison camp].

Mafela Trust, *Report of the Mafela Trust Research Team* (Bulawayo, The Trust, 1990).

Manungo, K. 'The Role of Peasants in the Struggle for Zimbabwe' (Harare, unpubl., 1988).

_____. 'The Role Peasants Played in the Zimbabwe War of Liberation, with Special Emphasis on Chiweshe District' (Ohio, Univ. of Ohio, Ph.D. thesis, 1991).

Maringapasi, B. D. 'The Development of ZANLA Strategy of Guerrilla Warfare, 1964–1979' (Harare, Univ. of Zimbabwe, History Dept., BA Hons. Diss., 1983).

Martin, D. and Johnson, P. *The Struggle for Zimbabwe: The Chimurenga War* (Harare, Zimbabwe Publishing House; London, Faber, 1981).

McLaughlin, J. 'Avila Mission: A turning point in church relations with the state and with the liberation forces' in N. Bhebe and T. Ranger (eds.), *Society in Zimbabwe's Liberation War: Volume Two* (Harare, Univ. of Zimbabwe Publications, forthcoming).

_____. 'The Catholic Church and Zimbabwe's War of Liberation' (Harare, Univ. of Zimbabwe, D.Phil. thesis, 1991).

Mnangagwa, E. D. 'The Formation of the Zimbabwe People's Army: ZIPA', in C. S. Banana (ed.), *Turmoil and Tenacity: Zimbabwe 1890–1990* (Harare, College Press, 1989), 143–6.

Moorcraft, P. and McLaughlin, P. *Chimurenga: The War in Rhodesia, 1965–1980* (Alberton, Galago, 1985).

Moore, D. 'The Contradictory Construction of Hegemony in Zimbabwe: Politics, Ideology and Class in the Formation of a New African State' (Toronto, York Univ., Ph.D. thesis, 1990).

_____. 'Hamba kahle, Kamba', *Southern African Review of Books* (July/Oct., 1991), 16–17.

_____. 'The ideological formation of the Zimbabwean ruling class', *Journal of Southern African Studies* (1991), XVII, 472–95.

_____. 'What was left of liberation in Zimbabwe? Socialist struggles within the struggle for independence', in L. Cliffe, P. Roberts and S. Ishemo (eds.), *Liberation Struggles and Postcolonial Development in Africa* (London, forthcoming).

Moore-King, B. *White Man — Black War* (Harare, Baobab, 1989).

Moyo, A. and Hallencreutz, C. (eds.), *Church and State in Zimbabwe* (Gweru, Mambo, 1988).

Mugabe, R. 'Zimbabwe African National Union Central Committee Report', *Zimbabwe News* (1985), XVI, 1–12.

Neuberg, A. *Armed Insurrection* (London, 1970 [originally published in German in 1928]).

Nkomo, J. *Nkomo: The Story of My Life* (London, Methuen, 1984).

Nyasha, and Rose, 'Four years of armed struggle in Zimbabwe', in M. Davies (ed.), *Third World Second Sex* (London, Zed, 1983).

Nyathi, A. and Hoffman, J. *Tomorrow is Built Today: Experiences of War, Colonialism and the Struggle for Collective Co-operatives in Zimbabwe* (Harare, Anvil, 1990).

Pandya, P. *Mao Tse Tung and Chimurenga: An Investigation in ZANU's Strategies* (Cape Town, Skotaville, 1988).

Ranger, T. *Peasant Consciousness and Guerrilla War in Zimbabwe* (Harare, Zimbabwe Publishing House; London, James Currey, 1985).

——. 'The changing of the old guard: Robert Mugabe and the revival of ZANU', *Journal of Southern African Studies* (1980), VII, 71–90.

Reid-Daly, R. and Stiff, P. *Selous Scouts: Top Secret War* (Alberton, Galago, 1982).

Reynolds, P. 'After war: Healers and children's trauma in Zimbabwe', *Africa* (1990), LX.

——. 'Children of tribulation: The need to heal and the means to heal war trauma', *Africa* (1990), LX, i.

Rhodesia, *Annual Report of the Secretary for African Education for the Year Ended 31st December 1977* (Salisbury, Govt. Printer, 1978).

Rhodesia, *Annual Report of the Secretary for Education for the Year Ended 31st December 1978* (Salisbury, Govt. Printer, 1979).

Ridell, R. C. 'Zimbabwe's land problem: The central issue', in W. H. Morris-Jones (ed.), *From Rhodesia to Zimbabwe: Behind and Beyond Lancaster House* (London, Cass, 1980), 1–13.

Moyo, S. 'The Socio-economic Status and Needs of Ex-Combatants: The Case of Masvingo Province' (Harare, Zimbabwe Institute of Development Studies, 1985).

Sarkesian, S. 'African military regimes: Institutionalized instability or cohesive development?', in S. Simmon (ed.), *The Military Régime and Security in the Third World: Domestic and International Impact* (Boulder, Westview, 1978).

Saul, J. S. 'Transforming the struggle in Zimbabwe', in his *State and Revolution in Eastern Africa* (London, Heinemann, 1979), 107–22.

Sithole, M. *Zimbabwe: Struggles within the Struggle* (Salisbury, Rujeko, 1979).

Smith, D. and Simpson, C. *Mugabe* (Salisbury, Sphere, 1981).

Staunton, I. (ed.), *Mothers of the Revolution* (Harare, Baobab, 1990).

Stiff, P. *See You in November: Rhodesia's No-holds Barred Intelligence War* (Alberton, Galago, 1985).

——. *Selous Scouts: Rhodesian War — A Pictorial Account* (Alberton, Galago, 1984).

Sylvester, C., 'Simultaneous revolutions: The Zimbabwean case', *Journal of Southern African Studies* (1990), XVI, 452–75.

Trewhela, P. 'The Kissinger/Vorster/Kaunda Detente: Genesis of the Swapo "Spy-Drama" Part II', *Searchlight South Africa* (1991), II, 46–7.

Tshabangu, O. *The March 11 Movement in ZAPU: Revolution within the Revolution for Zimbabwe* (York (UK), Tiger Press Publications, 1979).

Vo-Nguyen-Giap, *People's War: People's Army* (Hanoi, Foreign Languages Publishing House, 1961).

Werbner, R. *Tears of The Dead: The Social Biography of an African Family* (Edinburgh, Edinburgh Univ. Press, 1991).

Zambia, *Report of the Special International Commission on the Assassination of Herbert Wiltshire Chitepo* (Lusaka, Govt. Printer, 1976).

ZANU, *Mwenje No. 2: ZANU Political Programme* (Lusaka, ZANU, 1973).

ZAPU, *Our Path to Liberation* (Lusaka, ZAPU, 1977).

_____. *The Turning Point* (Lusaka, ZAPU, 1979).

Zimbabwe, 'The Fallen Heroes of Zimbabwe' (Harare, Prime Minister's Office, 1983).

Zimbabwe, *A Guide to Heroes' Acre . . . Some Basic Facts about Zimbabwe's Heroes and Heroes' Acre* (Harare, Ministry of Information, 1986).

Zimbabwe, *Report on the National Disability Survey of Zimbabwe* (Harare, Ministry of Labour and Social Services and Unicef, 1983).

Newspapers and Magazines

Africa News	Durham
Africa Now	London
Chimurenga	Stockholm
The Chronicle	Bulawayo
Daily Mail	Lusaka
Daily Telegraph	London
Facts and Reports	Amsterdam
Financial Gazette	Harare
Financial Times	London
The Herald	Harare
Horizon	Harare
Moto	Gweru
Parade	Harare
Review of the Press, British Zimbabwe	
Society	Harare
Southscan	London
Sunday Mail	Harare
Sunday News	Bulawayo

INDEX